The San Remo Manual is a contemporary restatement – together with some progressive development – of the law applicable to armed conflicts at sea, and has been drafted by an international group of specialists in international law and naval experts convened by the International Institute of Humanitarian Law. The last such restatement was undertaken by the Institute of International Law in 1913, and for the most part treaty law has not incorporated developments in the law since 1907. The accompanying Explanation is written in the form of a commentary and indicates the sources used by the experts for each of the provisions of the Manual and the discussion that led to their adoption. The work is based on treaty law of continuing validity and State practice and takes into account developments in related areas of international law, in particular, the effect of the UN Charter, the 1982 Law of the Sea Convention, air law and environmental law.

The Manual and Explanation represent a unique effort of experts from different parts of the world to establish the present state of the law. This document will be of major contemporary, future and historical importance, and will help shape generally accepted international law regulating armed conflicts at sea. There is no other book like it.

The Explanation was authored by a team of experts: Professor Salah El-Din Amer, Vice-Admiral James H. Doyle Jr, Commander William J. Fenrick, Mr Christopher Greenwood, Professor Wolff Heintschel von Heinegg, Professor Horace B. Robertson Jr, Mr Gert-Jan F. Van Hegelsom, and Ms Louise Doswald-Beck, who also acted as Editor and co-ordinator of the drafting work.

SAN REMO MANUAL

on

INTERNATIONAL LAW APPLICABLE TO ARMED CONFLICTS AT SEA

INTERNATIONAL INSTITUTE OF HUMANITARIAN LAW

SAN REMO MANUAL
on
INTERNATIONAL LAW APPLICABLE
TO ARMED CONFLICTS AT SEA

Prepared by
International Lawyers and Naval Experts
convened by the HIIHL

Editor

Louise Doswald-Beck

GROTIUS PUBLICATIONS

CAMBRIDGE
UNIVERSITY PRESS

CAMBRIDGE UNIVERSITY PRESS
Cambridge, New York, Melbourne, Madrid, Cape Town, Singapore, São Paulo

Cambridge University Press
The Edinburgh Building, Cambridge CB2 2RU, UK

Published in the United States of America by Cambridge University Press, New York

www.cambridge.org
Information on this title: www.cambridge.org/9780521551885

First published 1995
Re-issued in this digitally printed version 2005

A catalogue record for this publication is available from the British Library

Library of Congress Cataloguing in Publication data

San Remo manual on international law applicable to armed conflicts at
sea / prepared by international lawyers and naval experts
convened by the International Institute of Humanitarian Law; edited
by Louise Doswald-Beck,
p.   cm.
At head of title: International Institute of Humanitarian Law.
ISBN 0 521 55188 9 (hardcover). – ISBN 0 521 55864 6 (pbk.)
1. War, Maritime (International law) I. Doswald-Beck, Louise.
II. International Institute of Humanitarian Law.
JX5211.S26   1995
341.6′3 – dc20 95-8065 CIP

ISBN-13 978-0-521-55188-5 hardback
ISBN-10 0-521-55188-9 hardback

ISBN-13 978-0-521-55864-8 paperback
ISBN-10 0-521-55864-6 paperback

CONTENTS

FOREWORD

The International Institute of Humanitarian Law, at the initiative of its President, Professor J. Patrnogic, Professor N. Ronzitti from the University of Pisa (Italy) and Professor A. Goldie from the University of Syracuse (USA), began in 1987 a series of meetings of international lawyers and naval experts on the subject of the need for a modernisation of the law applicable to armed conflict at sea. At the second meeting, the experts suggested to the Institute that they work on the development of a manual. The intensive work over the following years led to the adoption of the San Remo Manual.

This document is a contemporary restatement of the law, together with some progressive development, which takes into account recent State practice, technological developments and the effect of related areas of the law, in particular, the United Nations Charter, the 1982 Law of the Sea Convention, air law and environmental law. The last restatement of the law of armed conflict at sea was undertaken by the Institute of International Law in 1913. Developments in the law since that date have for the most part not been incorporated into treaty law, with the exception of the Second Geneva Convention which is essentially limited to the protection of the wounded, sick and shipwrecked at sea, and does not address the whole question of the law on the conduct of hostilities at sea. The Manual and the related Explanation represent a unique effort of experts from different parts of the world to establish the present state of the law based on State practice and treaty law of continuing validity.

We would like to thank all participants and co-sponsors of this project, in particular, the rapporteurs and authors of the Explanation.

We are mostly indebted to the work of Ms Doswald-Beck, the Editor and co-ordinator of the drafting work, for her invaluable contribution to the realisation of this important project of the Institute.

Much appreciation is also owed to the work of Dr Genesio, Secretary-General of the Institute, and to the administrative staff.

This Manual and Explanation was made possible by the positive approach and flexibility of the participants which helped foster consensus as far as possible. It is hoped that this effort will have the desired result of a better comprehension and a wider knowledge and observance of the law applicable to armed conflicts at sea as well as acting as a basis for possible future developments.

Ambassador Hector Gros Espiell
President
International Institute of Humanitarian Law

SAN REMO MANUAL
on
INTERNATIONAL LAW APPLICABLE
TO ARMED CONFLICTS AT SEA

Prepared by

International Lawyers and Naval Experts

convened by the IIHL

Adopted in June 1994

CONTENTS

Contents

PART IV METHODS AND MEANS OF WARFARE AT SEA

PART V MEASURES SHORT OF ATTACK: INTERCEPTION, VISIT, SEARCH, DIVERSION AND CAPTURE

PART VI PROTECTED PERSONS, MEDICAL TRANSPORTS AND MEDICAL AIRCRAFT

ANNEX: SERIES OF MEETINGS AND CONTRIBUTIONS TO THE PROJECT

INTRODUCTORY NOTE

The San Remo Manual was prepared during the period 1988–94 by a group of legal and naval experts participating in their personal capacity in a series of Round Tables convened by the International Institute of Humanitarian Law. The purpose of the Manual is to provide a contemporary restatement of international law applicable to armed conflicts at sea. The Manual includes a few provisions which might be considered progressive developments in the law but most of its provisions are considered to state the law which is currently applicable. The Manual is viewed by the participants of the Round Tables as being in many respects a modern equivalent to the Oxford Manual on the Laws of Naval War Governing the Relations Between Belligerents adopted by the Institute of International Law in 1913. A contemporary manual was considered necessary because of developments in the law since 1913 which for the most part have not been incorporated into recent treaty law, the Second Geneva Convention of 1949 being essentially limited to the protection of the wounded, sick and shipwrecked at sea. In particular, there has not been a development for the law of armed conflict at sea similar to that for the law of armed conflict on land with the conclusion of Protocol I of 1977 additional to the Geneva Conventions of 1949. Although some of the provisions of Additional Protocol I affect naval operations, in particular those supplementing the protection given to medical vessels and aircraft in the Second Geneva Convention of 1949, Part IV of the Protocol, which protects civilians against the effects of hostilities, is only applicable to naval operations which affect civilians and civilian objects on land.

A preliminary Round Table on International Humanitarian Law Applicable to Armed Conflicts at Sea, held in San Remo in 1987 and convened by the International Institute of Humanitarian Law, in co-operation with the Institute of International Law of the University of Pisa (Italy) and the University of Syracuse (USA), undertook an initial review of the law. The Madrid Round Table, convened by the International Institute of Humanitarian Law in 1988, developed a plan of action to draft a contemporary restatement of the law of armed conflict at sea. In conformity with its mandate to prepare developments in international humanitarian law, the International Committee of the Red Cross supported this project throughout. In order to implement the Madrid Plan of Action, the Institute held annual Round Tables which met in Bochum in 1989, in Toulon in 1990, in Bergen in 1991, in Ottawa in 1992, in Geneva in 1993 and finally in Livorno in 1994. Basing themselves on thorough reports made by rapporteurs between the meetings, comments thereto by participants and careful discussion during the meetings, these groups drafted the Manual which was adopted in Livorno in June 1994.

The related Explanation was prepared by a core group of experts who had also been the rapporteurs for the Round Tables. The Manual should be read together with this Explanation for a full understanding of the Manual's provisions.

The Authentic text of the Manual is English.

PART I

GENERAL PROVISIONS

Section I Scope of application of the law

1   The parties to an armed conflict at sea are bound by the principles and rules of international humanitarian law from the moment armed force is used.

2   In cases not covered by this document or by international agreements, civilians and combatants remain under the protection and authority of the principles of international law derived from established custom, from the principles of humanity and from the dictates of the public conscience.

Section II Armed conflicts and the law of self-defence

3   The exercise of the right of individual or collective self-defence recognised in Article 51 of the Charter of the United Nations is subject to the conditions and limitations laid down in the Charter, and arising from general international law, including in particular the principles of necessity and proportionality.

4   The principles of necessity and proportionality apply equally to armed conflict at sea and require that the conduct of hostilities by a State should not exceed the degree and kind of force, not otherwise prohibited by the law of armed conflict, required to repel an armed attack against it and to restore its security.

5   How far a State is justified in its military actions against the enemy will depend upon the intensity and scale of the armed attack for which the enemy is responsible and the gravity of the threat posed.

6   The rules set out in this document and any other rules of international humanitarian law shall apply equally to all parties to the conflict. The equal application of these rules to all parties to the conflict shall not be affected by the international responsibility that may have been incurred by any of them for the outbreak of the conflict.

Section III Armed conflicts in which the Security Council has taken action

7   Notwithstanding any rule in this document or elsewhere on the law of neutrality, where the Security Council, acting in accordance with its powers under Chapter VII of the Charter of the United Nations, has identified one or more of the parties

to an armed conflict as responsible for resorting to force in violation of international law, neutral States:

(a)   are bound not to lend assistance other than humanitarian assistance to that State; *and*

(b)   may lend assistance to any State which has been the victim of a breach of the peace or an act of aggression by that State.

8   Where, in the course of an international armed conflict, the Security Council has taken preventive or enforcement action involving the application of economic measures under Chapter VII of the Charter, Member States of the United Nations may not rely upon the law of neutrality to justify conduct which would be incompatible with their obligations under the Charter or under decisions of the Security Council.

9   Subject to paragraph 7, where the Security Council has taken a decision to use force, or to authorise the use of force by a particular State or States, the rules set out in this document and any other rules of international humanitarian law applicable to armed conflicts at sea shall apply to all parties to any such conflict which may ensue.

Section IV Areas of naval warfare

10   Subject to other applicable rules of the law of armed conflict at sea contained in this document or elsewhere, hostile actions by naval forces may be conducted in, on or over:

(a)   the territorial sea and internal waters, the land territories, the exclusive economic zone and continental shelf and, where applicable, the archipelagic waters, of belligerent States;

(b)   the high seas; *and*

(c)   subject to paragraphs 34 and 35, the exclusive economic zone and the continental shelf of neutral States.

11   The parties to the conflict are encouraged to agree that no hostile actions will be conducted in marine areas containing:

(a)   rare or fragile ecosystems; *or*

(b)   the habitat of depleted, threatened or endangered species or other forms of marine life.

12   In carrying out operations in areas where neutral States enjoy sovereign rights, jurisdiction, or other rights under general international law, belligerents shall have due regard for the legitimate rights and duties of those neutral States.

Section V Definitions

13   For the purposes of this document:

(a)   'international humanitarian law' means international rules, established by treaties or custom, which limit the right of parties to a conflict to use the methods or means of warfare of their choice, or which protect States not party to the conflict or persons and objects that are, or may be, affected by the conflict;

(b)   'attack' means an act of violence, whether in offence or in defence;

(c)   'collateral casualties' or 'collateral damage' means the loss of life of, or injury to civilians or other protected persons, and damage to or the destruction of the natural environment or objects that are not in themselves military objectives;

(d)   'neutral' means any State not party to the conflict;

(e)   'hospital ships, coastal rescue craft and other medical transports' means vessels that are protected under the Second Geneva Convention of 1949 and Additional Protocol I of 1977;

(f)   'medical aircraft' means an aircraft that is protected under the Geneva Conventions of 1949 and Additional Protocol I of 1977;

(g)   'warship' means a ship belonging to the armed forces of a State bearing the external marks distinguishing the character and nationality of such a ship, under the command of an officer duly commissioned by the government of that State and whose name appears in the appropriate service list or its equivalent, and manned by a crew which is under regular armed forces discipline;

(h)   'auxiliary vessel' means a vessel, other than a warship, that is owned by or under the exclusive control of the armed forces of a State and used for the time being on government non-commercial service;

(i)   'merchant vessel' means a vessel, other than a warship, an auxiliary vessel, or a State vessel such as a customs or police vessel, that is engaged in commercial or private service;

(j)   'military aircraft' means an aircraft operated by commissioned units of the armed forces of a State having the military marks of that State, commanded by a member of the armed forces and manned by a crew subject to regular armed forces discipline;

(k)   'auxiliary aircraft' means an aircraft, other than a military aircraft, that is owned by or under the exclusive control of the armed forces of a State and used for the time being on government non-commercial service;

(l)   'civil aircraft' means an aircraft other than a military, auxiliary, or State aircraft such as a customs or police aircraft, that is engaged in commercial or private service;

(m)   'civil airliner' means a civil aircraft that is clearly marked and engaged in carrying civilian passengers in scheduled or non-scheduled services along Air Traffic Service routes.

PART II

REGIONS OF OPERATIONS

Section I Internal waters, territorial sea and archipelagic waters

14   Neutral waters consist of the internal waters, territorial sea, and, where applicable, the archipelagic waters, of neutral States. Neutral airspace consists of the airspace over neutral waters and the land territory of neutral States.

15   Within and over neutral waters, including neutral waters comprising an international strait and waters in which the right of archipelagic sea lanes passage may be exercised, hostile actions by belligerent forces are forbidden. A neutral State must take such measures as are consistent with Section II of this Part, including the exercise of surveillance, as the means at its disposal allow, to prevent the violation of its neutrality by belligerent forces.

16   Hostile actions within the meaning of paragraph 15 include, *inter alia*:

   (a)   attack on or capture of persons or objects located in, on or over neutral waters or territory;

   (b)   use as a base of operations, including attack on or capture of persons or objects located outside neutral waters, if the attack or seizure is conducted by belligerent forces located in, on or over neutral waters;

   (c)   laying of mines; *or*

   (d)   visit, search, diversion or capture.

17   Belligerent forces may not use neutral waters as a sanctuary.

18   Belligerent military and auxiliary aircraft may not enter neutral airspace. Should they do so, the neutral State shall use the means at its disposal to require the aircraft to land within its territory and shall intern the aircraft and its crew for the duration of the armed conflict. Should the aircraft fail to follow the instructions to land, it may be attacked, subject to the special rules relating to medical aircraft as specified in paragraphs 181–183.

19   Subject to paragraphs 29 and 33, a neutral State may, on a non-discriminatory basis, condition, restrict or prohibit the entrance to or passage through its neutral waters by belligerent warships and auxiliary vessels.

20   Subject to the duty of impartiality, and to paragraphs 21 and 23–33, and under such regulations as it may establish, a neutral State may, without jeopardising its neutrality, permit the following acts within its neutral waters:

   (a)   passage through its territorial sea, and where applicable its archipelagic waters, by warships, auxiliary vessels and prizes of belligerent States; warships, auxiliary vessels and prizes may employ pilots of the neutral State during passage;

   (b)   replenishment by a belligerent warship or auxiliary vessel of its food, water and fuel sufficient to reach a port in its own territory; *and*

   (c)   repairs of belligerent warships or auxiliary vessels found necessary by the neutral State to make them seaworthy; such repairs may not restore or increase their fighting strength.

21   A belligerent warship or auxiliary vessel may not extend the duration of its passage through neutral waters, or its presence in those waters for replenishment or repair, for longer than 24 hours unless unavoidable on account of damage or the stress of weather. The foregoing rule does not apply in international straits and waters in which the right of archipelagic sea lanes passage is exercised.

22   Should a belligerent State be in violation of the regime of neutral waters, as set out in this document, the neutral State is under an obligation to take the measures necessary to terminate the violation. If the neutral State fails to terminate the violation of its neutral waters by a belligerent, the opposing belligerent must so notify the neutral State and give that neutral State a reasonable time to terminate the violation by the belligerent. If the violation of the neutrality of the State by the belligerent constitutes a serious and immediate threat to the security of the opposing belligerent and the violation is not terminated, then that belligerent may, in the absence of any feasible and timely alternative, use such force as is strictly necessary to respond to the threat posed by the violation.

Section II International straits and archipelagic sea lanes

General rules

23   Belligerent warships and auxiliary vessels and military and auxiliary aircraft may exercise the rights of passage through, under or over neutral international straits and of archipelagic sea lanes passage provided by general international law.

24   The neutrality of a State bordering an international strait is not jeopardised by the transit passage of belligerent warships, auxiliary vessels, or military or auxiliary aircraft, nor by the innocent passage of belligerent warships or auxiliary vessels through that strait.

25   The neutrality of an archipelagic State is not jeopardised by the exercise of archipelagic sea lanes passage by belligerent warships, auxiliary vessels, or military or auxiliary aircraft.

26 Neutral warships, auxiliary vessels, and military and auxiliary aircraft may exercise the rights of passage provided by general international law through, under and over belligerent international straits and archipelagic waters. The neutral State should, as a precautionary measure, give timely notice of its exercise of the rights of passage to the belligerent State.

Transit passage and archipelagic sea lanes passage

27 The rights of transit passage and archipelagic sea lanes passage applicable to international straits and archipelagic waters in peacetime continue to apply in times of armed conflict. The laws and regulations of States bordering straits and archipelagic States relating to transit passage and archipelagic sea lanes passage adopted in accordance with general international law remain applicable.

28 Belligerent and neutral surface ships, submarines and aircraft have the rights of transit passage and archipelagic sea lanes passage through, under, and over all straits and archipelagic waters to which these rights generally apply.

29 Neutral States may not suspend, hamper, or otherwise impede the right of transit passage nor the right of archipelagic sea lanes passage.

30 A belligerent in transit passage through, under and over a neutral international strait, or in archipelagic sea lanes passage through, under and over neutral archipelagic waters, is required to proceed without delay, to refrain from the threat or use of force against the territorial integrity or political independence of the neutral littoral or archipelagic State, or in any other manner inconsistent with the purposes of the Charter of the United Nations, and otherwise to refrain from any hostile actions or other activities not incident to their transit. Belligerents passing through, under and over neutral straits or waters in which the right of archipelagic sea lanes passage applies are permitted to take defensive measures consistent with their security, including launching and recovery of aircraft, screen formation steaming, and acoustic and electronic surveillance. Belligerents in transit or archipelagic sea lanes passage may not, however, conduct offensive operations against enemy forces, nor use such neutral waters as a place of sanctuary nor as a base of operations.

Innocent passage

31 In addition to the exercise of the rights of transit and archipelagic sea lanes passage, belligerent vessels and auxiliary vessels may, subject to paragraphs 19 and 21, exercise the right of innocent passage through neutral international straits and archipelagic waters in accordance with general international law.

32 Neutral vessels may likewise exercise the right of innocent passage through belligerent international straits and archipelagic waters.

33 The right of non-suspendable innocent passage ascribed to certain international straits by international law may not be suspended in time of armed conflict.

Section III Exclusive economic zone and continental shelf

34   If hostile actions are conducted within the exclusive economic zone or on the continental shelf of a neutral State, belligerent States shall, in addition to observing the other applicable rules of the law of armed conflict at sea, have due regard for the rights and duties of the coastal State, *inter alia,* for the exploration and exploitation of the economic resources of the exclusive economic zone and the continental shelf and the protection and preservation of the marine environment. They shall, in particular, have due regard for artificial islands, installations, structures and safety zones established by neutral States in the exclusive economic zone and on the continental shelf.

35   If a belligerent considers it necessary to lay mines in the exclusive economic zone or the continental shelf of a neutral State, the belligerent shall notify that State, and shall ensure, *inter alia,* that the size of the minefield and the type of mines used do not endanger artificial islands, installations and structures, nor interfere with access thereto, and shall avoid so far as practicable interference with the exploration or exploitation of the zone by the neutral State. Due regard shall also be given to the protection and preservation of the marine environment.

Section IV High seas and sea-bed beyond national jurisdiction

36   Hostile actions on the high seas shall be conducted with due regard for the exercise by neutral States of rights of exploration and exploitation of the natural resources of the sea-bed, and ocean floor, and the subsoil thereof, beyond national jurisdiction.

37   Belligerents shall take care to avoid damage to cables and pipelines laid on the sea-bed which do not exclusively serve the belligerents.

PART III

BASIC RULES AND
TARGET DISCRIMINATION

Section I Basic rules

38   In any armed conflict the right of the parties to the conflict to choose methods or means of warfare is not unlimited.

39   Parties to the conflict shall at all times distinguish between civilians or other protected persons and combatants and between civilian or exempt objects and military objectives.

40   In so far as objects are concerned, military objectives are limited to those objects which by their nature, location, purpose or use make an effective contribution to military action and whose total or partial destruction, capture or neutralisation, in the circumstances ruling at the time, offers a definite military advantage.

41   Attacks shall be limited strictly to military objectives. Merchant vessels and civil aircraft are civilian objects unless they are military objectives in accordance with the principles and rules set forth in this document.

42   In addition to any specific prohibitions binding upon the parties to a conflict, it is forbidden to employ methods or means of warfare which:

    (a)   are of a nature to cause superfluous injury or unnecessary suffering; *or*

    (b)   are indiscriminate, in that:

        (i)   they are not, or cannot be, directed against a specific military objective; *or*

        (ii)   their effects cannot be limited as required by international law as reflected in this document.

43   It is prohibited to order that there shall be no survivors, to threaten an adversary therewith or to conduct hostilities on this basis.

44   Methods and means of warfare should be employed with due regard for the natural environment taking into account the relevant rules of international law. Damage to or destruction of the natural environment not justified by military necessity and carried out wantonly is prohibited.

45   Surface ships, submarines and aircraft are bound by the same principles and rules.

Section II Precautions in attack

46   With respect to attacks, the following precautions shall be taken:

(a)   those who plan, decide upon or execute an attack must take all feasible measures to gather information which will assist in determining whether or not objects which are not military objectives are present in an area of attack;

(b)   in the light of the information available to them, those who plan, decide upon or execute an attack shall do everything feasible to ensure that attacks are limited to military objectives;

(c)   they shall furthermore take all feasible precautions in the choice of methods and means in order to avoid or minimise collateral casualties or damage; *and*

(d)   an attack shall not be launched if it may be expected to cause collateral casualties or damage which would be excessive in relation to the concrete and direct military advantage anticipated from the attack as a whole; an attack shall be cancelled or suspended as soon as it becomes apparent that the collateral casualties or damage would be excessive.

Section VI of this Part provides additional precautions regarding civil aircraft.

Section III Enemy vessels and aircraft exempt from attack

Classes of vessels exempt from attack

47   The following classes of enemy vessels are exempt from attack:

(a)   hospital ships;

(b)   small craft used for coastal rescue operations and other medical transports;

(c)   vessels granted safe conduct by agreement between the belligerent parties including:

(i)   cartel vessels, e.g., vessels designated for and engaged in the transport of prisoners of war;

(ii)   vessels engaged in humanitarian missions, including vessels carrying supplies indispensable to the survival of the civilian population, and vessels engaged in relief actions and rescue operations;

(d)   vessels engaged in transporting cultural property under special protection;

(e)   passenger vessels when engaged only in carrying civilian passengers;

(f)   vessels charged with religious, non-military scientific or philanthropic missions, vessels collecting scientific data of likely military applications are not protected;

(g)   small coastal fishing vessels and small boats engaged in local coastal trade, but they are subject to the regulations of a belligerent naval commander operating in the area and to inspection;

(h)   vessels designed or adapted exclusively for responding to pollution incidents in the marine environment;

(i)   vessels which have surrendered;

(j)   life rafts and life boats.

Conditions of exemption

48   Vessels listed in paragraph 47 are exempt from attack only if they:

(a)   are innocently employed in their normal role;

(b)   submit to identification and inspection when required; *and*

(c)   do not intentionally hamper the movement of combatants and obey orders to stop or move out of the way when required.

Loss of exemption

Hospital ships

49   The exemption from attack of a hospital ship may cease only by reason of a breach of a condition of exemption in paragraph 48 and, in such a case, only after due warning has been given naming in all appropriate cases a reasonable time limit to discharge itself of the cause endangering its exemption, and after such warning has remained unheeded.

50   If after due warning a hospital ship persists in breaking a condition of its exemption, it renders itself liable to capture or other necessary measures to enforce compliance.

51   A hospital ship may only be attacked as a last resort if:

(a)   diversion or capture is not feasible;

(b)   no other method is available for exercising military control;

(c)   the circumstances of non-compliance are sufficiently grave that the hospital ship has become, or may be reasonably assumed to be, a military objective; *and*

(d)   the collateral casualties or damage will not be disproportionate to the military advantage gained or expected.

All other categories of vessels exempt from attack

52   If any other class of vessel exempt from attack breaches any of the conditions of its exemption in paragraph 48, it may be attacked only if:

(a)   diversion or capture is not feasible;

(b)   no other method is available for exercising military control;

(c)   the circumstances of non-compliance are sufficiently grave that the vessel has become, or may be reasonably assumed to be, a military objective; *and*

(d)   the collateral casualties or damage will not be disproportionate to the military advantage gained or expected.

Classes of aircraft exempt from attack

53   The following classes of enemy aircraft are exempt from attack:

(a)   medical aircraft;

(b)   aircraft granted safe conduct by agreement between the parties to the conflict; *and*

(c)   civil airliners.

Conditions of exemption for medical aircraft

54   Medical aircraft are exempt from attack only if they:

(a)   have been recognised as such;

(b)   are acting in compliance with an agreement as specified in paragraph 177;

(c)   fly in areas under the control of own or friendly forces; *or*

(d)   fly outside the area of armed conflict.

In other instances, medical aircraft operate at their own risk.

Basic rules and target discrimination

Conditions of exemption for aircraft granted safe conduct

55 Aircraft granted safe conduct are exempt from attack only if they:

    (a)   are innocently employed in their agreed role;

    (b)   do not intentionally hamper the movements of combatants; *and*

    (c)   comply with the details of the agreement, including availability for inspection.

Conditions of exemption for civil airliners

56 Civil airliners are exempt from attack only if they:

    (a)   are innocently employed in their normal role; *and*

    (b)   do not intentionally hamper the movements of combatants.

Loss of exemption

57 If aircraft exempt from attack breach any of the applicable conditions of their exemption as set forth in paragraphs 54–56, they may be attacked only if:

    (a)   diversion for landing, visit and search, and possible capture, is not feasible;

    (b)   no other method is available for exercising military control;

    (c)   the circumstances of non-compliance are sufficiently grave that the aircraft has become, or may be reasonably assumed to be, a military objective; *and*

    (d)   the collateral casualties or damage will not be disproportionate to the military advantage gained or anticipated.

58 In case of doubt whether a vessel or aircraft exempt from attack is being used to make an effective contribution to military action, it shall be presumed not to be so used.

Section IV Other enemy vessels and aircraft

Enemy merchant vessels

59 Enemy merchant vessels may only be attacked if they meet the definition of a military objective in paragraph 40.

60   The following activities may render enemy merchant vessels military objectives:

   (a)   engaging in belligerent acts on behalf of the enemy, e.g., laying mines, minesweeping, cutting undersea cables and pipelines, engaging in visit and search of neutral merchant vessels or attacking other merchant vessels;

   (b)   acting as an auxiliary to an enemy's armed forces, e.g., carrying troops or replenishing warships;

   (c)   being incorporated into or assisting the enemy's intelligence gathering system, e.g., engaging in reconnaissance, early warning, surveillance, or command, control and communications missions;

   (d)   sailing under convoy of enemy warships or military aircraft;

   (e)   refusing an order to stop or actively resisting visit, search or capture;

   (f)   being armed to an extent that they could inflict damage to a warship; this excludes light individual weapons for the defence of personnel, e.g., against pirates, and purely deflective systems such as 'chaff'; *or*

   (g)   otherwise making an effective contribution to military action, e.g., carrying military materials.

61   Any attack on these vessels is subject to the basic rules set out in paragraphs 38–46.

Enemy civil aircraft

62   Enemy civil aircraft may only be attacked if they meet the definition of a military objective in paragraph 40.

63   The following activities may render enemy civil aircraft military objectives:

   (a)   engaging in acts of war on behalf of the enemy, e.g., laying mines, minesweeping, laying or monitoring acoustic sensors, engaging in electronic warfare, intercepting or attacking other civil aircraft, or providing targeting information to enemy forces;

   (b)   acting as an auxiliary aircraft to an enemy's armed forces, e.g., transporting troops or military cargo, or refuelling military aircraft;

   (c)   being incorporated into or assisting the enemy's intelligence-gathering system, e.g., engaging in reconnaissance, early warning, surveillance, or command, control and communications missions;

(d)   flying under the protection of accompanying enemy warships or military aircraft;

(e)   refusing an order to identify itself, divert from its track, or proceed for visit and search to a belligerent airfield that is safe for the type of aircraft involved and reasonably accessible, or operating fire control equipment that could reasonably be construed to be part of an aircraft weapon system, or on being intercepted clearly manoeuvring to attack the intercepting belligerent military aircraft;

(f)   being armed with air-to-air or air-to-surface weapons; *or*

(g)   otherwise making an effective contribution to military action.

64   Any attack on these aircraft is subject to the basic rules set out in paragraphs 38–46.

Enemy warships and military aircraft

65   Unless they are exempt from attack under paragraphs 47 or 53, enemy warships and military aircraft and enemy auxiliary vessels and aircraft are military objectives within the meaning of paragraph 40.

66   They may be attacked, subject to the basic rules in paragraphs 38–46.

Section V Neutral merchant vessels and civil aircraft

Neutral merchant vessels

67   Merchant vessels flying the flag of neutral States may not be attacked unless they:

(a)   are believed on reasonable grounds to be carrying contraband or breaching a blockade, and after prior warning they intentionally and clearly refuse to stop, or intentionally and clearly resist visit, search or capture;

(b)   engage in belligerent acts on behalf of the enemy;

(c)   act as auxiliaries to the enemy's armed forces;

(d)   are incorporated into or assist the enemy's intelligence system;

(e)   sail under convoy of enemy warships or military aircraft; *or*

(f)   otherwise make an effective contribution to the enemy's military action, e.g., by carrying military materials, and it is not feasible for the attacking forces to first place passengers and crew in a place of safety. Unless circumstances do not permit, they are to be given a warning, so that they can re-route, off-load, or take other precautions.

68   Any attack on these vessels is subject to the basic rules in paragraphs 38–46.

69   The mere fact that a neutral merchant vessel is armed provides no grounds for attacking it.

Neutral civil aircraft

70   Civil aircraft bearing the marks of neutral States may not be attacked unless they:

(a)   are believed on reasonable grounds to be carrying contraband, and, after prior warning or interception, they intentionally and clearly refuse to divert from their destination, or intentionally and clearly refuse to proceed for visit and search to a belligerent airfield that is safe for the type of aircraft involved and reasonably accessible;

(b)   engage in belligerent acts on behalf of the enemy;

(c)   act as auxiliaries to the enemy's armed forces;

(d)   are incorporated into or assist the enemy's intelligence system; *or*

(e)   otherwise make an effective contribution to the enemy's military action, e.g., by carrying military materials, and, after prior warning or interception, they intentionally and clearly refuse to divert from their destination, or intentionally and clearly refuse to proceed for visit and search to a belligerent airfield that is safe for the type of aircraft involved and reasonably accessible.

71   Any attack on these aircraft is subject to the basic rules in paragraphs 38–46.

Section VI Precautions regarding civil aircraft

72   Civil aircraft should avoid areas of potentially hazardous military activity.

73   In the immediate vicinity of naval operations, civil aircraft shall comply with instructions from the belligerents regarding their heading and altitude.

74   Belligerents and neutral States concerned, and authorities providing air traffic services, should establish procedures whereby commanders of warships and military aircraft are aware on a continuous basis of designated routes assigned to or flight plans filed by civil aircraft in the area of military operations, including information on communication channels, identification modes and codes, destination, passengers and cargo.

75 Belligerent and neutral States should ensure that a Notice to Airmen (NOTAM) is issued providing information on military activities in areas potentially hazardous to civil aircraft, including activation of danger areas or temporary airspace restrictions. This NOTAM should include information on:

    (a) frequencies upon which the aircraft should maintain a continuous listening watch;

    (b) continuous operation of civil weather-avoidance radar and identification modes and codes;

    (c) altitude, course and speed restrictions;

    (d) procedures to respond to radio contact by the military forces and to establish two-way communications; *and*

    (e) possible action by the military forces if the NOTAM is not complied with and the civil aircraft is perceived by those military forces to be a threat.

76 Civil aircraft should file the required flight plan with the cognisant Air Traffic Service, complete with information as to registration, destination, passengers, cargo, emergency communication channels, identification modes and codes, updates en route and carry certificates as to registration, airworthiness, passengers and cargo. They should not deviate from a designated Air Traffic Service route or flight plan without Air Traffic Control clearance unless unforeseen conditions arise, e.g., safety or distress, in which case appropriate notification should be made immediately.

77 If a civil aircraft enters an area of potentially hazardous military activity, it should comply with relevant NOTAMs. Military forces should use all available means to identify and warn the civil aircraft, by using, *inter alia*, secondary surveillance radar modes and codes, communications, correlation with flight plan information, interception by military aircraft, and, when possible, contacting the appropriate Air Traffic Control facility.

PART IV

METHODS AND MEANS OF WARFARE AT SEA

Section I Means of warfare

Missiles and other projectiles

78 Missiles and projectiles, including those with over-the-horizon capabilities, shall be used in conformity with the principles of target discrimination as set out in paragraphs 38–46.

Torpedoes

79 It is prohibited to use torpedoes which do not sink or otherwise become harmless when they have completed their run.

Mines

80 Mines may only be used for legitimate military purposes including the denial of sea areas to the enemy.

81 Without prejudice to the rules set out in paragraph 82, the parties to the conflict shall not lay mines unless effective neutralisation occurs when they have become detached or control over them is otherwise lost.

82 It is forbidden to use free-floating mines unless:

   (a) they are directed against a miliary objective; *and*

   (b) they become harmless within an hour after loss of control over them.

83 The laying of armed mines or the arming of pre-laid mines must be notified unless the mines can only detonate against vessels which are military objectives.

84 Belligerents shall record the locations where they have laid mines.

85   Mining operations in the internal waters, territorial sea or archipelagic waters of a belligerent State should provide, when the mining is first executed, for free exit of shipping of neutral States.

86   Mining of neutral waters by a belligerent is prohibited.

87   Mining shall not have the practical effect of preventing passage between neutral waters and international waters.

88   The minelaying States shall pay due regard to the legitimate uses of the high seas by, *inter alia*, providing safe alternative routes for shipping of neutral States.

89   Transit passage through international straits and passage through waters subject to the right of archipelagic sea lanes passage shall not be impeded unless safe and convenient alternative routes are provided.

90   After the cessation of active hostilities, parties to the conflict shall do their utmost to remove or render harmless the mines they have laid, each party removing its own mines. With regard to mines laid in the territorial seas of the enemy, each party shall notify their position and shall proceed with the least possible delay to remove the mines in its territorial sea or otherwise render the territorial sea safe for navigation.

91   In addition to their obligations under paragraph 90, parties to the conflict shall endeavour to reach agreement, both among themselves and, where appropriate, with other States and with international organisations, on the provision of information and technical and material assistance, including in appropriate circumstances joint operations, necessary to remove minefields or otherwise render them harmless.

92   Neutral States do not commit an act inconsistent with the laws of neutrality by clearing mines laid in violation of international law.

Section II Methods of warfare

Blockade

93   A blockade shall be declared and notified to all belligerents and neutral States.

94   The declaration shall specify the commencement, duration, location, and extent of the blockade and the period within which vessels of neutral States may leave the blockaded coastline.

95   A blockade must be effective. The question whether a blockade is effective is a question of fact.

96   The force maintaining the blockade may be stationed at a distance determined by military requirements.

97　A blockade may be enforced and maintained by a combination of legitimate methods and means of warfare provided this combination does not result in acts inconsistent with the rules set out in this document.

98　Merchant vessels believed on reasonable grounds to be breaching a blockade may be captured. Merchant vessels which, after prior warning, clearly resist capture may be attacked.

99　A blockade must not bar access to the ports and coasts of neutral States.

100　A blockade must be applied impartially to the vessels of all States.

101　The cessation, temporary lifting, re-establishment, extension or other alteration of a blockade must be declared and notified as in paragraphs 93 and 94.

102　The declaration or establishment of a blockade is prohibited if:

(a)　it has the sole purpose of starving the civilian population or denying it other objects essential for its survival; *or*

(b)　the damage to the civilian population is, or may be expected to be, excessive in relation to the concrete and direct military advantage anticipated from the blockade.

103　If the civilian population of the blockaded territory is inadequately provided with food and other objects essential for its survival, the blockading party must provide for free passage of such foodstuffs and other essential supplies, subject to:

(a)　the right to prescribe the technical arrangements, including search, under which such passage is permitted; *and*

(b)　the condition that the distribution of such supplies shall be made under the local supervision of a Protecting Power or a humanitarian organisation which offers guarantees of impartiality, such as the International Committee of the Red Cross.

104　The blockading belligerent shall allow the passage of medical supplies for the civilian population or for the wounded and sick members of armed forces, subject to the right to prescribe technical arrangements, including search, under which such passage is permitted.

Zones

105　A belligerent cannot be absolved of its duties under international humanitarian law by establishing zones which might adversely affect the legitimate uses of defined areas of the sea.

106   Should a belligerent, as an exceptional measure, establish such a zone:

(a)   the same body of law applies both inside and outside the zone;

(b)   the extent, location and duration of the zone and the measures imposed shall not exceed what is strictly required by military necessity and the principle of proportionality;

(c)   due regard shall be given to the rights of neutral States to legitimate uses of the seas;

(d)   necessary safe passage through the zone for neutral vessels and aircraft shall be provided:

(i)   where the geographical extent of the zone significantly impedes free and safe access to the ports and coasts of a neutral State;

(ii)   in other cases where normal navigation routes are affected, except where military requirements do not permit; *and*

(e)   the commencement, duration, location and extent of the zone, as well as the restrictions imposed, shall be publicly declared and appropriately notified.

107   Compliance with the measures taken by one belligerent in the zone shall not be construed as an act harmful to the opposing belligerent.

108   Nothing in this Section should be deemed to derogate from the customary belligerent right to control neutral vessels and aircraft in the immediate vicinity of naval operations.

Section III Deception, ruses of war and perfidy

109   Military and auxiliary aircraft are prohibited at all times from feigning exempt, civilian or neutral status.

110   Ruses of war are permitted. Warships and auxiliary vessels, however, are prohibited from launching an attack whilst flying a false flag, and at all times from actively simulating the status of:

(a)   hospital ships, small coastal rescue craft or medical transports;

(b)   vessels on humanitarian missions;

(c)   passenger vessels carrying civilian passengers;

(d)   vessels protected by the United Nations flag;

(e)   vessels guaranteed safe conduct by prior agreement between the parties, including cartel vessels;

(f)   vessels entitled to be identified by the emblem of the red cross or red crescent; *or*

(g)   vessels engaged in transporting cultural property under special protection.

111   Perfidy is prohibited. Acts inviting the confidence of an adversary to lead it to believe that it is entitled to, or is obliged to accord, protection under the rules of international law applicable in armed conflict, with intent to betray that confidence, constitute perfidy. Perfidious acts include the launching of an attack while feigning:

(a)   exempt, civilian, neutral or protected United Nations status;

(b)   surrender or distress by, e.g., sending a distress signal or by the crew taking to life rafts.

PART V

MEASURES SHORT OF ATTACK: INTERCEPTION, VISIT, SEARCH, DIVERSION AND CAPTURE

Section I Determination of enemy character of vessels and aircraft

112 The fact that a merchant vessel is flying the flag of an enemy State or that a civil aircraft bears the marks of an enemy State is conclusive evidence of its enemy character.

113 The fact that a merchant vessel is flying the flag of a neutral State or a civil aircraft bears the marks of a neutral State is *prima facie* evidence of its neutral character.

114 If the commander of a warship suspects that a merchant vessel flying a neutral flag in fact has enemy character, the commander is entitled to exercise the right of visit and search, including the right of diversion for search under paragraph 121.

115 If the commander of a military aircraft suspects that a civil aircraft with neutral marks in fact has enemy character, the commander is entitled to exercise the right of interception and, if circumstances require, the right to divert for the purpose of visit and search.

116 If, after visit and search, there is reasonable ground for suspicion that the merchant vessel flying a neutral flag or a civil aircraft with neutral marks has enemy character, the vessel or aircraft may be captured as prize subject to adjudication.

117 Enemy character can be determined by registration, ownership, charter or other criteria.

Section II Visit and search of merchant vessels

Basic rules

118 In exercising their legal rights in an international armed conflict at sea, belligerent warships and military aircraft have a right to visit and search merchant vessels outside neutral waters where there are reasonable grounds for suspecting that they are subject to capture.

31

119   As an alternative to visit and search, a neutral merchant vessel may, with its consent, be diverted from its declared destination.

Merchant vessels under convoy of accompanying neutral warships

120   A neutral merchant vessel is exempt from the exercise of the right of visit and search if it meets the following conditions:

(a)   it is bound for a neutral port;

(b)   it is under the convoy of an accompanying neutral warship of the same nationality or a neutral warship of a State with which the flag State of the merchant vessel has concluded an agreement providing for such convoy;

(c)   the flag State of the neutral warship warrants that the neutral merchant vessel is not carrying contraband or otherwise engaged in activities inconsistent with its neutral status; *and*

(d)   the commander of the neutral warship provides, if requested by the commander of an intercepting belligerent warship or military aircraft, all information as to the character of the merchant vessel and its cargo as could otherwise be obtained by visit and search.

Diversion for the purpose of visit and search

121   If visit and search at sea is impossible or unsafe, a belligerent warship or military aircraft may divert a merchant vessel to an appropriate area or port in order to exercise the right of visit and search.

Measures of supervision

122   In order to avoid the necessity of visit and search, belligerent States may establish reasonable measures for the inspection of cargo of neutral merchant vessels and certification that a vessel is not carrying contraband.

123   The fact that a neutral merchant vessel has submitted to such measures of supervision as the inspection of its cargo and grant of certificates of non-contraband cargo by one belligerent is not an act of unneutral service with regard to an opposing belligerent.

124   In order to obviate the necessity for visit and search, neutral States are encouraged to enforce reasonable control measures and certification procedures to ensure that their merchant vessels are not carrying contraband.

Section III Interception, visit and search of civil aircraft

Basic rules

125 In exercising their legal rights in an international armed conflict at sea, belligerent military aircraft have a right to intercept civil aircraft outside neutral airspace where there are reasonable grounds for suspecting they are subject to capture. If, after interception, reasonable grounds for suspecting that a civil aircraft is subject to capture still exist, belligerent military aircraft have the right to order the civil aircraft to proceed for visit and search to a belligerent airfield that is safe for the type of aircraft involved and reasonably accessible. If there is no belligerent airfield that is safe and reasonably accessible for visit and search, a civil aircraft may be diverted from its declared destination.

126 As an alternative to visit and search:

(a)   an enemy civil aircraft may be diverted from its declared destination;

(b)   a neutral civil aircraft may be diverted from its declared destination with its consent.

Civil aircraft under the operational control of an accompanying neutral military aircraft or warship

127 A neutral civil aircraft is exempt from the exercise of the right of visit and search if it meets the following conditions:

(a)   it is bound for a neutral airfield;

(b)   it is under the operational control of an accompanying:

    (i)   neutral military aircraft or warship of the same nationality; *or*

    (ii)   neutral military aircraft or warship of a State with which the flag State of the civil aircraft has concluded an agreement providing for such control;

(c)   the flag State of the neutral military aircraft or warship warrants that the neutral civil aircraft is not carrying contraband or otherwise engaged in activities inconsistent with its neutral status; *and*

(d)   the commander of the neutral military aircraft or warship provides, if requested by the commander of an intercepting belligerent military aircraft, all information as to the character of the civil aircraft and its cargo as could otherwise be obtained by visit and search.

Measures of interception and supervision

128 Belligerent States should promulgate and adhere to safe procedures for intercepting civil aircraft as issued by the competent international organisation.

129 Civil aircraft should file the required flight plan with the cognisant Air Traffic Service, complete with information as to registration, destination, passengers, cargo, emergency communication channels, identification modes and codes, updates en route and carry certificates as to registration, airworthiness, passengers and cargo. They should not deviate from a designated Air Traffic Service route or flight plan without Air Traffic Control clearance unless unforeseen conditions arise, e.g., safety or distress, in which case appropriate notification should be made immediately.

130 Belligerents and neutrals concerned, and authorities providing air traffic services should establish procedures whereby commanders of warships and military aircraft are continuously aware of designated routes assigned to and flight plans filed by civil aircraft in the area of military operations, including information on communication channels, identification modes and codes, destination, passengers and cargo.

131 In the immediate vicinity of naval operations, civil aircraft shall comply with instructions from the combatants regarding their heading and altitude.

132 In order to avoid the necessity of visit and search, belligerent States may establish reasonable measures for the inspection of the cargo of neutral civil aircraft and certification that an aircraft is not carrying contraband.

133 The fact that a neutral civil aircraft has submitted to such measures of supervision as the inspection of its cargo and grant of certificates of non-contraband cargo by one belligerent is not an act of unneutral service with regard to an opposing belligerent.

134 In order to obviate the necessity for visit and search, neutral States are encouraged to enforce reasonable control measures and certification procedures to ensure that their civil aircraft are not carrying contraband.

Section IV Capture of enemy vessels and goods

135 Subject to the provisions of paragraph 136, enemy vessels, whether merchant or otherwise, and goods on board such vessels may be captured outside neutral waters. Prior exercise of visit and search is not required.

136 The following vessels are exempt from capture:

  (a) hospital ships and small craft used for coastal rescue operations;

  (b) other medical transports, so long as they are needed for the wounded, sick and shipwrecked on board;

(c)   vessels granted safe conduct by agreement between the belligerent parties including:

    (i)   cartel vessels, e.g., vessels designated for and engaged in the transport of prisoners of war; *and*

    (ii)   vessels engaged in humanitarian missions, including vessels carrying supplies indispensable to the survival of the civilian population, and vessels engaged in relief actions and rescue operations;

(d)   vessels engaged in transporting cultural property under special protection;

(e)   vessels charged with religious, non-military scientific or philanthropic missions; vessels collecting scientific data of likely military applications are not protected;

(f)   small coastal fishing vessels and small boats engaged in local coastal trade, but they are subject to the regulations of a belligerent naval commander operating in the area and to inspection; *and*

(g)   vessels designed or adapted exclusively for responding to pollution incidents in the marine environment when actually engaged in such activities.

137   Vessels listed in paragraph 136 are exempt from capture only if they:

(a)   are innocently employed in their normal role;

(b)   do not commit acts harmful to the enemy;

(c)   immediately submit to identification and inspection when required; *and*

(d)   do not intentionally hamper the movement of combatants and obey orders to stop or move out of the way when required.

138   Capture of a merchant vessel is exercised by taking such vessel as prize for adjudication. If military circumstances preclude taking such a vessel as prize at sea, it may be diverted to an appropriate area or port in order to complete capture. As an alternative to capture, an enemy merchant vessel may be diverted from its declared destination.

139   Subject to paragraph 140, a captured enemy merchant vessel may, as an exceptional measure, be destroyed when military circumstances preclude taking or sending such a vessel for adjudication as an enemy prize, only if the following criteria are met beforehand:

(a)   the safety of passengers and crew is provided for; for this purpose, the ship's boats are not regarded as a place of safety unless the safety of the passengers and crew is assured in the prevailing sea and weather conditions by the proximity of land or the presence of another vessel which is in a position to take them on board;

(b)   documents and papers relating to the prize are safeguarded; *and*

(c)   if feasible, personal effects of the passengers and crew are saved.

140   The destruction of enemy passenger vessels carrying only civilian passengers is prohibited at sea. For the safety of the passengers, such vessels shall be diverted to an appropriate area or port in order to complete capture.

Section V Capture of enemy civil aircraft and goods

141   Subject to the provisions of paragraph 142, enemy civil aircraft and goods on board such aircraft may be captured outside neutral airspace. Prior exercise of visit and search is not required.

142   The following aircraft are exempt from capture:

(a)   medical aircraft; *and*

(b)   aircraft granted safe conduct by agreement between the parties to the conflict.

143   Aircraft listed in paragraph 142 are exempt from capture only if they:

(a)   are innocently employed in their normal role;

(b)   do not commit acts harmful to the enemy;

(c)   immediately submit to interception and identification when required;

(d)   do not intentionally hamper the movement of combatants and obey orders to divert from their track when required; *and*

(e)   are not in breach of a prior agreement.

144   Capture is exercised by intercepting the enemy civil aircraft, ordering it to proceed to a belligerent airfield that is safe for the type of aircraft involved and reasonably accessible and, on landing, taking the aircraft as a prize for adjudication. As an alternative to capture, an enemy civil aircraft may be diverted from its declared destination.

145   If capture is exercised, the safety of passengers and crew and their personal effects must be provided for. The documents and papers relating to the prize must be safeguarded.

Section VI Capture of neutral merchant vessels and goods

146 Neutral merchant vessels are subject to capture outside neutral waters if they are engaged in any of the activities referred to in paragraph 67 or if it is determined as a result of visit and search or by other means, that they:

(a) are carrying contraband;

(b) are on a voyage especially undertaken with a view to the transport of individual passengers who are embodied in the armed forces of the enemy;

(c) are operating directly under enemy control, orders, charter, employment or direction;

(d) present irregular or fraudulent documents, lack necessary documents, or destroy, deface or conceal documents;

(e) are violating regulations established by a belligerent within the immediate area of naval operations; *or*

(f) are breaching or attempting to breach a blockade.

Capture of a neutral merchant vessel is exercised by taking such vessel as prize for adjudication.

147 Goods on board neutral merchant vessels are subject to capture only if they are contraband.

148 Contraband is defined as goods which are ultimately destined for territory under the control of the enemy and which may be susceptible for use in armed conflict.

149 In order to exercise the right of capture referred to in paragraphs 146(a) and 147, the belligerent must have published contraband lists. The precise nature of a belligerent's contraband list may vary according to the particular circumstances of the armed conflict. Contraband lists shall be reasonably specific.

150 Goods not on the belligerent's contraband list are 'free goods', that is, not subject to capture. As a minimum, 'free goods' shall include the following:

(a) religious objects;

(b) articles intended exclusively for the treatment of the wounded and sick and for the prevention of disease;

(c) clothing, bedding, essential foodstuffs, and means of shelter for the civilian population in general, and women and children in particular, provided there is not serious reason to believe that such goods will be diverted to other purpose, or that a definite military advantage would accrue to the enemy by their substitution for enemy goods that would thereby become available for military purposes;

(d)   items destined for prisoners of war, including individual parcels and collective relief shipments containing food, clothing, educational, cultural, and recreational articles;

(e)   goods otherwise specifically exempted from capture by international treaty or by special arrangement between belligerents; *and*

(f)   other goods not susceptible for use in armed conflict.

151   Subject to paragraph 152, a neutral vessel captured in accordance with paragraph 146 may, as an exceptional measure, be destroyed when military circumstances preclude taking or sending such a vessel for adjudication as an enemy prize, only if the following criteria are met beforehand:

(a)   the safety of passengers and crew is provided for; for this purpose the ship's boats are not regarded as a place of safety unless the safety of the passengers and crew is assured in the prevailing sea and weather conditions, by the proximity of land, or the presence of another vessel which is in a position to take them on board;

(b)   documents and papers relating to the captured vessel are safeguarded; *and*

(c)   if feasible, personal effects of the passengers and crew are saved.

Every effort should be made to avoid destruction of a captured neutral vessel. Therefore, such destruction shall not be ordered without there being entire satisfaction that the captured vessel can neither be sent into a belligerent port, nor diverted, nor properly released. A vessel may not be destroyed under this paragraph for carrying contraband unless the contraband, reckoned either by value, weight, volume or freight, forms more than half the cargo. Destruction shall be subject to adjudication.

152   The destruction of captured neutral passenger vessels carrying civilian passengers is prohibited at sea. For the safety of the passengers, such vessels shall be diverted to an appropriate port in order to complete capture provided for in paragraph 146.

Section VII Capture of neutral civil aircraft and goods

153   Neutral civil aircraft are subject to capture outside neutral airspace if they are engaged in any of the activities in paragraph 70 or if it is determined as a result of visit and search or by any other means, that they:

(a)   are carrying contraband;

(b)   are on a flight especially undertaken with a view to the transport of individual passengers who are embodied in the armed forces of the enemy;

(c)   are operating directly under enemy control, orders, charter, employment or direction;

(d)   present irregular or fraudulent documents, lack necessary documents, or destroy, deface or conceal documents;

(e)   are violating regulations established by a belligerent within the immediate area of naval operations; *or*

(f)   are engaged in a breach of blockade.

154   Goods on board neutral civil aircraft are subject to capture only if they are contraband.

155   The rules regarding contraband as prescribed in paragraphs 148–150 shall also apply to goods on board neutral civil aircraft.

156   Capture is exercised by intercepting the neutral civil aircraft, ordering it to proceed to a belligerent airfield that is safe for the type of aircraft involved and reasonably accessible and, on landing and after visit and search, taking it as prize for adjudication. If there is no belligerent airfield that is safe and reasonably accessible, a neutral civil aircraft may be diverted from its declared destination.

157   As an alternative to capture, a neutral civil aircraft may, with its consent, be diverted from its declared destination.

158   If capture is exercised, the safety of passengers and crew and their personal effects must be provided for. The documents and papers relating to the prize must be safeguarded.

PART VI

PROTECTED PERSONS, MEDICAL TRANSPORTS AND MEDICAL AIRCRAFT

General rules

159 Except as provided for in paragraph 171, the provisions of this Part are not to be construed as in any way departing from the provisions of the Second Geneva Convention of 1949 and Additional Protocol I of 1977 which contain detailed rules for the treatment of the wounded, sick and shipwrecked and for medical transports.

160 The parties to the conflict may agree, for humanitarian purposes, to create a zone in a defined area of the sea in which only activities consistent with those humanitarian purposes are permitted.

Section I Protected persons

161 Persons on board vessels and aircraft having fallen into the power of a belligerent or neutral shall be respected and protected. While at sea and thereafter until determination of their status, they shall be subject to the jurisdiction of the State exercising power over them.

162 Members of the crews of hospital ships may not be captured during the time they are in the service of these vessels. Members of the crews of rescue craft may not be captured while engaging in rescue operations.

163 Persons on board other vessels or aircraft exempt from capture listed in paragraphs 136 and 142 may not be captured.

164 Religious and medical personnel assigned to the spiritual and medical care of the wounded, sick and shipwrecked shall not be considered prisoners of war. They may, however, be retained as long as their services for the medical or spiritual needs of prisoners of war are needed.

165 Nationals of an enemy State, other than those specified in paragraphs 162–164, are entitled to prisoner-of-war status and may be made prisoners of war if they are:

(a)   members of the enemy's armed forces;

(b)   persons accompanying the enemy's armed forces;

(c)   crew members of auxiliary vessels or auxiliary aircraft;

(d)   crew members of enemy merchant vessels or civil aircraft not exempt from capture, unless they benefit from more favourable treatment under other provisions of international law; *or*

(e)   crew members of neutral merchant vessels or civil aircraft that have taken a direct part in the hostilities on the side of the enemy, or served as an auxiliary for the enemy.

166   Nationals of a neutral State:

(a)   who are passengers on board enemy or neutral vessels or aircraft are to be released and may not be made prisoners of war unless they are members of the enemy's armed forces or have personally committed acts of hostility against the captor;

(b)   who are members of the crew of enemy warships or auxiliary vessels or military aircraft or auxiliary aircraft are entitled to prisoner-of-war status and may be made prisoners of war;

(c)   who are members of the crew of enemy or neutral merchant vessels or civil aircraft are to be released and may not be made prisoners of war unless the vessel or aircraft has committed an act covered by paragraphs 60, 63, 67 or 70, or the member of the crew has personally committed an act of hostility against the captor.

167   Civilian persons other than those specified in paragraphs 162–166 are to be treated in accordance with the Fourth Geneva Convention of 1949.

168   Persons having fallen into the power of a neutral State are to be treated in accordance with Hague Conventions V and XIII of 1907 and the Second Geneva Convention of 1949.

Section II Medical transports

169   In order to provide maximum protection for hospital ships from the moment of the outbreak of hostilities, States may beforehand make general notification of the characteristics of their hospital ships as specified in Article 22 of the Second Geneva Convention of 1949. Such notification should include all available information on the means whereby the ship may be identified.

170   Hospital ships may be equipped with purely deflective means of defence, such as chaff and flares. The presence of such equipment should be notified.

171 In order to fulfil most effectively their humanitarian mission, hospital ships should be permitted to use cryptographic equipment. The equipment shall not be used in any circumstances to transmit intelligence data nor in any other way to acquire any military advantage.

172 Hospital ships, small craft used for coastal rescue operations and other medical transports are encouraged to implement the means of identification set out in Annex I of Additional Protocol I of 1977.

173 These means of identification are intended only to facilitate identification and do not, of themselves, confer protected status.

Section III Medical aircraft

174 Medical aircraft shall be protected and respected as specified in the provisions of this document.

175 Medical aircraft shall be clearly marked with the emblem of the red cross or red crescent, together with their national colours, on their lower, upper and lateral surfaces. Medical aircraft are encouraged to implement the other means of identification set out in Annex I of Additional Protocol I of 1977 at all times. Aircraft chartered by the International Committee of the Red Cross may use the same means of identification as medical aircraft. Temporary medical aircraft which cannot, either for lack of time or because of their characteristics, be marked with the distinctive emblem should use the most effective means of identification available.

176 Means of identification are intended only to facilitate identification and do not, of themselves, confer protected status.

177 Parties to the conflict are encouraged to notify medical flights and conclude agreements at all times, especially in areas where control by any party to the conflict is not clearly established. When such an agreement is concluded, it shall specify the altitudes, times and routes for safe operation and should include means of identification and communications.

178 Medical aircraft shall not be used to commit acts harmful to the enemy. They shall not carry any equipment intended for the collection or transmission of intelligence data. They shall not be armed, except for small arms for self-defence, and shall only carry medical personnel and equipment.

179 Other aircraft, military or civilian, belligerent or neutral, that are employed in the search for, rescue or transport of the wounded, sick and shipwrecked, operate at their own risk, unless pursuant to prior agreement between the parties to the conflict.

180 Medical aircraft flying over areas which are physically controlled by the opposing belligerent, or over areas the physical control of which is not clearly established, may be ordered to land to permit inspection. Medical aircraft shall obey any such order.

181 Belligerent medical aircraft shall not enter neutral airspace except by prior agreement. When within neutral airspace pursuant to agreement, medical aircraft shall comply with the terms of the agreement. The terms of the agreement may require the aircraft to land for inspection at a designated airport within the neutral State. Should the agreement so require, the inspection and follow-on action shall be conducted in accordance with paragraphs 182–183.

182 Should a medical aircraft, in the absence of an agreement or in deviation from the terms of an agreement, enter neutral airspace, either through navigational error or because of an emergency affecting the safety of the flight, it shall make every effort to give notice and to identify itself. Once the aircraft is recognised as a medical aircraft by the neutral State, it shall not be attacked but may be required to land for inspection. Once it has been inspected, and if it is determined in fact to be a medical aircraft, it shall be allowed to resume its flight.

183 If the inspection reveals that the aircraft is not a medical aircraft, it may be captured, and the occupants shall, unless agreed otherwise between the neutral State and the parties to the conflict, be detained in the neutral State where so required by the rules of international law applicable in armed conflict, in such a manner that they cannot again take part in the hostilities.

ANNEX

SERIES OF MEETINGS AND
CONTRIBUTIONS TO THE PROJECT

Preliminary Round Table on International Humanitarian Law Applicable to Armed Conflicts at Sea
San Remo, 15–17 June 1987
In co-operation with the University of Pisa, Italy and Syracuse University, NY, USA

Round Table of Experts on International Humanitarian Law Applicable to Armed Conflicts at Sea
Madrid, 26–29 September 1988
In collaboration with the Humanitarian Law Study Centre of the Spanish Red Cross

MEETINGS OF EXPERTS FOLLOWING THE MADRID
PLAN OF ACTION

First Meeting: Bochum, 10–14 November 1989
In collaboration with the Institute of Peacekeeping Law and Humanitarian Law, Ruhr University, Bochum and the German Red Cross in the Federal Republic of Germany

Second Meeting: Toulon, 19–23 October 1990
In collaboration with the Mediterranean Institute of Strategic Studies, Université de Toulon et du Var and the French Red Cross

Third Meeting: Bergen, 20–24 September 1991
In collaboration with the Norwegian Navy School of Tactics and the Norwegian Red Cross

Fourth Meeting: Ottawa, 25–28 September 1992
In collaboration with the Canadian Department of National Defence and the Canadian Red Cross

Fifth Meeting: Geneva, 23–28 September 1993
In collaboration with the International Committee of the Red Cross

Final Meeting: Livorno 9–12 June 1994
In collaboration with the Institute of Naval Warfare of the Italian Navy

FINANCIAL CONTRIBUTORS

Financial contributions were made by the governments of Sweden, Switzerland and Italy.

RAPPORTEURS AND AUTHORS

Rapporteurs

Ms Louise Doswald-Beck
Commander William Fenrick
Mr Christopher Greenwood
Professor Wolff Heintschel von Heinegg
Professor Horace Robertson, Jr, Rear Admiral, US Navy (ret.)
Mr Gert-Jan F. Van Hegelsom

Authors of special reports

Professor Salah El-Din Amer
Vice-Admiral James H. Doyle, Jr, US Navy (ret.)
Captain J. Ashley Roach
Professor Dietrich Schindler

Authors of background papers

Lieutenant-Colonel Kim Carter
Professor Wolff Heintschel von Heinegg

Members of the harmonisation group and authors of the Explanation

Professor Salah El-Din Amer
Ms Louise Doswald-Beck
Vice-Admiral James Doyle, Jr, Rear Admiral, US Navy (ret.)
Commander William Fenrick
Mr Christopher Greenwood
Professor Wolff Heintschel von Heinegg
Professor Horace Robertson, Jr, Rear Admiral, US Navy (ret.)
Mr Gert-Jan F. Van Hegelsom

Editor and co-ordinator of drafting

Ms Louise Doswald-Beck

PARTICIPANTS

All participants attended in their personal capacity and not as representatives of the institutions with which they are associated (the names of which are given for information)

Professor Salah El-Din Amer
Cairo University
Cairo
Egypt

Professor Louis Balmond
Institut Méditerranéen d'Etudes
   Stratégiques
Faculty of Law, Université de Toulon et
   du Var
La Garde
France

Captain Jack F. T. Bayliss
Chief Naval Judge Advocate
Greenwich, London
Great Britain

Professor Ove Bring
Faculty of Law, University of Uppsala
Uppsala
Sweden

Captain di Freg. (CM) Fabio Caffio
Statsmaggiore Defese
Rome
Italy

Lieutenant-Colonel Kim Carter
Office of the Judge Advocate General
Department of National Defence
Ottawa
Canada

Mr Gérald Cauderay
Technical Adviser
International Committee of the Red
   Cross
Geneva
Switzerland

Mr Jeffrey Chan Wah Teck
Legal Services
Singapore
Republic of Singapore

Admiral (ret.) Giovanni Clara
Italian Navy
Livorno
Italy

Captain François Cluzel
Ministry of Defence
Paris
France

Dr Arne Willy Dahl
Office of the Judge Advocate General
Oslo
Norway

Mr Ige F. Dekker
Twente University
Wagennizer
The Netherlands

Professor Yoram Dinstein
Faculty of Law, Tel Aviv University
Tel Aviv
Israel

Ms Louise Doswald-Beck
Senior Legal Adviser
International Committee of the Red
   Cross
Geneva
Switzerland

Vice-Admiral (ret.) James H. Doyle, Jr
United States Navy
Bethesda, MD
USA

Major Chang Hong Feng
Chinese People's Liberation Army
Beijing
China

Commander William J. Fenrick
Office of the Judge Advocate General
National Defence Headquarters
Ottawa, Ontario
Canada

Dr Horst Fischer
Institut für Friedenssicherungsrecht und
  Humanitäres Völkerrecht
Ruhr University, Bochum
Bochum
Germany

Dr Dieter Fleck
Ministry of Defence
Bonn
Germany

Capitano di Vascello (CM) Pietro
  Francucci
Ministero Difesa-Marina
Rome
Italy

Rear-Admiral Carlos Alberto Frasch
Argentine Navy
Buenos Aires
Argentina

Dr Hans-Peter Gasser
Senior Legal Adviser
International Committee of the Red
  Cross
Geneva
Switzerland

Dr Ugo Genesio
Secretary General
International Institute of Humanitarian
  Law
San Remo
Italy

Dr Andrea Gioia
Pisa University
Pisa
Italy

Mr Blaise Godet
Federal Department of Foreign Affairs
Bern
Switzerland

† Professor Frederick Goldie
Syracuse University
Fayetteville
USA

Professor Leslie C. Green
University of Alberta
Edmonton, Alberta
Canada

Mr Christopher Greenwood
Magdalene College
University of Cambridge
Cambridge
Great Britain

Professor Wolff Heintschel von Heinegg
Institut für Friedenssicherungsrecht und
  Humanitäres Völkerrecht
Ruhr University, Bochum
Bochum
Germany

Dr Geoffrey Heng
International Law Branch
Ministry of Defence Legal Services
Singapore
Republic of Singapore

Dr Cdr Patrick Huyghe
Belgian Navy
De Haan
Belgium

Ms Marie Jacobsson
Ministry for Foreign Affairs
Stockholm
Sweden

Commandant Bertrand Joire-Noulens
Direction Centrale du Commissariat de la
  Marine
Paris
France

Professor Frits Kalshoven
Leyden University
Leiden
The Netherlands

Captain Valery Sergeievitch Knyazev
Russian Navy
Moscow
Russia

Dr Erik Kussbach
Federal Ministry of Foreign Affairs
Vienna
Austria

Captain Johnathan B. R. L. Langdon
Chief Naval Judge Advocate
Greenwich
Great Britain

Captain Shaun Lyons
Chief Naval Judge Advocate
Greenwich
Great Britain

Professor Akira Mayama
Konan University
Kobe
Japan

Professor Djamchid Momtaz
Tehran University
Tehran
Iran

Professor Jovica Patrnogic
Hon. President
International Institute of Humanitarian
    Law
San Remo
Italy

Dr Harry Post
Institute of Public International Law
Utrecht University
Utrecht
The Netherlands

Captain Jan Reksten
Royal Norwegian Navy Training
    Establishment
Haakonsvern
Norway

Captain J. Ashley Roach
Office of the Legal Adviser
US Department of State
Washington
USA

Professor Horace B. Robertson, Jr
Rear Admiral, United States Navy (ret.)
Duke University School of Law
Durham
USA

Professor Natalino Ronzitti
Mission Permanente d'Italie
Geneva
Switzerland

Rear Admiral Frank Rosenius
Kustflottan, HMS Visborg
Harsfjarden
Sweden

Mr Dimitri B. Rurikov
Ministry of Foreign Affairs
Moscow
Russia

Professor Dietrich Schindler
Zurich University
Switzerland

Professor Ivan A. Shearer
Faculty of Law, University of Sydney
Sydney
Australia

Mr Gert-Jan Van Hegelsom
Directorate of Legal Affairs
Ministry of Defence
The Hague
The Netherlands

Professor G. Venturini
University of Studies Milan
Istituto di Diritto e Politica
    Internazionale
Milan
Italy

Professor Raúl Emilio Vinuesa
Facultad de Derecho, Buenos Aires
   University
Buenos Aires
Argentina

Professor Dr B. Vukas
Faculty of Law, Zagreb University
Zagreb
Republic of Croatia

Professor George K. Walker
Wake Forest University School of Law
Winston-Salem, NC
USA

Commander Zhaozhong Zhang
Naval Research Centre
Chinese Navy
Beijing
China

ASSOCIATED EXPERTS AND OBSERVERS

Mr E. Aaro
Naval Tactical School of Haakonsvern
Norway

Captain Kimito Abo
JMSDF Staff College Research Dept
Tokyo
Japan

Captain (N) Robin W. Allen
Maritime Command Headquarters
Halifax
Canada

Professor Harry H. Almond
National Defense University
Washington, DC
USA

Professor Masahiko Asada
Faculty of Law, Okayama University
Okayama
Japan

Dr Stefania Baldini
International Institute of Humanitarian
   Law
San Remo
Italy

Sir Frank D. Berman
Foreign and Commonwealth Office
London
Great Britain

Judge Advocate General Odd Blomdal
Oslo
Norway

Professor Remigiusz Bierzanek
Polish Red Cross
Warsaw
Poland

Botho, Prince of Sayn-Wittgenstein-
   Hohenstein
President
German Red Cross
Bonn
Germany

Mr Antoine Bouvier
International Committee of the Red
   Cross
Geneva
Switzerland

Professor Pierre Bringuier
Université de Rennes
Rennes
France

Professor Lucius Caflisch
Directorate of Public International Law
Foreign Affairs Department
Berne
Switzerland

50

Ms Annick Chalifour
Canadian Red Cross Society
Ottawa
Canada

Professor John G. Crabb
Ferney-Voltaire
France

Captain Téo José de Figueiredo
Brazilian Navy
Rome
Italy

Professor Andrea De Guttry
University of Pisa
Italy

Colonel Frédéric de Mulinen
Director of Military Courses
International Institute of Humanitarian
   Law
San Remo
Italy

Professor Ingrid Detter de Lupis
University of Stockholm
Sweden

Colonel (ret.) Robert Duval
Institut Méditerranéen d'Etudes
   Stratégiques
Faculty of Law, Université de Toulon et
   du Var
Toulon
France

Commander Carl G. Dybeck
Swedish Defence Staff
Stockholm
Sweden

Mr Philippe Eberlin
International Committee of the Red
   Cross
Geneva
Switzerland

Dr T. Eitel
International Law Department
Ministry of Foreign Affairs
Bonn
Germany

Professor José Luis Fernandez Flores
Magistrado Tribunal Supremo
Madrid
Spain

Commander Jean-Louis Fillon
Chef du Bureau du Droit de la Mer
Marine Nationale
Paris
France

Captain Roald Gjelsten
Office of the Judge Advocate General
Oslo
Norway

Commodore P. K. Goel, VSM
Naval Headquarters
New Delhi
India

Mr Juan Carlos Gonzales Barral
Cruz Roja Española
Madrid
Spain

Professor Edward Gordon
The George Washington University
Washington DC
USA

Ambassador Hector Gros Espiell
President
International Institute of Humanitarian
   Law
San Remo
Italy

Mr Theodore Halkiopoulos
Ministry for Foreign Affairs
Athens
Greece

Captain Jaime Harris
Chilean Navy
Valparaiso
Chile

Dr Stein Hegdal
Office of the Judge Advocate General
Oslo
Norway

Mr E. Hildan
Norwegian Shipowners'Association
Oslo
Norway

Professor K. Ipsen
Institut für Friedenssicherungsrecht und
   Humanitäres Völkerrecht
Ruhr University Bochum
Bochum
Germany

Ms Gertrud Ivri
Myrdal Foundation
Stockholm
Sweden

Commander (N) Heinz Dieter Jopp
Ministry of Defence
Bonn
Germany

Professor Paul Kerdiles
Institut Méditerranéen d'Etudes
   Stratégiques
Université de Toulon et du Var
La Garde
France

Mr Thomas Klemp
German Red Cross
Bonn
Germany

Professor Dr R. Lagoni
Institut für Seerecht und Seehandelsrecht
Hamburg University
Hamburg
Germany

Professor Ruth Lapidoth
The Hebrew University
Jerusalem
Israel

Dr Salvatore E. La Rosa
Genoa
Italy

Professor Teofil Lesko
Military Political Academy
Warsaw
Poland

Professor Howard S. Levie
St Louis University
St Louis
USA

Professor Vaughan Lowe
Cambridge University
Cambridge
England

Mr Eric Lucas
Direction Centrale du Commissariat de la
   Marine
Paris
France

Dir. M. Lutken
Naval Tactical School of Haakonsvern
Norway

Captain Ken MacMillan
Department of National Defence
Canada

Sr Eduardo Mallea
Consulado Argentino en Madrid
Madrid
Spain

Ms Sally Mallison
The George Washington University
Washington DC
USA

Mr Thomas Mallison
The George Washington University
Washington DC
USA

Mr Rou Manabe
Ministry of Foreign Affairs
Tokyo
Japan

Captain V. Y. Markov
Naval Force of Russia
Moscow
Russia

Captain Julius Marwoto
Embassy of the Republic of Indonesia
in Rome
Rome
Italy

Professor Akira Mayama
Konan University
Kobe
Japan

Professor Mustapha Mehedi
University of Oran
Oran
Algeria

Professor Samuel Menefee
University of Virginia
Charlottesville
USA

Captain Dr R. A. Moreno
Argentine Navy
Buenos Aires
Argentina

Mr Yoshitoshi Nakamura
Ministry of Foreign Affairs
Tokyo
Japan

Professor Konstantin Obradovic
Institute of International Politics and
    Economy
Belgrade
Yugoslavia

Commander Oguguo
Nigerian Navy
Lagos
Nigeria

Major Steven Ong
Headquarters of the Navy
Singapore
Republic of Singapore

Professor Manuel Perez Gonzalez
Complutense University
Madrid
Spain

Dr Glen Plant
Centre for Environmental Law and
    Policy
London School of Economics and
    Political Science
London
Great Britain

Captain Freg. Raimondo Pollastrini
Istituto di Guerra Marittima
Livorno
Italy

Mr Eugene Prokhorov
Ministry of Foreign Affairs
Moscow
Russia

Captain Lahsene Reghal
Navy Officer
Algiers
Algeria

Captain José Agustin Reilly
Fuerzas Armadas Argentinas
Buenos Aires
Argentina

Professor Michael Reisman
Yale Law School
Yale
USA

Professor Dr E. Riedel
Phillips-Universität Marburg
Marburg
Germany

Mr José Luis Rodriguez Villasante
Spanish Navy
Madrid
Spain

Dr C. G. Roelofsen
State University of Utrecht
Utrecht
The Netherlands

Mr Ilya Rogachev
Ministry of Foreign Affairs
Moscow
Russia

Commander Luiz Guilherme Sa de
    Gusmão
Escola de Guerra Naval
Rio de Janeiro
Brasil

Captain José Sanchez Silva
Escuela Militar de Estudios Juridicos de
    Defensa
Madrid
Spain

Mr Yves Sandoz
Director
International Committee of the Red
    Cross
Geneva
Switzerland

Mr L. Skorpen Hansen
Naval Tactical School of Haakonsvern
Norway

† Professor Waldemar A. Solf
Washington College of Law Institute
Alexandria
USA

Mr Laurent Stefanini
Ministry of Foreign Affairs
Paris
France

Dipl. Ing. Hans Jürgen Stein
Siemens AG
Unterschleissheim
Germany

Major Wei Ming Tan
Ministry of Defence Legal Services
Singapore
Republic of Singapore

Professor Tadashi Tanaka
Daito Bunka University
Tokyo
Japan

Major Ronnie Tay
Legal Services Naval Staff
Singapore
Republic of Singapore

Rear-Admiral (ret.) Jean Thery
Institut Méditerranéen d'Etudes
    Stratégiques
Faculty of Law, Université de Toulon et
    du Var
La Garde
France

Lieutenant Commander Fredrik Thuesen
Royal Norwegian Navy Training
    Establishment
Haakonsvern
Norway

Captain Guillermo Valenzuela
Dirección General del Personal de la
    Armada
Valparaiso
Chile

Generale Pietro Verri
International Institute of Humanitarian
   Law
San Remo
Italy

Mr A. Vestrheim
Office of the Judge Advocate General
Oslo
Norway

Captain Alex Waghorn Jarpa
Chilean Naval Mission
London
Great Britain

Major Feng Wei
Military Legislative Affairs Bureau
Beijing
China

Professor Bodgan Wierzbicki
Warsaw University
Bialystok
Poland

Mr Georg Witschel
Ministry of Foreign Affairs
Bonn
Germany

Major Lui Tuck Yew
Singapore Navy
Republic of Singapore

Colonel Janye Zhu
Chinese People's Liberation Army
Beijing
China

ADMINISTRATIVE AND SECRETARIAL STAFF

Ms Alessandra Armando
International Institute of Humanitarian
   Law
San Remo
Italy

Ms Patricia Di Pietro
International Institute of Humanitarian
   Law
San Remo
Italy

Ms Paola Perazzoli
International Institute of Humanitarian
   Law
San Remo
Italy

Ms Janine Rossier
International Committee of the Red
         Cross
Geneva
Switzerland

SAN REMO MANUAL
on
INTERNATIONAL LAW APPLICABLE
TO ARMED CONFLICTS AT SEA

Prepared by

International Lawyers and Naval Experts

convened by the IIHL

Adopted in June 1994

EXPLANATION

Editor

Louise Doswald-Beck

Authors

Professor Salah El-Din Amer
Ms Louise Doswald-Beck
Vice-Admiral James H. Doyle, Jr, US Navy (ret.)
Commander William J. Fenrick
Mr Christopher Greenwood
Professor Wolff Heintschel von Heinegg
Professor Horace B. Robertson, Jr, Rear-Admiral, US Navy (ret.)
Mr Gert-Jan F. Van Hegelsom

CONTENTS

Contents

INTRODUCTION

Background

The San Remo Manual was prepared during the period 1988–94 by a group of legal and naval experts participating in their personal capacity in a series of Round Tables convened for this purpose by the International Institute of Humanitarian Law. A preliminary Round Table on International Humanitarian Law Applicable to Armed Conflicts at Sea, held in San Remo in 1987 on the initiative of the International Institute of Humanitarian Law, in co-operation with the University of Pisa and the University of Syracuse in New York, discussed the need for a modernisation of the law applicable to armed conflicts at sea. The Declaration adopted at that meeting noted that:

> new technologies and methods of warfare, new developments in the law of armed conflict and in the law of the sea and the increased possibilities of grave harm to the environment as a result of armed conflict at sea, require study in the light of the principles [of international law applicable in armed conflict] ...

It was only in the subsequent meeting at Madrid, convened by the International Institute of Humanitarian Law with the support of the Spanish Red Cross in 1989, that participants decided on a plan of action to study systematically these issues and to draft a restatement of the contemporary law applicable to armed conflicts at sea together with some proposals for progressive development.

Motivation for the development of the Manual

The Round Table of Madrid felt the need to embark on such a project for a number of interconnected reasons. First, treaty law on the conduct of hostilities at sea is not only fragmentary but also mostly dates back to 1907, thus requiring an assessment of the continuing validity of its provisions in the light of later developments in customary law. Other instruments of importance, namely, the unratified London Declaration concerning the Laws of Naval War of 1909 and the Oxford Manual on the Laws of Naval War Governing the Relations Between Belligerents adopted by the Institute of International Law in 1913 reflected the customary law of that time but could not be relied on as a reliable guide to contemporary law.

Secondly, new technology and modern methods and means of warfare have put into question the continuing viability of the whole of the traditional legal regime which was based on nineteenth-century conditions. The traditional law on the conduct of hostilities at sea took into account humanitarian needs and neutral interests, by specifying rules on visit, search and capture of merchant vessels and the protection of passengers and crew, in ways which were suitable for sailing ships and means of warfare used in earlier centuries. A modern restatement of the law needs to apply the principles and basic rules of international humanitarian law to modern naval warfare, whilst taking into account factors which are specific to naval warfare, in particular, measures of economic warfare related to the taking of prizes and the effect of belligerent naval operations on neutrals.

Thirdly, the law applicable to armed conflict on land had been updated by Protocols I and II of 1977 additional to the Geneva Conventions of 1949. Although some provisions of Additional Protocol I affect naval operations, in particular those supplementing the protection given to medical vessels and aircraft in the Second Geneva Convention of 1949, Part IV of the Protocol, which protects civilians against the effects of hostilities, is only applicable to naval operations which affect civilians and civilian objects on land. The participants believed that it was necessary to establish the extent to which changes in the law of land warfare have nevertheless affected State practice in relation to principles and rules applicable to armed conflict at sea.

Fourthly, given the important developments in other branches of international law since the beginning of this century, namely, the law of the sea, the United Nations Charter, environmental law and air law, it was considered essential to evaluate the extent to which the law applicable to armed conflicts at sea is affected by such developments.

Finally, as all these factors have had the effect of introducing a great deal of uncertainty in the present state of the law, with the result that discussions on the subject have tended to concentrate on the many areas of controversy, it was decided that the most productive approach would be to discuss one aspect of the law at a time, to concentrate first on identifying areas of agreement and drafting these results and then to try to find possible common ground on controversial subjects.

Purpose and nature of the Manual

The participants in Madrid hoped that the results of such an endeavour by a group of specialists in international law and naval experts from different countries would aid the dissemination and the comprehension of the contemporary law, and would encourage the drafting of national naval manuals with a certain uniformity.

Given the extent of uncertainty in the law, they decided that it was premature to think in terms of a draft treaty, but rather that it was more appropriate to work on a document that would be a modern equivalent of the Oxford Manual of 1913 which should in itself promote a better comprehension and development of the law. Thus the Manual is not meant to be a binding document but it is of course not excluded that some or all of it could serve as a basis for diplomatic conferences at a later stage.

The International Committee of the Red Cross, which has the internationally recognised mandate of preparing developments in international humanitarian law, actively supported this project.

The Madrid Plan of Action

The Plan of Action as adopted at Madrid read as follows:

Plan of action for the promotion of the law of armed conflicts at sea in particular international humanitarian law applicable in armed conflicts at sea, 1989–1992

I Subjects to be dealt with in each future meeting of experts

1   Military objectives in the law of naval warfare:
    (i)   The principle of distinction;
    (ii)   Legal status of the merchant ship in the law of naval warfare:
        (a)   when is it a military objective?
        (b)   other matters, e.g., the effect of arming;
    (iii)   Target identification, including the enhanced risk of perfidy.

2   Methods and means of combat in naval warfare:
    (i)   Mines, missiles, torpedoes and other weapon systems;
    (ii)   State practice in relation to exclusion zones.

3   Protection of different categories of victims of armed conflicts at sea:
    –   rescue
    –   transport of civilians and prisoners of war
    –   communications of hospital ships
    –   identification of hospital ships and rescue craft and other protected craft
    –   any others

4   Visit, search and seizure – conditions of applicability.

5   Regions of operations in naval warfare (different maritime areas).

II Method of work, organisation and form of future meetings

1   Each meeting is to last approximately five days and comprise not more than 20 experts, bearing in mind fair geographical representation.

2   The desired result of each meeting is to draft a type of 'restatement' of accepted law governing the subject, possibly together with some proposals.

3   In preparation of the meeting, one or more persons is to prepare a report on the law governing the subject and, if suitable, some proposals. The purpose of this is that the reports could be used as a basis for discussion. These reports should be distributed to the other participants three months in advance.

4   Notice is to be given in due time (approximately one year) for each meeting as well as the request to prepare a report.

5   The meetings listed are not in a definitive chronological order.

It should be noted that although the participants agreed to the adoption of this plan, many of them at the time were very sceptical as to whether this project would be a success given the difficulties involved. It is for this reason that the Plan of Action was worded relatively restrictively and did not include all the subjects that are in fact now covered in the Manual. It will be noted in this regard that the work terminated in 1994 and not in 1992 as originally envisaged. The success of the operation as it developed encouraged the participants to draft a more extensive manual than that originally planned although it is not an exhaustive indication of the law. In particular, it does not deal with the whole question of State responsibility for violations of the law and war criminality nor with means of implementation and enforcement of the law. Participants felt that the general rules of international humanitarian law applicable to armed conflicts on land and international law in general also applied here, and they decided not to embark on a Part dealing with this subject in the Manual. The Manual also does not expressly deal with non-international armed conflicts, but, as will be seen in the explanation to paragraph 1 of the Manual, non-international armed conflicts are not expressly excluded, thus encouraging the application of the humanitarian rules contained in this Manual to possible naval operations undertaken during such conflicts. Of course, the provisions of this Manual are without any prejudice to international humanitarian law applicable to armed conflicts on land and to air combat over the land territory of the parties to the conflict.

The process

The Plan of Action already specified part of the process by which it was expected to draft the Manual, but of course the actual process was more detailed. All the Round Tables were convened by the International Institute of Humanitarian Law and were held with the support of institutions in the cities in which they were held. In addition, support was given by the International Committee of the Red Cross throughout the process.

The first Round Table was held in Bochum, Germany, in November 1989 with the support of the Institute of Peacekeeping Law and Humanitarian Law of the Ruhr-Universität, Bochum, and the German Red Cross. The subject was the first on the Madrid Plan of Action, namely, *The Military Objective and the Principle of Distinction in the Law of Naval Warfare*. The Rapporteur who had been chosen for this topic was Commander William Fenrick (Ministry of Defence, Canada) who wrote for this Round Table an extensive report covering the historical background, existing treaty law and State practice, and at the end of the report proposed some conclusions. This report was sent to all the participants three months before the meeting and the participants were invited to submit comments to the report. These comments were in turn sent to all the participants before the meeting. During the meeting itself, each of the main issues dealt with by the Rapporteur was assigned to a working session and a discussion leader was appointed for each working session. The task of the discussion leader was to make a short introductory statement to the session in order to structure the discussion. For this purpose, he analysed the opinions of the Rapporteur on the issue to be discussed in that working session and the comments on that issue that had been sent by the participants. On the basis of this, he then proposed the topics needing discussion and the method and order of such discussion. After discussion in plenary, during which the participants concentrated on identifying points of agreement or possible accommodation, the discussion leader was given the task of making an initial draft of the conclusions of that working session. Towards the end of the Round Table, all the discussion leaders, the Rapporteur and the Editor met as a drafting group in order to draft the overall conclusions of that Round Table. The results of the drafting group were submitted to the Round Table as a whole at the last session and agreed alterations made.

It was noted at Bochum that the results of the first Round Table were bound to be provisional as most of the law governing armed conflict at sea is interlinked, and that therefore modifications would need to be made at later stages in the light of subsequent discussions on other subjects. This was indeed done at later Round Tables, which followed exactly the same procedure that had proved so useful at Bochum.

The Second Round Table met in Toulon, France, in October 1990 with the support of the Institut Méditerranéen d'Etudes Stratégiques, the University of Toulon and the French Red Cross. The subject discussed was *Methods and Means of Combat in Naval Warfare* and the Rapporteur was Mr Gert-Jan F. Van Hegelsom (Ministry of Defence, The Netherlands).

The Third Round Table was held in Bergen, Norway, in September 1991 with the support of the Norwegian Navy School of Tactics and the Norwegian Red Cross. Two subjects were discussed at this meeting. The first was *Visit, Search, Diversion and Capture* for which the Rapporteur was Dr. Wolff Heintschel von Heinegg (Ruhr–Universität, Bochum). The second subject was *The Effect of the United Nations Charter on the Law of Naval Warfare* which did not expressly feature on the Madrid Plan of Action but the participants decided that it was essential to deal with it given the extensive discussions that inevitably occurred on this topic. The special Rapporteur appointed for this subject was Mr Christopher Greenwood (Cambridge University).

A major procedural decision was made by the Round Table at Bergen, namely, that it was essential to draft a commentary that should appear at the same time as the Manual itself. The reason for this decision was that the readers of the Manual need an explanation of the legal bases and the reasoning underlying the adoption of the provisions of the Manual and that this commentary (later termed the 'Explanation') should also indicate those provisions which were the subject of disagreement between the participants. It was also decided that the commentary should include an indication of those provisions which are in the nature of a progressive development of the law as well as those which are the result of a certain compromise between participants. The Rapporteurs agreed to be responsible for drafting this commentary for those parts of the Manual for which they had initially submitted the main report.

The Fourth Round Table was held in Ottawa, Canada, in September 1992 with the support of the Department of National Defence and the Canadian Red Cross. The subject discussed was *Regions of Operations of Naval Warfare – Different Maritime Areas* and the Rapporteur was Professor Horace Robertson (Rear-Admiral, US Navy (ret.), Duke University).

After the meeting of the Round Table at Ottawa, the Rapporteurs met with the Editor in order to embark on the first of a series of 'harmonisation meetings'. This harmonisation group undertook the task of harmonising the terminology used in the various documents adopted at the end of each Round Table, deciding on a logical order of paragraphs, and reviewing the commentary that was written by the Rapporteurs for the Explanation. The first meeting of the harmonisation group also decided to accept the offer of Vice-Admiral James Doyle, US Navy (ret.) to prepare a special report together with proposals on the law applicable to aircraft during naval operations, in particular with regard to military operations affecting civil aircraft. The Round Table in Bergen had simply accepted that the provisions applicable to merchant vessels applied *mutatis mutandis* to civil aircraft, on the understanding that this subject needed subsequent examination and proper formulation.

The Fifth Round Table was held in Geneva in September 1993 in cooperation with the International Committee of the Red Cross. The principal subject discussed was the *Protection of Victims of Armed Conflicts at Sea* and the Rapporteur was Ms Louise Doswald-Beck (International Committee of the Red Cross). Also discussed at this session were two subjects which the Round Table in Ottawa decided needed further study, namely, the protection of the environment and the question whether a distinction should be made, for the purposes of the Manual, between 'neutrality' and 'non-belligerency'. A special report and a background paper on the environment were prepared by Professor Salah El-Din Amer (Cairo University) and Lieutenant-Colonel Kim Carter (Ministry of Defence, Canada) respectively. A special report and a background paper on the question of neutrality and non-belligerency were written by Professor Dietrich Schindler (University of Zurich) and Dr Wolff Heintschel von Heinegg respectively. We must note here with gratitude that Professor Schindler wrote the commentary to paragraph 13(1) on this subject in the Explanation.

A second meeting of the harmonisation group took place in Geneva after the Round Table and a third more lengthy meeting took place in Geneva at the headquarters of the ICRC in March 1994 in order to finalise the harmonised text of the Manual, including the draft paragraphs relating to civil aircraft, and to finalise the Explanation. Both documents were then sent to all participants in preparation for the final Round Table in Livorno.

The Round Table in Livorno, held in June 1994 with the support of the Istituto di Guerra Marittima of the Italian Navy, first had the task of deciding on the inclusion or otherwise of contentious paragraphs or words that remained in square brackets from earlier meetings. A particular group of squared brackets that appeared in various places throughout the text related to the choice between 'due regard' or 'respect' as the standard to be observed by parties to the armed conflict in relation to the peacetime rights of neutrals in areas of belligerent operations and to the protection of the environment in such areas. A special paper on the use of these terms in international humanitarian law treaties and in law of the sea treaties was prepared by Captain Ashley Roach (Department of State, USA) in order to facilitate discussion in Livorno.

The Round Table in Livorno then had the task of deciding on whether it approved of the paragraphs on aircraft proposed by the harmonisation group, before making one last review of the entire text to determine whether any adjustments were needed. After approval of the text, the participants decided to accept the Explanation written by the harmonisation group, but without formal approval of the latter text as such, as the Explanation was accepted as being the responsibility of the authors.

The participants

The Madrid Plan of Action proposed that the work be undertaken by a group of about twenty experts, taking into account geographical representation. In practice about twenty-five experts personally attended all or most of the meetings, but each meeting was attended by about forty persons. The difference in numbers is due to several factors. First, some specialist experts were invited to some of the meetings in order to contribute their expertise to a specific issue. Secondly, interested observers attended some of the meetings and sometimes participated in discussions. Thirdly, some persons attended by virtue of their function, for example the senior Judge Advocates of certain navies (although, as with all participants, they attended in their personal capacity), but the individuals changed from time to time. Finally, some individuals attended only the first one or two meetings or only the last one or two meetings, but nevertheless made useful contributions to the work.

As the title page of the Manual indicates, the participants were a mixture of specialists in international law and naval experts, the latter comprising both operational and non-operational personnel. Overall, about a third of the participants were academic personnel and the others were governmental personnel attending in their personal capacity.

Sources used to determine the content of the Manual

Apart from existing treaties, a great deal of stress was placed on State practice during this century, in particular practice since the Second World War, in order to establish the content of contemporary international customary law. This practice comprised actual behaviour during conflicts by belligerents and reactions by neutrals as well as the content of recently drafted national manuals. Some reference was also made to the writings of publicists as a subsidiary source and, where appropriate, note was taken of any relevant judicial decisions. Of particular value also was the advice and practical information given by naval practitioners who participated in the Round Tables.

Innovations in the content of the Manual

The San Remo Manual differs in many respects from the Oxford Manual of 1913, and contains some elements that may at first sight seem surprising. The most obvious point in this respect is the inclusion of two Sections in Part I relating to the *jus ad bellum*, namely, Section II on the law of self-defence and Section III on the situation applicable where the United Nations Security Council has taken action. After very extensive debate on this issue, the majority of participants were of the opinion that some indication of the effect of the United Nations Charter was necessary. The principal reason for this decision was the recognition of the fact that the traditional law of war, which came into operation during a formal state of war, gave belligerents extensive powers over neutral shipping which could continue to be exercised until a formal peace treaty was concluded. It needed to be established whether these rules remain valid in whole or in part in the post-Charter era, in which conflicts are not usually legally characterised as war, and in which the resort to force is limited to self-defence or as provided for by the United Nations Charter. The direct reference to the rules of the United Nations Charter in Part I of the Manual indicates that the Round Table fully took into account its legal effects in order to conclude that many of the traditional rules continue to be applicable despite the absence of a formal state of war and that the law applies equally to all belligerents irrespective of which belligerent is guilty of aggression. The majority of participants were also of the opinion, as reflected in the Manual, that the rights of belligerents are affected by the restraints of the law of self-defence and that this will affect the rights of belligerents to make full use of all the methods of naval warfare that the traditional law automatically allowed once a state of war existed. This is particularly the case with regard to the institution of various measures of economic warfare against neutral shipping, such as the capture of contraband, and other measures affecting the economic interests of neutral nations, such as the institution of a blockade. These participants thought that the requirements of the law of self-defence, namely, necessity and proportionality, would have the effect of limiting the extent to which such measures could be taken, thus having a restraining influence on the effect of the war. It was also thought important to indicate the situation of neutrals once the Security Council has taken a decision under Chapter VII, and that forces implementing enforcement action by the United Nations are bound to respect the rules of international humanitarian law.

Closely linked with this issue is the designation given in the Manual to States that are not party to the conflict. It will be noticed that the Round Table decided to make reference to such as States as 'neutral' as is the case in the four Geneva Conventions of 1949, rather than as 'neutral or other State which is not party to the conflict' as used in Additional Protocol I of 1977. The participants carefully debated whether there should be a distinction made between rules applicable to 'non-belligerents' and those applicable to 'neutrals' and decided that such a distinction should not be recognised for the purposes of the Manual as the designation of a State as 'neutral' or 'non-belligerent' would be inevitably arbitrary and this would therefore introduce extreme uncertainty with regard to the rules applicable to the shipping of States not party to the conflict and to the protection of the waters of such States.

A new element of major importance in this Manual compared with the traditional law is the introduction of the concept of the 'military objective'. In the traditional law, the only ships which could be attacked on sight were belligerent warships and auxiliaries, but a number of military measures could be taken against both belligerent and neutral shipping which helped the enemy's war effort, but which only in certain specific instances and subject to certain conditions allowed destruction of the vessels concerned. The introduction this century of new means of warfare, in particular submarines and aircraft, has led to difficulty with regard to the implementation of the traditional law and to attacks on merchant shipping by these means. Based on recent State practice, and on the concept of the military objective found in Additional Protocol I, the Round Table decided to introduce this concept into naval operations in order to limit the lawfulness of attacks to merchant vessels which directly help the military action of the enemy, whilst retaining the possibility of traditional measures short of attack in relation to other defined vessels. The purpose of this measure is to take into account modern means of warfare and genuine military needs, whilst respecting the gains made since the Second World War in international humanitarian law applicable to land warfare which provides protection for civilian persons and objects.

Another innovation is the inclusion of paragraphs on the rules applicable to zones which belligerents might establish and which adversely affect the use by others of certain areas of the sea (often referred to as 'exclusion zones'). There was a certain amount of controversy amongst the participants as to whether rules applicable to such zones should be included in the Manual, for it was feared that doing so could encourage the belief that they are clearly lawful. The majority of participants, however, thought that it was more useful to be pragmatic in this regard as such zones have been established and would probably continue to be used. Therefore, they thought it wise to specify certain criteria and restrictions so as to prevent the abusive establishment of zones as well as behaviour within the zone that would contravene international humanitarian law.

A major innovation of importance is the clarification of which military operations may be carried out in certain parts of the sea, taking into account the new peacetime legal regimes applicable to certain sea areas which have been established over the last few decades. It is also noteworthy that the Round Table attempted to take into account developments in environmental law, although the extent to which many of these treaties are formally applicable during armed conflict is uncertain, as well as the need to pay due regard to the needs of the environment in general.

Finally, it may be noted that many provisions in the Manual relate to aircraft which are either involved in naval operations, or which may be affected by naval action. There was a certain amount of uncertainty as to the extent to which the peacetime law of civil aviation is formally applicable to armed conflicts and therefore the attempt was made to marry as pragmatically as possible military considerations, including the requirements of international humanitarian law, with international civil aviation rules. It was decided that although the Manual relates to international law applicable to armed conflicts at sea, aircraft are in practice involved to a great degree in such operations, and that therefore an academic approach which would not refer to aircraft would be impracticable and not reflect reality. Of course, the provisions on aircraft in the Manual do not refer to air operations over land.

Related publications

A full report of the San Remo meeting held in 1987 is reproduced in volume 14, number 4, of the *Syracuse Journal of International Law and Commerce*, 1988.

The reports and special papers prepared for the Round Tables and the comments thereto submitted in writing by the participants have been published in the original English in the *Bochumer Schriften zur Friedensicherung und zum Humanitären Völkerrecht*, edited by Professor Wolff Heintschel von Heinegg.

Language

All the work relating to the development of the Manual and the Explanation was in English and is the original language of these documents.

Louise Doswald-Beck
Editor

ABBREVIATIONS

AC	Appeal Cases (Great Britain)
AJIL	American Journal of International Law
Ann. Dig.	Annual Digest of Public International Law Cases
API, **Additional Protocol I**	1977 Protocol Additional to the Geneva Conventions of 12 August 1949, and relating to the Protection of Victims of International Armed Conflicts
BVR	Beyond visual range
Canadian Manual, **Canadian Draft Manual**	Canadian forces law of armed conflict manual (second draft)
Certain Conventional **Weapons Convention**	1980 United Nations Convention on Prohibitions or Restrictions on the Use of Certain Conventional Weapons Which May be Deemed to be Excessively Injurious or to Have Indiscriminate Effects
Chicago Convention	1944 Convention on International Civil Aviation
Enmod Convention	1976 Convention on the Prohibition of Military or any Other Hostile Use of Environmental Modification Techniques
EPIL	Encyclopaedia of Public International Law
GCI, **First Geneva Convention**	1949 Geneva Convention (I) for the Amelioration of the Condition of Wounded and Sick in Armed Forces in the Field
GCII, **Second Geneva Convention**	1949 Geneva Convention (II) for the Amelioration of the Wounded, Sick and Shipwrecked Members of Armed Forces at Sea
GCIII, **Third Geneva Convention**	1949 Geneva Convention (III) relative to the Treatment of Prisoners of War

GCIV, **Fourth Geneva Convention**	1949 Geneva Convention (IV) relative to the Protection of Civilian Persons in Time of War
German Manual	Humanitarian Law in Armed Conflicts – Manual – (English translation of German tri-service manual *ZDv 15/2 Humanitäres Völkerrecht in bewaffneten Konflikten – Handbuch*)
HRAW	1923 Hague Rules of Aerial Warfare
ICAO	International Civil Aviation Organisation
ICJ	International Court of Justice
ICRC	International Committee of the Red Cross
ILR	International Law Reports
IMO	International Maritime Organisation
ITU	International Telecommunication Union
LlPC	Lords Prize Cases
LNTS	League of Nations Treaty Series
LOS Convention	1982 United Nations Convention on the Law of the Sea
LRTWC	UN War Crimes Commission, Law Reports of Trials of War Criminals
NOTAM	Notice to Airmen
NWP9	US Navy, The Commander's Handbook on the Law of Naval Operations
NWP9A	US Navy, Annotated Supplement to the Commander's Handbook on the Law of Naval Operations, NWP9 (REV.A)/FMFM 1-10
OTH	Over the horizon
RGDIP	Revue général de droit international public
RIAA	Reports of International Arbitral Awards
UN	United Nations
WVR	Wörterbuch des Völkerrechts

PART I

GENERAL PROVISIONS

Section I Scope of application of the law

1　　**The parties to an armed conflict at sea are bound by the principles and rules of international humanitarian law from the moment armed force is used.**

1.1　　International humanitarian law, as defined in paragraph 13 of this document, applies to all armed conflicts from the moment that force is used and therefore its application does not depend on a 'state of war' nor on attaining a particular threshold of intensity of the hostilities. Reference in this regard can be made to the ICRC Commentary to Article 2 of the Geneva Conventions which defines the use of the word 'armed conflict' for the purposes of the application of the law as follows:

> Any difference arising between two States and leading to the intervention of members of the armed forces is an armed conflict within the meaning of Article 2, even if one of the Parties denies the existence of a state of war. It makes no difference how long the conflict lasts, or how much slaughter takes place.[1]

The purpose for the application of the law from the moment that any force is used is in order to assure that the rules providing limits on the conduct of hostilities and protection for non-State parties and protected persons and objects are indeed implemented and that parties cannot absolve themselves of these rules by denying that an armed conflict exists.

Therefore, in the naval context, any clash between the naval forces of two or more States may be said to be an armed conflict within this definition. However, it should be noted that although the provisions of this Manual are primarily meant to apply to international armed conflicts at sea, this has intentionally not been expressly indicated in paragraph 1 in order not to dissuade the implementation of these rules in non-international armed conflicts involving naval operations.

1　*ICRC Commentary on Geneva Convention II for the Amelioration of the Condition of Wounded, Sick and Shipwrecked Members of Armed Forces at Sea*, 1960 (ed.) Jean S. Pictet, p. 28. Although Article 2 of the Geneva Conventions only refers expressly to armed conflicts in which a state of war is not recognised by one of the parties, it has generally been interpreted as applying to an armed conflict in which none of the parties regard themselves as being in a state of war.

1.2   International humanitarian law includes for the purposes of this document both the law on the conduct of hostilities (sometimes referred to as 'Hague Law") and the law on the protection of victims of armed conflicts (so-called 'Geneva Law"). It therefore incorporates the rules applicable to armed conflict at sea contained in international customary law and treaties such as the Hague Conventions of 1907, the Geneva Protocol of 1925, the Geneva Conventions of 1949 and their Additional Protocols of 1977. The provisions in this document are obviously without prejudice to the rules applicable to land warfare and do not affect the rules regarding aerial warfare above belligerent territory.

1.3   Although it is clear that parties to a conflict are bound to respect the protective rules of international humanitarian law from the moment armed force is used, it is less clear if all the traditional rules relating to the duties of neutral States automatically come into operation at the same time. This relates in particular to the traditional rights of belligerents with regard to economic warfare against neutral merchant shipping and the duties of neutrals with regard to the use by belligerents of the sea areas under the jurisdiction of neutral States. It is implicit in the present text that their application is not dependent on the existence of a formal state of war. State practice, particularly since the Second World War, suggests, however, that they are not automatically applicable in their entirety as soon as fighting breaks out. Thus, the rules considered in paragraphs 18–22, 93–104 and 118–158 have not generally been treated as automatically applicable to any conflict, irrespective of its scale or duration. However, it is clear that once measures of economic warfare against neutral shipping or aircraft are carried out by a belligerent, the rules indicated in this document must be respected.

2   **In cases not covered by this document or by international agreements, civilians and combatants remain under the protection and authority of the principles of international law derived from established custom, from the principles of humanity and from the dictates of the public conscience.**

2.1   This provision is a modern version of the famous 'Martens Clause' which appeared in the Preamble to Hague Convention No IV respecting the Laws and Customs of War on Land, 1907, and in Article 1(2) of Additional Protocol I. Its presence here serves as a reminder that the mere fact that an issue is not addressed by a specific provision of the text does not mean that it is not regulated by international law nor that a belligerent enjoys a free hand.

Section II Armed conflicts and the law of self-defence

<u>Preliminary remark</u>

Paragraphs 3–5 form a whole and are to be read together.

3   **The exercise of the right of individual or collective self-defence recognised in Article 51 of the Charter of the United Nations is subject to the conditions and limitations laid down in the Charter, and arising from general international law, including in particular the principles of necessity and proportionality.**

3.1   Unlike the other provisions in the present text, this paragraph is concerned solely with the *jus ad bellum*. It is based upon the view, which met with general agreement, that, in the absence of some form of United Nations authorisation (a matter which is considered in Section III), the principal ground on which a State is justified in resorting to armed force is in exercise of the right of self-defence. This right is not created by Article 51 of the United Nations Charter, which describes the right as 'inherent', but is derived from customary international law and preserved by the Charter. Paragraph 3 makes clear that a State which uses force in exercise of the right of self-defence must comply with the requirements of Article 51, which provides:

> Nothing in the present Charter shall impair the inherent right of individual or collective self-defence if an armed attack occurs against a member of the United Nations, until the Security Council has taken measures necessary to maintain international peace and security. Measures taken by members in the exercise of this right of self-defence shall be immediately reported to the Security Council and shall not affect the authority and responsibility of the Security Council to take at any time such action as it deems necessary in order to maintain or restore international peace and security.

3.2   There was some discussion of the precise nature of those requirements, in particular of the question what degree of action on the part of the Security Council was sufficient to constitute 'measures necessary to maintain international peace and security' and thus to preclude further action in self-defence. The view of the majority of participants, however, was that it was not necessary for a text dealing with the laws of naval warfare to take a position on these questions. Nor does the text take a position on the controversial question whether there is a right of anticipatory self-defence. The provisions of the Charter are therefore dealt with only in so far as they have repercussions on the conduct of hostilities at sea.

3.3   In addition to the requirements expressly laid down by Article 51 of the Charter, the exercise of the right of self-defence is also subject to the principles of necessity and proportionality. These principles are derived from customary international law and were an inherent part of the right of self-defence before the adoption of the Charter. Their continued application after 1945 was reaffirmed by the International Court of Justice in the *Case Concerning Military and Paramilitary Activities in and Against Nicaragua*[2] and was recognised by both parties in that case.

2   ICJ Reports, 1986, p. 3, para. 194; 76 ILR 1 at p. 437.

The effect of these principles is that a State which is the victim of an armed attack is entitled to resort to force against the attacker but only to the extent necessary to defend itself and to achieve such defensive goals as repelling the attack, recovering territory and removing threats to its future security. These principles do not require that a State which is attacked use only the degree and kind of force that has been used against it but that the force employed by the State acting in self-defence be proportionate to what is required for the achievement of legitimate objectives of self-defence.

4   **The principles of necessity and proportionality apply equally to armed conflict at sea and require that the conduct of hostilities by a State [3] should not exceed the degree and kind of force, not otherwise prohibited by the law of armed conflict, required to repel an armed attack against it and to restore its security.**

4.1   The view of the Rapporteur was that this paragraph followed inevitably from paragraph 3. Once it is accepted that the right of self-defence is subject to the limitations imposed by the principles of necessity and proportionality, he maintained that it followed that a State resorting to force in exercise of the right of self-defence had to comply both with the law of armed conflict *jus in bello* and with the principle that it must not use excessive force. That view attracted sufficient support to be reflected in paragraph 4 of this document.

4.2   In effect, this paragraph enshrines two principles:

(a)   a State which resorts to force in exercise of the right of self-defence must not exceed the degree and kind of force necessary to achieve those goals which the right of self-defence permits it to achieve by force, namely repelling the attack against it, recovering territory which had been lost as a result of the armed attack and restoring its security against a repetition of the armed attack. According to this principle, even if the degree and kind of force used by a State is not incompatible with the law of armed conflict (in that it is directed only against military objectives and employs only methods and means of warfare which are not prohibited), it will still be unlawful if it exceeds what is necessary to achieve those goals, since it will no longer fall within the right of self-defence;

(b)   conversely, the fact that an act may be a necessary and proportionate measure of self-defence cannot justify it if it involves a violation of the laws of armed conflict.

4.3   The second principle was accepted by all participants without question. The first principle, however, was challenged by several participants who argued that the rules of the *jus ad bellum* applied only until the outbreak of an armed conflict. Once a State became engaged in an armed conflict, it was argued, that State was subject only to the law of armed conflict and the law of neutrality. This is because the law of armed conflict contains its own principles of necessity and proportionality, the effect of which is summed up in the following passage from the United States Navy's *The Commander's Handbook on the Law of Naval Operations*:

---

3   The use of the singular includes the plural where appropriate throughout this document.

(1)   Only that degree and kind of force, not otherwise prohibited by the law of armed conflict, required for the partial or complete submission of the enemy with a minimum expenditure of time, life and physical resources may be applied.

(2)   The employment of any kind or degree of force not required for the purpose of the partial or complete submission of the enemy with a minimum expenditure of time, life and physical resources is prohibited.[4]

4.4   This passage and the principles set out in paragraph 4 of this document are similar in that both regard as unlawful the employment of force which is not necessary for the defeat of the enemy, even if the degree and kind of force employed is not otherwise inconsistent with the law of armed conflict. Where they differ is that the passage quoted from *The Commander's Handbook* insists only that the degree and kind of force used must not exceed what is necessary for the partial or complete submission of the enemy. It does not address the question whether the State concerned is entitled to seek the partial or complete submission of the enemy, since it treats that as a question for the *jus ad bellum*. Paragraph 4 of this document, however, is based upon the assumption that a State exercising the right of self-defence will be entitled only to seek to achieve those goals which fall within the concept of self-defence and which are discussed above. Whether that will include seeking the partial or complete submission of the enemy will depend upon the circumstances of each case and is considered in the commentary to paragraph 5.

4.5   The application of the principles set out in paragraph 4 was the subject of some further controversy. The disagreement centred on whether the principles of necessity and proportionality are applicable in a strategic sense only, or also on a tactical level. Those in favour of the latter approach thought that the application of the principles of necessity and proportionality could affect hostilities at all levels of the conflict in that they would restrict the choice of targets, the use of methods and means of warfare and measures taken against neutral shipping taken not only in accordance with the rules of international humanitarian law, but also in accordance with whether they would be necessary and proportionate to the needs of self-defence of the parties. Those participants who were not in favour of this approach were of the opinion that the principles of necessity and proportionality cannot affect tactical behaviour once an action in self-defence has commenced and that these principles rather affect only strategic decisions on how to achieve the needs of self-defence.

4.6   The paragraph as worded does not specify whether its implementation may affect tactical decisions, but in any event, once the needs of self-defence are met, that is, the armed attack has been repelled and the security of the attacked party restored, further hostile actions are not necessary. Therefore the fact that a state of war is still technically in being, or that there has been no formal peace treaty or formal termination of the conflict, will not justify further hostilities if they are not necessary for the security of the party concerned.

---

4   US Department of the Navy, Office of the Chief of Naval Operations, *The Commander's Handbook on the Law of Naval Operations* (NWP9A) (Washington: US Government Printer's Office, 1989), para. 5.2 [hereinafter *The Commander's Handbook*].

5   How far a State is justified in its military actions against the enemy will depend upon the intensity and scale of the armed attack for which the enemy is responsible and the gravity of the threat posed.

5.1   This paragraph also proved controversial. The majority of participants considered that there were circumstances in which the scale of an armed attack, the threat which it posed and the likelihood of further threats to the security of the State which was attacked, even if the immediate attack were repelled, might be such that it would be a legitimate measure of self-defence for the victim of that attack to seek the total defeat of the armed forces of its enemy. For many of the members of that majority this conclusion was a prerequisite of their acceptance of the principles enshrined in paragraph 4. Therefore, they were prepared to accept the notion that the law of self-defence limited the freedom to conduct hostilities only on the basis that, if the circumstances so required, a State might be entitled in self-defence to seek the total defeat of its enemy, although they accepted that this would be an exceptional situation.

5.2   A minority of participants, however, took the view that a State was never entitled under modern international law to seek the total defeat of its enemy, since it considered that that could never be justified by reference to criteria of self-defence, on the basis that the defence of one State could never require the total submission of another.

6   The rules set out in this document and any other rules of international humanitarian law shall apply equally to all parties to the conflict. The equal application of these rules to all parties to the conflict shall not be affected by the international responsibility that may have been incurred by any of them for the outbreak of the conflict.

6.1   The principle that the *jus in bello* applies equally to both sides in an armed conflict, irrespective of which State is the aggressor, is now well established in international law. It was affirmed by various war crimes tribunals in the trials which followed the Second World War and has been accepted by almost all States in the conflicts which have occurred since 1945. The question whether the laws of armed conflict should apply to both sides in a conflict without distinguishing between aggressor and victim was extensively debated during the Diplomatic Conference of 1974–77, which reaffirmed the principle of equal application by including in the Preamble to Additional Protocol I a paragraph which reads:

> Reaffirming further that the provisions of the Geneva Conventions and of this Protocol must be fully applied in all circumstances to all persons who are protected by those instruments, without any adverse distinction based on the nature or origin of the armed conflict or on the causes espoused by or attributed to the Parties to the conflict.

6.2   This principle is given effect in paragraph 6 of this document, which was adopted without dissent.

Section III Armed conflicts in which the Security Council has taken action

7   Notwithstanding any rule in this document or elsewhere in the law of neutrality, where the Security Council, acting in accordance with its powers under Chapter VII of the Charter of the United Nations, has identified one or more of the parties to an armed conflict as responsible for resorting to force in violation of international law, neutral States:

(a)   are bound not to lend assistance other than humanitarian assistance to that State; *and*

(b)   may lend assistance to any State which has been the victim of a breach of the peace or an act of aggression by that State.

7.1   This paragraph deals with the situation in which the Security Council, acting under Chapter VII of the United Nations Charter, has made a determination under Article 39 that there is a threat to the peace, breach of the peace or act of aggression and has identified the State or States responsible for that situation but has not taken action in the form of imposing economic sanctions or deciding upon military measures. In such a situation, the resolution passed by the Council is binding upon all Member States, which have a duty under Article 25 of the Charter to accept and carry out the Security Council's decision. The precise implications of this duty, in such a situation, are not entirely clear but it seems that Member States not involved in the conflict are subject to certain duties which override the law of neutrality, namely that they must not give assistance to the State or States identified by the Security Council as responsible for resorting to force in violation of international law and they may, without violating the law of neutrality, lend assistance to the State which has been the victim of attack and to any State co-operating with it in the exercise of the right of collective self-defence. The position of non-Member States is more complex but has to be viewed in the light of Article 2(6) of the Charter.

8   Where, in the course of an international armed conflict, the Security Council has taken preventive or enforcement action involving the application of economic measures under Chapter VII of the Charter, Member States of the United Nations may not rely upon the law of neutrality to justify conduct which would be incompatible with their obligations under the Charter or under decisions of the Security Council.

8.1   Article 25 of the United Nations Charter provides that:

The Members of the United Nations agree to accept and carry out the decisions of the Security Council in accordance with the present Charter.

Decisions taken by the Security Council within its powers under Chapter VII of the Charter thus impose legal obligations upon all Member States.

8.2   Article 103 of the United Nations Charter provides that:

> In the event of a conflict between the obligations of the Members of the United Nations under the present Charter and their obligations under any other international agreement, their obligations under the present Charter shall prevail.

Paragraph 8 is an application of the principle laid down in Article 103 in that it makes clear that a Member State of the United Nations cannot rely upon the law of neutrality as an excuse for not implementing mandatory economic sanctions imposed by the Security Council under Article 41 of the Charter upon one of the parties to an armed conflict. In other words, the fact that the law of neutrality would permit a neutral State to engage in certain kinds of trade with both belligerents, provided that it did not discriminate between them, will not justify a Member of the United Nations in engaging in trade contrary to the terms of a Security Council resolution imposing economic sanctions.

9   Subject to paragraph 7, where the Security Council has taken a decision to use force, or to authorise the use of force by a particular State or States, the rules set out in this document and any other rules of international humanitarian law applicable to armed conflicts at sea shall apply to all parties to any such conflict which may ensue.

9.1   This paragraph merely emphasises the point, now well established, that international humanitarian law, including that applicable to armed conflict at sea, applies with equal strength to naval forces fighting under the flag of the United Nations, when the United Nations has taken a decision to use force under Article 42 of the Charter, or with the authority of the United Nations, for example, when the Security Council has authorised the taking of enforcement action by a regional organisation or an *ad hoc* coalition of States.[5]

Section IV Areas of naval warfare

10   Subject to other applicable rules of the law of armed conflict at sea contained in this document or elsewhere, hostile actions by naval forces may be conducted in, on or over:

> **(a)   the territorial sea and internal waters, the land territories, the exclusive economic zone and continental shelf and, where applicable, the archipelagic waters, of the belligerent States;**
>
> **(b)   the high seas; *and***
>
> **(c)   subject to paragraphs 34 and 35, the exclusive economic zone and the continental shelf of neutral States.**

---

[5]   See also the resolutions adopted by the Institut de droit international at its 1971 (Zagreb) and 1975 (Wiesbaden) sessions.

10.1   As originally formulated by the Rapporteur for the Ottawa (1992) session of the Round Table, the draft paragraph read as follows:

> Subject to other applicable rules of the law of armed conflict at sea, hostile operations by naval forces may be conducted on the high seas, the territorial sea and internal waters, the land territories, and where applicable the archipelagic waters, of the belligerent, any co-belligerent and the enemy. For this purpose, the high seas include the exclusive economic zone and the waters and airspace above the continental shelf.

10.2   The first sentence of the Rapporteur's formulation, except for the reference to archipelagic waters, repeated well-established customary international law.[6] The provision in the first sentence concerning archipelagic waters reflected the fact that under the UN Convention on the Law of the Sea, the sovereignty of an archipelagic State extends to its archipelagic waters in the same sense as to its territorial sea, subject only to exceptions for archipelagic sea lanes passage and the preservation of certain rights and activities of immediately adjacent neighbouring States.[7] It also reflected the fact that several recently promulgated national naval operational manuals have treated archipelagic waters the same as the territorial sea for application of rules affecting neutral and belligerent rights.[8]

10.3   The second sentence of the Rapporteur's formulation reflected the provisions of the LOS Convention concerning the exclusive economic zone, which, while recognising coastal State sovereign rights and jurisdiction for certain economic purposes, prohibit subjecting it to coastal State sovereignty and preserve the rights of other States for freedom of navigation and overflight and other internationally lawful uses of the sea related to these freedoms.[9]

10.4   During the discussions at the Round Table several participants felt that the provision proposed by the Rapporteur did not adequately differentiate between the exclusive economic zone and the high seas in general. Although all but one of the participants accepted that belligerents are permitted to conduct hostile actions within the exclusive economic zone of a neutral State, several participants stated the view that the provision as to the exclusive economic zone should be separated out and include an explicit proviso that such actions were subject to the rights and duties of the coastal State in the zone, which are now stated in paragraphs 34 and 35. The paragraph was

---

6   See US Department of the Navy, Office of Chief of Naval Operations, *The Law of Naval Warfare* (NWIP 10-2), para. 430 (Washington: US Government Printer's Office, 1955); C. John Colombos, *The International Law of the Sea*, p. 528 (6th edn, New York: David McKay Company Inc., 1967).

7   United Nations Convention on the Law of the Sea, 10 December 1982, UN Pub. Sales No. E. 83, vol. 5 (1983) [hereinafter LOS Convention], Part IV.

8   See NWP9A, *The Commander's Handbook* para. 7.3.b; German Federal Ministry of Defence, *Humanitarian Law in Armed Conflicts – Manual* (Bonn: 1992), DSK VV207320067, para. 1010 [hereinafter German Manual]. The Canadian Draft Manual contains inconsistent provisions, which will apparently be clarified as it is further revised. Compare para. 706 with para. 1509. Canadian Forces, *Law of Armed Conflict Manual* (Second draft, Ottawa: undated) [hereinafter Canadian Manual].

9   LOS Convention, Arts. 56–58, 88–115.

therefore divided into three subparagraphs, one pertaining to land and water areas subject to the sovereignty or other forms of jurisdiction of the belligerents, the second being the high seas, and the third the exclusive economic zone and continental shelf of neutral States.

10.5   As implied above, one participant would have excluded all hostile activities from the exclusive economic zones and continental shelves of neutral States.

10.6   With respect to the high seas, the Round Table wished to emphasise that it did not accept the interpretations of some publicists that the LOS Convention's Articles 88 and 301, reserving the high seas for peaceful purposes, prohibit naval warfare on the high seas. See Part II of the Manual and the commentary thereto.

11   The parties to the conflict are encouraged to agree that no hostile actions will be conducted in marine areas containing:

(a)   rare or fragile ecosystems; *or*

(b)   the habitat of depleted, threatened or endangered species or other forms of marine life.

11.1   The growing number of treaty rules, international resolutions and constitutional provisions laying down the obligation of the State to protect the environment demonstrates at the very least that there is a general recognition of a need to protect the marine environment, and a duty upon every State to protect and to preserve the marine environment.

11.2   In the 1982 LOS Convention nearly fifty Articles are devoted to the protection of the marine environment. Flag States still retain the jurisdiction to prescribe rules of law and other regulations for their ships, but certain minimum standards are imposed upon them. It is also provided that States are responsible for the fulfilment of their international obligations concerning the protection and preservation of the marine environment.

11.3   According to Article 192 of the LOS Convention, 'States have the obligation to protect and preserve the marine environment'.

11.4   Discussions during the Geneva session of the Round Table in 1993 introduced the idea of including provisions referring to fragile ecosystems as well as the habitat of depleted, threatened or endangered species and other forms of marine life. Although the consensus of the participants was that this subject should be addressed in the text, there was a lack of consensus for creating a legal prohibition against engaging in hostile actions in such sensitive areas. Accordingly, paragraph 11 was drafted in hortatory rather than mandatory language. In this form it received the approval of the Round Table. There was then a consensus on a new paragraph dealing with the subject-matter: the new paragraph 11.

11.5   This new paragraph is a reflection of paragraph 5 of Article 194 of the LOS Convention, which stipulates that: 'The measures taken in accordance with this Part shall include those necessary to protect and preserve rare or fragile ecosystems as well as the habitat of depleted, threatened or endangered species and other forms of marine life'.

11.6   It is obvious that paragraph 11 does not impose an obligation upon the States parties to an armed conflict at sea not to conduct their hostile actions in marine areas containing the protected species, but rather to encourage them to agree, on a mutual basis, not to use the marine areas containing such species as a theatre of operations in naval warfare. This soft-law guideline, in time of armed conflict at sea, reflects the general rules of peacetime international environmental law. It was recognised that the most crucial areas where this might occur would be in the exclusive economic zone or the continental shelf. A consensus developed, however, that the principle should be stated in general terms and for all areas.

11.7   In the light of the encouragement stated in this paragraph, belligerents may wish to refer to existing and future international instruments identifying and protecting such marine areas, for guidance regarding the nature and location of such areas. Examples may include relevant areas featuring in the World Heritage List established by the 1972 Convention for the Protection of the World Cultural and Natural Heritage.

12   In carrying out operations in areas where neutral States enjoy sovereign rights, jurisdiction, or other rights under general international law, belligerents shall have due regard for the legitimate rights and duties of those neutral States.

12.1   The Rapporteur did not propose a paragraph that corresponds to this paragraph of the Round Table's draft, although he did suggest a similar paragraph with respect to belligerent operations in the exclusive economic zone or waters above the continental shelf of a neutral State. (These provisions are now included in paragraph 34.) During the course of the discussions, however, a number of members expressed concern that the draft should emphasise the duty of a belligerent to conduct its operations, no matter where occurring, in such a manner as not to interfere unduly with the rights of neutral States which might have correlative rights in the same area. Although it was recognised that the most crucial areas where this might occur would be in the exclusive economic zone or the continental shelf, a consensus developed that the principle should be stated in general terms and for all areas, regardless of whether neutral rights were based on jurisdictional claims (for example, exclusive economic zone, continental shelf) or universal rights flowing from the general law of the sea (for example, the high seas). Such rights also included those involving activities in the 'Area'.[10] It was also pointed out by several participants that some States had not formally claimed exclusive economic zones but may have established exclusive fishery zones or the like. Paragraph 12 reflects this consensus.

10   See LOS Convention, Part XI.

12.2   During the discussions at the Ottawa session and elsewhere, there was substantial debate as to whether the operative standard for belligerents in carrying out their duties should be 'due regard' or 'respect' for the rights of neutrals. A substantial majority favoured the term 'due regard' since it was already accepted in the general law of the sea and reflected the balance that should exist between the rights of belligerents to conduct hostile activities in the oceans and the rights of neutrals to carry out their legitimate activities in the same areas. A minority felt that a higher burden should be placed on the belligerent and that 'respect' more adequately conveyed this meaning. Accordingly, square brackets were used to indicate that further discussion of this issue was required. After the receipt of a special report on this issue at the final session in Livorno, further debate occurred. Two considerations in favour of the 'due regard' standard seemed to be decisive in the debate. The first of these was that, as brought out in the special report, the term 'due regard' generally used throughout the law of the sea was more appropriate in a document tied so closely to the law of the sea as well as the law of armed conflict. The second was that the term 'respect', as used in other documents dealing with international humanitarian law, conveyed the sense of an absolute and affirmative duty to protect the physical integrity of protected persons and objects. Thus, to use it in a situation in which a balancing of rights was involved created the danger of prejudicing the meaning of that term in other areas of international humanitarian law. Accordingly, the 'due regard' standard was adopted here and at other places in the text where the issue had been preserved.

12.3   There was also considerable discussion at the Ottawa Round Table concerning the belligerent duty to have 'due regard for' the marine environment. It was ultimately decided that the environment should be left for a subsequent session of the Round Table. This discussion was held during the 1993 Geneva session of the Round Table, and the results of that discussion are reflected in paragraphs 11, 13(c), 34, 35 and 44 of the Manual.

12.4   The reader should also refer to the commentary on paragraphs 34–37.

Section V Definitions

13   **For the purposes of this document:**

(a) **'international humanitarian law' means international rules, established by treaties or custom, which limit the right of parties to a conflict to use the methods or means of warfare of their choice, or which protect States not party to the conflict or persons and objects that are, or may be, affected by the conflict;**

(b) **'attack' means an act of violence, whether in offence or in defence;**

(c) **'collateral casualties' or 'collateral damage' means the loss of life of, or injury to civilians or other protected persons, and damage to or the destruction of the natural environment or objects that are not in themselves military objectives;**

(d) 'neutral' means any State not party to the conflict;

(e) 'hospital ships, coastal rescue craft and other medical transports' means vessels that are protected under the Second Geneva Convention of 1949 and Additional Protocol I of 1977;

(f) 'medical aircraft' means an aircraft that is protected under the Geneva Conventions of 1949 and Additional Protocol I of 1977;

(g) 'warship' means a ship belonging to the armed forces of a State bearing the external marks distinguishing the character and nationality of such a ship, under the command of an officer duly commissioned by the government of that State and whose name appears in the appropriate service list or its equivalent, and manned by a crew which is under regular armed forces discipline;

(h) 'auxiliary vessel' means a vessel, other than a warship, that is owned by or under the exclusive control of the armed forces of a State and used for the time being on government non-commercial service;

(i) 'merchant vessel' means a vessel, other than a warship, an auxiliary vessel, or a State vessel such as a customs or police vessel, that is engaged in commercial or private service;

(j) 'military aircraft' means an aircraft operated by commissioned units of the armed forces of a State having the military marks of that State, commanded by a member of the armed f orces and manned by a crew subject to regular armed forces discipline;

(k) 'auxiliary aircraft' means an aircraft, other than a military aircraft, that is owned by or under the exclusive control of the armed forces of a State and used for the time being on government non-commercial service;

(l) 'civil aircraft' means an aircraft other than a military, auxiliary, or State aircraft such as a customs or police aircraft, that is engaged in commercial or private service;

(m) 'civil airliner' means a civil aircraft that is clearly marked and engaged in carrying civilian passengers in scheduled or non-scheduled services along Air Traffic Service routes.

13.1 (a) 'international humanitarian law'

This is defined in this document as rules of international law, including treaty or customary law, which regulate the conduct of hostilities, protect States not party to the conflict and provide protection for civilian persons and objects, those *hors de combat*, and other objects that are entitled to special protection during armed conflict.

13.2   This part of international law was traditionally called the 'law of war' and since the conclusion of the United Nations Charter the 'law of armed conflict'. Both these terms are still used. A more recent appellation for the same body of law is 'international humanitarian law'. When this term was first used, it was frequently referred to as applying exclusively to so-called 'Geneva Law', that is, the law protecting victims of armed conflicts as contained in the four Geneva Conventions of 1949. The law on the conduct of hostilities continued to be referred to as the 'law of war', 'the law of armed conflict' or 'Hague Law'. More recently, however, the practice has developed to include within the definition of 'international humanitarian law' both the law on the conduct of hostilities and the law on the protection of victims. An example of this is the Statute of the International Tribunal for the Prosecution of Persons Responsible for Serious Violations of International Humanitarian Law Committed in the Territory of the Former Yugoslavia since 1991, which was established pursuant to Security Council Resolution 827. The Statute refers to rules found in both the Geneva Conventions and rules on the conduct of hostilities found in the Hague Conventions.[11]

13.3   The term therefore includes *inter alia* the customary law applicable to armed conflict at sea and the relevant provisions in the Hague Conventions of 1907, the Geneva Gas Protocol of 1925, the Geneva Conventions of 1949 and their Additional Protocols of 1977.

13.4   For the purposes of this document, the term also includes measures of economic warfare directed against enemy or neutral vessels or aircraft, and provisions relating to neutral rights and duties in so far as these rules relate to conduct at sea or the treatment of captured persons. It does not include rules relating to the adjudication of prizes which in any event are not specifically included in this document.

13.5   **(b)   'attack'**
This definition is inspired by Article 49(1) of Additional Protocol I of 1977 which reads as follows:

> 'Attacks' means acts of violence against the adversary, whether in offence or in defence.

13.6   The purpose of the definition is to make it quite clear that references to 'attack' in humanitarian law are not to be confused with the concept of an armed attack as referred to in Article 2(4) of the United Nations Charter. Therefore the rules of humanitarian law relating to attacks apply to all acts of violence irrespective of whether they are being carried out as part of an act of aggression, in self-defence, or as part of a collective security action. Conversely, the definition makes it clear that the concept of 'attack' is not linked to the tactical concept of attack as opposed to a

---

11   Security Council document S/25704, 3 May 1993, Annex to the Report of the Secretary General pursuant to paragraph 2 of Security Council Resolution 808 (1993). It may also be noted that the ICRC includes the law on the conduct of hostilities in its definition of international humanitarian law: see 'Action by the International Committee of the Red Cross in the event of breaches of international humanitarian law', *International Review of the Red Cross*, March–April 1981.

tactical defensive measure. Therefore acts that may be perceived as tactically defensive, such as the laying of mines, are 'attacks' for the purposes of the law.

13.7   The reason for the difference between the definition of 'attack' in Additional Protocol I and the definition adopted here, is that acts of violence in land warfare are only carried out against the 'enemy', whereas in naval warfare, it is lawful to carry out acts of violence against neutral shipping or neutral aircraft in certain limited situations, as indicated in paragraphs 67 and 70 of the Manual.

13.8   (c)   **'collateral casualties' or 'collateral damage'**
It has long been recognised in customary law that when attacking military objectives, persons or objects which may not be directly attacked may nevertheless be incidentally affected. This will either occur because of errors when targeting, insufficient accuracy of the means used or because such incidental effects are inevitable around the target attacked. The law requires that such incidental effects are not excessive in relation to the value of the military objective attacked (see para 46(d)). The terms 'collateral casualties' and 'collateral damage' are both used in order to underline the fact that this rule applies to both persons and objects.

13.9   This definition is similar to Article 51(5)(b) of Additional Protocol I which only speaks of civilians and civilian objects as it appears in the section relating to the civilian population. However, in practice the rule extends to damage or injury caused to all persons or objects that may not be directly attacked, and therefore this definition has included other protected persons (for example, the wounded, sick, shipwrecked), all objects that are not military objectives and the natural environment.

13.10   It is the first time that the natural environment is included in the definition of 'collateral damage' in an international humanitarian law text, but this has been done intentionally so that the rules relating to collateral damage apply also to the natural environment. However, the experts agreed that when making an assessment on whether an attack would cause excessive collateral damage, probable incidental damage to civilian lives should be considered with more care than that to the environment. The standard will not therefore be the same. However, a commander should nevertheless consider the impact of his attack on the environment in the light of the need for the attack on the military objective concerned on the one hand, and the likely effect on the other.

13.11   (d)   **'neutral'**
This definition corresponds to the definition of neutrality traditionally used in international law. The question has been raised whether it still applies in present-day international law. It has been contended that the prohibition to use force in international relations, laid down in the UN Charter, gives States the right to discriminate against the aggressor and thereby to depart from the law of neutrality. Under Article 51 of the Charter, States have the right of individual or collective self-defence if an armed attack occurs against a member of the United Nations. It is argued that, by virtue of the right of collective self-defence, States may not only enter the war on the victim's side but may also assist the victim of attack by lesser means, such as the supply of arms.

13.12   Others have denied such a right. They contend that, in the absence of an authoritative determination of the aggressor by the Security Council, a belligerent is not obliged to accept being discriminated against. They also argue that States have practically never invoked Article 51 of the Charter when discriminating against a belligerent. They furthermore state that the law of neutrality, like the *jus in bello*, applies without regard to who is the aggressor and whom the victim of aggression. Both sides recognise, however, that a belligerent may not use military force against a State which discriminates against it unless this State has committed an armed attack against it or has become a party to the conflict.

13.13   The controversy referred to does not affect the Manual. All the rules on neutrals contained in it apply to all States not party to the conflict, even to those which may consider themselves authorised to depart from certain rules of neutrality. This is generally agreed upon with respect to the rules on the protection of neutral merchant vessels from attack (paragraphs 67–69), the protection of neutral waters and the freedom of neutral navigation (paragraphs 14–35; 80–92; 105–108), blockade (paragraphs 93–104), and the visit, search, diversion and capture of neutral merchant vessels (paragraphs 112–124, 146–152).

13.14   Some doubts have been expressed with respect to the rules of paragraphs 14–22 on the use of neutral waters by belligerents. They put a duty on neutral States to prevent belligerents from using their internal waters, their territorial sea and their archipelagic waters for hostile actions (paragraphs 15–18). They furthermore oblige neutral States to take the measures necessary to terminate violations of their neutral waters (paragraphs 15 and 22). In so far as neutrals are free to permit or to restrict certain uses of their waters by belligerents they must do so on a non-discriminatory basis (paragraphs 19–21). These provisions must be considered as being applicable to all States not party to the conflict, even if one assumes that these States have a right to discriminate against the aggressor, for, if a State permits a party to the conflict to use its waters for belligerent purposes, or if it tolerates such use, the respective waters become part of the region of operations. They therefore lose their inviolability as neutral waters. The aggrieved belligerent may attack enemy warships or other enemy military objectives in these areas (see paragraph 22).

13.15   (e) **'hospital ships, coastal rescue craft and other medical transports'**
The combined effect of the Second Geneva Convention (GCII) and Additional Protocol I (API) means that the following classes of vessels are included in this definition:

13.16   **Hospital ships** are:

(i)   vessels built or equipped by a party to the conflict specially and solely with a view to assisting either military and/or civilian wounded, sick or shipwrecked;[12]

(ii)   vessels of the same nature used by national Red Cross or Red Crescent societies, officially recognised relief societies or by private persons, provided that the party to the conflict on which they depend has given them an official commission;[13]

---

12   GCII Art. 22 and API Art. 22.
13   GCII Art. 24 and API Art. 22.

(iii)   vessels of the same nature used by neutral States, their national Red Cross or Red Crescent societies, officially recognised relief societies, private persons of neutral countries or impartial international humanitarian organisations, provided that they have placed themselves under the control of one of the parties to the conflict with the authorisation of this party and with the previous consent of their own government.[14]

13.17   **Coastal rescue craft** are shore-based craft employed by the State or by officially recognised lifeboat institutions in order to rescue either military and/or civilian wounded, sick or shipwrecked. They are protected by virtue of Article 27 GCII and Article 22 API.

Article 27 GCII speaks of 'small craft' used for 'coastal rescue operations'. However, the craft concerned do not have to be particularly small (that is, less than a certain tonnage) to be covered, for the term used is rather indicative to recognise the protection of these rescue craft which tend to be relatively small. Similarly, their rescue operations do not have to be confined to the coast but can take place far out to sea if the vessel has this capacity. The term coastal indicates rather that the craft are shore-based and are not lifeboats of ships nor craft that accompany a flotilla to be used for rescue operations.

13.18   **Other medical transports** are other classes of vessels that are protected by virtue of GCII or API.

Medical transports are defined in API as:

> any means of transportation, whether military or civilian, permanent or temporary, assigned exclusively to medical transportation and under the control of a competent authority of a Party to the conflict.[15]

Medical transportation is defined as:

> the conveyance by land, water or air of the wounded, sick, shipwrecked, medical personnel, religious personnel, medical equipment or medical supplies protected by the Conventions and by this Protocol.[16]

The vessels that fall into this category are as follows:

(i)   *Life boats:* the life boats and small craft of hospital ships.[17]

(ii)   *Ships chartered to transport medical equipment:* these are vessels that are specially chartered to transport equipment exclusively intended for the treatment of the wounded and sick members of the armed forces or for the prevention of disease.[18] One may also assume that equipment destined for the treatment of the civilian population would be similarly covered, for although they are not included in the wording of Article

14   GCII Art. 25 and API Art. 22.
15   API Art. 8(g).
16   API Art. 8(f).
17   GCII Art. 26 and API Art. 22.
18   GCII Art. 38.

38 of GCII, they would fall within the definition of a 'medical transport' as defined in API.

(iii)   *Other medical ships and craft:* these are all other vessels that fall into the definition of 'medical transports' as indicated in Article 8 of API quoted above. The important condition to fall into this category is that the vessel is exclusively involved in the conveyance of the wounded, sick, shipwrecked, medical and/or religious personnel, medical equipment or supplies. Whether this exclusive use is temporary or permanent is immaterial for the purposes of this definition.

13.19   *Neutral vessels that have charitably taken on board the wounded, sick or shipwrecked or collected the dead* do not fall into the definition of 'hospital ship', 'coastal rescue craft' or 'other medical transport', but they do nevertheless fall into the definition of paragraph 12(d) of the Manual as they are protected (albeit temporarily) under Article 21 of the Second Geneva Convention. These vessels are protected from capture or attack for the length of time that they are carrying out this activity, although they are not protected from subsequent capture or attack if they undertake an activity that allows this, as indicated in paragraphs 146 and 67 respectively.

13.20   **(f)   'medical aircraft'**
This refers to aircraft, whether fixed wing or otherwise, that fall within the definition of medical transports as indicated in Article 8(g) of API and quoted above in the commentary to paragraph 13(e). Therefore this definition covers military or civilian aircraft that are exclusively assigned, either temporarily or permanently, to the transport of the wounded, sick, shipwrecked, medical and/or religious personnel, or medical equipment and supplies.

13.21   **(g)   'warship'**
This subparagraph reflects the well-established definition of a warship in international law. The 1907 Hague Convention VII,[19] the 1958 High Seas Convention,[20] and the 1982 Law of the Sea Convention[21] all require that a warship meets the criteria in this definition. Only warships can exercise belligerent rights. In some States, Coast Guard vessels belong to the armed forces and are considered warships. The term warship includes a submarine as well as a surface ship.

13.22   **(h)   'auxiliary vessel'**
Many States employ a class of vessels engaged in logistical support to their armed forces that are neither warships nor merchant vessels. The distinguishing criteria are that these vessels are either owned by or are under the exclusive control of the armed forces of a State *and* used for the time being on government non-commercial service in support of the armed forces, as, for example, transporting troops and military cargo. The ships may be manned entirely by civilians. The practice has been to define these ships as auxiliary vessels. An auxiliary vessel does not have the rights, duties and obligations of either a warship or a merchant vessel. An auxiliary vessel has the nationality of the State whose flag it is entitled to fly.

19   Arts. 2–5.
20   Art. 8(2).
21   Art. 29.

13.23 **(i)** **'merchant vessel'**
The term 'merchant vessel' has never had a precise meaning within the peacetime law of the sea that is satisfactory for the purposes of the law of armed conflict. This subparagraph attempts to provide that meaning in a way that is consistent with long-standing practice in the law of armed conflict and precisely differentiates between the four broad categories of vessels dealt with in this document, namely (1) hospital ships, coastal rescue craft and other medical transports, (2) warships, (3) auxiliary vessels and (4) merchant vessels. In other words it was the intent of the Round Table to provide that if a ship was not within one of the first three categories, it was a merchant vessel. In doing so, however, it was necessary to except from the term 'merchant vessel' those government vessels which, though usually manned by government employees, do not have functions which would make them auxiliary vessels. The Round Table also accepted the customary law rule that vessels used in private service, such as private yachts and pleasure craft, should also be included within the term 'merchant vessels'. Merchant vessels sail under the flag of one State only, and have the nationality of the State whose flag they are entitled to fly.[22]

13.24 **(j)** **'military aircraft'**
This subparagraph defining a military aircraft contains the same criteria as that for a warship in subparagraph (g). The criteria are also reflected in the 1923 Hague Rules of Aerial Warfare.[23] Military aircraft are 'state aircraft' under the 1944 Chicago Convention on International Civil Aviation.[24] Only military aircraft may exercise belligerent rights.

13.25 **(k)** **'auxiliary aircraft'**
This subparagraph corresponds to the definition of an auxiliary vessel in subparagraph (h). The same criteria apply in the case of an auxiliary aircraft. Auxiliary aircraft are considered 'state aircraft'.[25] States often employ auxiliary aircraft in the logistical support of their armed forces, such as transporting troops and military cargo. An auxiliary aircraft must bear an external mark indicating its nationality.[26]

13.26 **(l)** **'civil aircraft'**
This definition of civil aircraft is patterned after the definition of a merchant vessel in subparagraph (i). The key criterion is the employment in commercial or private service. Under the Chicago Convention civil aircraft are aircraft other than State aircraft, which are aircraft used in military, customs or police services.[27] In the 1923 Hague Rules of Aerial Warfare, civil aircraft are termed private aircraft; military and auxiliary aircraft are termed public aircraft.[28] The Chicago Convention prescribes that a civil aircraft engaged

---

22 LOS Convention, Arts. 91–92.
23 Arts. 2–3. The 1923 Hague Draft Rules of Aerial Warfare (HRAW) were never adopted in legally binding form, but at the time of their conclusion they were regarded as an authoritative attempt to clarify and formulate rules of air warfare, and largely corresponded to customary rules and general principles underlying the laws of war on land and sea. See Prefatory Note to the 1923 Hague Rules of Aerial Warfare, in *Documents on the Law of War*, Roberts and Guelff (eds.), 1982, p. 121.
24 Art. 3(b).
25 HRAW, Art. 2(b).
26 HRAW, Art. 5.
27 Art. 3.
28 Art. 2.

in international air navigation has the nationality of the State in which it is registered. Further, the civil aircraft can only be registered in one State and must bear the nationality and registration of that State.[29]

13.27 (m) 'civil airliner'

Civil airliners fall within the definition of civil aircraft in subparagraph (l) bearing its appropriate nationality and registration marks.[30] The phrase 'engaged in carrying civilian passengers' means that the passengers are actually on board the airliner. Therefore, an empty civil airliner parked on the tarmac, for example, does not fall within the definition in paragraph 13(m). Civil airliners are highlighted separately because of their world-wide employment in carrying civilian passengers in international navigation and the potential risks to innocent passengers in areas of armed conflict. Belligerents and neutrals can anticipate that civil airliners will be carrying passengers on international routes over water on scheduled and non-scheduled flights in practically all areas of the globe. Belligerent and neutral States will also be involved in providing regular air traffic services in their flight information region in accordance with ICAO regulations and procedures. All States must take special precautions to safeguard civil airliners and their passengers in areas of armed conflict and hazardous military operations. See paragraphs 72–77.

29   Arts. 17–20.
30   Chicago Convention, Art. 20.

PART II

REGIONS OF OPERATIONS

Section I Internal waters, territorial sea and archipelagic waters

Preliminary remarks

The paragraphs in this Part, together with paragraphs 10 and 12 of Part I of the Manual, were developed at the Ottawa (1992) session under the Madrid Plan of Action agenda item, *Theatre of Operations in Naval Warfare – Different Maritime Areas*. A session devoted to this subject was included in the Plan of Action in recognition of the changes that had been wrought in the jurisdictional areas or zones of the ocean since the customary rules for the conduct of armed conflict had crystallised during the nineteenth and early twentieth centuries. These changes were reflected in the 1982 United Nations Convention on the Law of the Sea[31] and included a broadening of the territorial sea from three to twelve nautical miles, the recognition of several new zones denominated as the contiguous zone, the exclusive economic zone, the continental shelf and archipelagic waters, and the recognition of special navigational rights in these zones and through international straits.[32] Although the 1982 United Nations Convention on the Law of the Sea is regarded as providing a peacetime regime for the law of the sea, the areas it defines subject to coastal State sovereignty or the exercise of other forms of national jurisdiction have a significant effect on the exercise of both belligerent and neutral rights during time of armed conflict. As stated by a noted authority on the law of the sea:

> To the extent one continues to divide public international law into the two classic categories – the laws of war and the laws of peace – the Convention on the Law of the Sea would doubtlessly fall within the latter category ...

> At the same time, the Convention does contain rules for dividing the oceans into different jurisdictional zones. Some of the rules of warfare and neutrality vary with the status of geographic areas ... The classic dichotomy in the law of the sea between internal waters and the territorial sea on the one hand, and the high seas on the other, has yielded to new subtleties and modalities, particularly in the regimes of straits, archipelagic waters, the exclusive economic zones and the continental shelf.[33]

31 See note 7.
32 LOS Convention, Parts I–VI
33 Bernard H. Oxman, 'The Regime of Warships Under the United Nations Convention on the Law of the Sea', *Virginia Journal of International Law*, vol. 24, p. 809, at p. 811 (1984).

The purpose of Part II of this Manual is to adapt the traditional doctrines and principles, particularly those dealing with the relationship of belligerents and neutrals under neutral jurisdiction, to these new divisions of the sea.

14   Neutral waters consist of the internal waters, territorial sea, and, where applicable, the archipelagic waters, of neutral States. Neutral airspace consists of the airspace over neutral waters and the land territory of neutral States.

14.1   With a slight change in wording to reflect the nomenclature of other parts of the Round Table's results, the first sentence of this paragraph is identical to that proposed by the Rapporteur on maritime areas. The second sentence, defining neutral airspace, was added at the final session in the interest of clarity, although, in a strict sense, this was unnecessary since under the general law of the sea, the coastal or archipelagic State sovereignty over its territorial sea and archipelagic waters extends to the superjacent airspace.[34]

14.2   In his introduction of this paragraph to the Round Table, the Rapporteur pointed out that there were two significant issues involved in its drafting. The first was that the rules governing belligerent–neutral behaviour were developed at a time when it was generally recognised that the breadth of the territorial sea was three nautical miles measured from a baseline which followed the sinuosities of the coast. As a result of changes in the law of the sea, as reflected in the 1982 LOS Convention, the breadth of the territorial sea was now generally accepted as twelve nautical miles which was often measured from straight baselines. The second issue was the development of the concept of archipelagic waters, also recognised in the 1982 LOS Convention, by which certain archipelagic States (for example, Indonesia, Philippines, Bahamas) might claim waters within 'archipelagic baselines' connecting the outermost points of outermost islands of the archipelago as subject to their sovereignty, that is, with a status essentially like the territorial sea. The consequence of these two developments was the incorporation into the territorial sea, archipelagic waters and territorial airspace of vast areas of the oceans and the superjacent airspace, which had formerly been high seas and international airspace. Should these areas be treated in the law of armed conflict in the same way that the narrow territorial sea had been treated – that is, off-limits to combat operations and as a base of operations by belligerents with a correlative duty on the part of neutral States to enforce their neutrality – strong belligerents would be tempted to violate such neutral waters and weak neutral States might be unable or unwilling to enforce their neutral duties. The result would likely be an increase in the tension between neutral and belligerent States and the likelihood of hostile operations within neutral waters.

14.3   The Rapporteur also pointed out, however, that all three of the contemporary naval operational manuals (US, Canada, Germany) appeared to draw the conclusion that archipelagic waters and the expanded territorial sea were to be treated in the same manner as had the narrow territorial sea under the traditional rules. Both the Canadian and United States manuals, however, recognised the difficulties posed.[35]

14.4   The Round Table's discussion of this paragraph inevitably merged with the next; accordingly, further comment is reserved for that paragraph.

---

34   LOS Convention, Arts. 2(2) and 49(2).
35   See NWP9, *The Commander's Handbook*, para. 7.3.6; Canadian Manual, para. 706(6).

15   **Within and over neutral waters, including neutral waters comprising an international strait and waters in which the right of archipelagic sea lanes passage may be exercised, hostile actions by belligerent forces are forbidden. A neutral State must take such measures as are consistent with Section II of this Part, including the exercise of surveillance, as the means at its disposal allow, to prevent the violation of its neutrality by belligerent forces.**

15.1   The basic principles stated in this paragraph are derived from Hague Convention (XIII) Concerning the Rights and Duties of Neutral Powers in Naval War,[36] Articles 1 and 25. Article 1 states that belligerents shall respect the sovereign rights of neutral States and shall abstain from acts that would constitute a violation of neutrality. Article 25 states that a neutral State must exercise such surveillance 'as the means at its disposal allow' to prevent violation of its territorial waters. These principles were included in the Rapporteur's report to the Round Table.

15.2   The discussion at the Round Table on the first sentence of this paragraph centred primarily on whether it was reasonable, in view of the large expanse of archipelagic waters of some States (Indonesia being the prime example), to treat archipelagic waters in the same way as the territorial sea for the purpose of excluding belligerent hostile actions when the archipelagic State was a neutral. After considerable debate and the expression of reservations by several participants that such a provision was impracticable and unenforceable, the Round Table agreed that the legal status of archipelagic waters dictated that, subject to later provisions as to archipelagic sea lanes passage, the archipelagic waters of neutral States should be equated to the territorial sea. In this conclusion they were persuaded in part by the fact that the three modern naval operational manuals accepted this categorisation.[37]

15.3   The second sentence of the paragraph was non-controversial and accepted without dissent. It should be noted, however, that the question of what action a belligerent may take if a neutral State's measures are unsuccessful in preventing or terminating a belligerent's misuse of the neutral's waters is addressed in paragraph 22. The question of what activities belligerent warships, military aircraft or naval formations may engage in while in transit passage or archipelagic sea lanes passage is examined in paragraph 30.

---

36   Convention (XIII) Concerning the Rights and Duties of Neutral Powers in Naval War, 18 October 1907, 36 Stat. 2415 (US); 100 British & Foreign State Papers (1906–7), pp. 448–54 (UK), reprinted in *American Journal of International Law*, vol. 2 (Supp.), p. 202 [cited hereinafter as Hague XIII]. Although Hague XIII has not received universal ratification, and a number of important States, including the United Kingdom, have never ratified it, most of its provisions are considered to be declaratory of customary law. Dietrich Schindler, 'Commentary [on Hague Convention XIII]', in N. Ronzitti (ed.), *The Law of Naval Warfare: A Collection of Agreements and Documents with Commentaries* (Dordrecht, Boston, London: Martinus Nijhoff Publishers, 1988), p. 211, at pp. 215, 221. For this reason both the Rapporteur and the Round Table treated its provisions as authoritative in the absence of State practice to the contrary.

37   See note 35.

16   **Hostile actions within the meaning of paragraph 15 include, *inter alia*:**

     (a)   **attack on or capture of persons or objects located in, on or over neutral waters or territory;**

     (b)   **use as a base of operations, including attack on or capture of persons or objects located outside neutral waters, if the attack or seizure is conducted by belligerent forces located in, on or over neutral waters;**

     (c)   **laying of mines; *or***

     (d)   **visit, search, diversion or capture.**

16.1   The provisions of this paragraph are derived principally from Hague XIII, Article 2 (act of hostility; visit, search and capture), Article 4 (prize courts), and Article 5 (base of operations). The final text adopted by the Round Table differed from that proposed by the Rapporteur in the following respects following the same subparagraph numbering:

(a)   The Rapporteur's proposal referred only to 'attack or seizure of enemy warships or military aircraft';

(b)   the Rapporteur's proposal stated merely to 'use as a base of operations';

(d)   the Rapporteur's proposal did not include 'diversion';

16.2   As is self-evident, the purpose of this paragraph is to give examples of belligerent actions which are forbidden within the meaning of paragraph 15. The use of the term '*inter alia*' makes it clear that the list of actions which are forbidden is illustrative and not exhaustive.

16.3   The provisions of this paragraph were non-controversial, and the changes adopted by the Round Table were accepted as clarifications of the Rapporteur's text with little discussion. The inclusion of 'diversion' in subparagraph (d) refers both to diversion of merchant vessels and civil aircraft to an appropriate area, port or airfield for visit and search, as provided for in paragraphs 121 and 125, and diversion of merchant vessels and civil aircraft to an alternate destination in lieu of visit and search, as provided for in paragraphs 119, 125 and 126. The provisions as to diversion to an alternate destination were adopted at a prior session of the Round Table as a codification of a progressive development in the law of economic warfare, particularly as it was practised in the 1990–91 Gulf War. See commentary to paragraphs 119, 121, 125 and 126.

16.4   As originally formulated by both the Rapporteur and provisionally adopted at the Ottawa session, paragraph 16 included a subparagraph (e) listing detention of a prize or establishment of a prize court. This provision was deleted as unnecessary at the final session of the Round Table because the list is illustrative.

17   **Belligerent forces may not use neutral waters as a sanctuary.**

17.1   Although Hague Convention XIII does not contain an explicit provision such as that suggested in paragraph 17, a number of its provisions, taken together, strongly imply that a belligerent force may not use neutral waters as a sanctuary. These include provisions concerning prolonging port stays (Article 14), restrictions on carrying out repairs (Article 17), prohibitions against using neutral waters for replenishment of supplies or crews (Article 18), and restrictions on replenishment of food and fuel (Articles 19 and 20). It was the decision of the Round Table to include an explicit provision against using neutral waters as a sanctuary. This was particularly important in view of the greatly expanded areas that might be encompassed within neutral waters by virtue of the recognition of expanded territorial seas and archipelagic waters.

18   **Belligerent military and auxiliary aircraft may not enter neutral airspace. Should they do so, the neutral State shall use the means at its disposal to require the aircraft to land within its territory and shall intern the aircraft and its crew for the duration of the armed conflict. Should the aircraft fail to follow the instructions to land, it may be attacked, subject to the special rules relating to medical aircraft as specified in paragraphs 181–183.**

18.1   Under the 1923 Hague Rules of Aerial Warfare, belligerent military aircraft were forbidden to enter the jurisdiction of a neutral State. Further, the neutral State was obliged to use all means to prevent such an entry and, if an entry occurred, to compel the belligerent military aircraft to land. The neutral State was then obliged to intern the aircraft, crew, and passengers.[38] Paragraph 18 reflects the substance of this customary rule and warns that if a belligerent military aircraft refuses to obey orders to land, it may be attacked. The rule also applies to belligerent auxiliary aircraft owned by or under the exclusive control of the armed forces of a State and used for the time being on government non-commercial service.[39]

18.2   Belligerent medical aircraft that enter the jurisdiction of a neutral State may *not* be attacked, but must be treated in accordance with paragraphs 181–183. Belligerent military aircraft that are exercising the rights of passage over neutral international straits and archipelagic sea lanes in accordance with paragraphs 23 and 26 are exempt from the rule in paragraph 18. It is assumed that belligerent military and auxiliary aircraft that have been granted safe conduct by agreement between the parties to the conflict and are exempt from attack in accordance with paragraph 53 will also have the agreement of the neutral concerned before entering that neutral's airspace.

38   HRAW, Art. 42.
39   These aircraft are defined in para. 13(k) of the Manual.

1 9   **Subject to paragraphs 29 and 33, a neutral State may, on a non-discriminatory basis, condition, restrict or prohibit the entrance to or passage through its neutral waters by belligerent warships and auxiliary vessels.**

19.1   Paragraph 19 is derived primarily from Hague Convention XIII but takes into account the practice of States in recent naval conflicts as well as the impact of the new divisions of the oceans flowing from the 1982 LOS Convention. Article 9 of Hague Convention XIII requires that a neutral State shall apply the conditions, restrictions and prohibitions for belligerent entry into its ports, roadsteads and territorial waters impartially to all belligerents. Although the Convention is silent as to whether a neutral State may prohibit passage of warships through its territorial sea, international practice in both World Wars establishes that it may do so, except for those parts of the territorial sea leading to or constituting an international strait.[40] On the other hand, a neutral State is not required to prohibit such passage, and, under Hague Convention XIII may allow 'mere' passage without jeopardising its neutrality.[41] The current United States operational manual adopts this position.[42] The Canadian Draft Manual on the other hand does not appear to recognise the right of neutral States to close their territorial seas to the passage of belligerent warships.[43] The provisions of the German Manual are somewhat unclear, at least in the English version.[44]

19.2   In view of the conflicting State practice and the ambiguity of treaty law, the Round Table adopted what it considered to be the better practice, which was to allow a neutral State discretion as to whether it would permit passage through its neutral waters. By also adopting paragraph 20(a), the Round Table ensured that if the neutral State chose to allow such passage, its neutrality would not be jeopardised.

19.3   As stated above (paragraph 19.1) Hague Convention XIII refers to 'mere' passage through the territorial sea. Modern usage, at least in a peacetime environment, is to use the term 'innocent' passage. Except for reference to 'nonsuspendable innocent passage through international straits', which is a term of art from the law of the sea applicable to certain categories of international straits not subject of the right of transit passage,[45] the Round Table's draft does not characterise passage through the territorial sea or archipelagic waters as either 'innocent' or 'mere'. The term 'innocent' was felt to be inappropriate, since its meaning within the peacetime regime is defined in terms of refraining from actions which might be harmful to the interests of a coastal State by virtue of such passage.[46] On the other hand, passage during armed conflict needs to be 'innocent' also in the sense of not engaging in actions which might be

40   H. A. Smith, *The Law and Custom of the Sea* (New York: Frederick A. Praeger, 2nd edn 1950), p. 153; Robert W. Tucker, US Naval War College International Law Studies, *The Law of War and Neutrality at Sea* (Washington: US Government Printer's Office, 1957), p. 232; NWIP 10-2 *The Law of Naval Warfare*, para. 443a, note 28.
41   Hague Convention XIII, Art. 10.
42   NWP9A, *The Commander's Handbook*, para. 7.3.4.1.
43   Canadian Manual, para. 1511(3).
44   German Manual, paras. 1126 and 1127. The former paragraph states that passage by warships and prizes through the territorial sea 'is no violation of neutrality' (citing Hague XIII, Art. 10). The latter paragraph states that the neutral State may 'altogether prohibit [warships] from remaining in its waters', but the context suggests that the reference is to warships that have remained in neutral waters for more than 24 hours.
45   See LOS Convention, Art. 45.
46   See LOS Convention, Art. 19.

harmful to the other belligerent. Since passage during armed conflict is subject to such conditions and restrictions as the coastal State may choose to apply, as well as those contained in the law of armed conflict as set forth in this Manual, use of the term 'passage', without modifiers, was felt to be adequate.

19.4   Although earlier texts such as Hague Convention XIII and national military manuals were largely silent as to the status of auxiliary vessels with respect to passage through neutral waters, in view of the widespread practice of employing civilian-manned ships in support of naval forces at sea and their close integration into such forces, the Round Table decided that they should be equated to warships in this respect. Later paragraphs within this text also adopt the same position with regard to other aspects of the law of armed conflict at sea.

19.5   The 'subject to' clause adopted as a part of paragraph 19 makes it clear that transit passage through international straits used for international navigation, non-suspendable innocent passage through international straits not subject to the right of transit passage, and archipelagic sea lanes passage through archipelagic waters may not be prohibited nor subjected to conditions or restrictions not permitted by the general law of the sea (Parts III and IV of the LOS Convention). As indicated in paragraph 27, the laws and regulations of States for such passage adopted in accordance with general international law continue to apply in time of armed conflict. For further amplification, see that paragraph and the commentary thereto.

20   **Subject to the duty of impartiality, and to paragraphs 21 and 23–33, and under such regulations as it may establish, a neutral State may, without jeopardising its neutrality, permit the following acts within its neutral waters:**

(a)   **passage through its territorial sea, and where applicable its archipelagic waters, by warships, auxiliary vessels and prizes of belligerent States; warships, auxiliary vessels and prizes may employ pilots of the neutral State during passage;**

(b)   **replenishment by a belligerent warship or auxiliary vessel of its food, water and fuel sufficient to reach a port in its own territory; *and***

(c)   **repairs of belligerent warships or auxiliary vessels found necessary by the neutral State to make them seaworthy; such repairs may not restore or increase their fighting strength.**

20.1   In a sense, this paragraph is the opposite side of the coin of paragraph 19. Paragraph 19 empowers a neutral State to condition, restrict or prohibit passage through its neutral waters; paragraph 20 tells a neutral State that it may allow certain categories of actions by warships, auxiliary vessels and their prizes without jeopardising its neutral status. It may allow such actions, however, only if it treats all belligerents impartially and subject to the restrictions contained in paragraphs 21 and 23–33, the former of which deals with the duration of stay within neutral waters, the latter with the rights of transit passage, archipelagic sea lanes passage, non-suspendable innocent passage and innocent passage in periods of armed conflict at sea.

20.2   Paragraph 20 is derived primarily from Hague Convention XIII, Article 9 (duty of impartiality), Article 10 (neutrality not affected by mere passage through territorial sea), Article 11 (employment of licensed pilots of neutral State), Article 17 (repairs in neutral waters), and Article 19 (revictualling and refuelling in neutral waters). The paragraphs adopted by the Round Table track the provisions of Hague Convention XIII except as follows:

(a)   Subparagraph (a): (1) consistent with other provisions within this Part, archipelagic waters are treated the same as the territorial sea; (2) the provision as to prizes is more restrictive than those contained in Hague Convention XIII. Under Hague Convention XIII, for example, prizes may be brought into ports and roadsteads for sequestration pending decision of a prize court.[47] The Round Table's formulation only allows *passage* through territorial waters and archipelagic waters.

(b)   Subparagraph (b): paragraph 20 replaces the ambiguous standard of Article 19 of Hague Convention XIII for 'revictualling' ('peace standard') with what the Round Table believed was a more objective and determinable standard ('sufficient to reach a port of its own territory'). It also replaces the rather cumbersome and ambiguous standard for refuelling with the same standard as for food and water.

(c)   Subparagraph (c): this paragraph does not change the sense of the language of Hague Convention XIII, Articles 17 and 18. The Round Table noted that it was a disputed point as to whether a belligerent was entitled to repair battle damage in neutral waters.[48] The Round Table's draft does not address this point, but it was the sense of the group, as reflected in subparagraph (c), that repairs should be limited to those necessary to make the warship seaworthy, and in no sense should they increase or restore the fighting strength of the warship.

20.3   For an explanation of the inclusion of auxiliary vessels and aircraft in this paragraph, see paragraph 19.4.

21   **A belligerent warship or auxiliary vessel may not extend the duration of its passage through neutral waters, or its presence in those waters for replenishment or repair, for longer than 24 hours unless unavoidable on account of damage or the stress of weather. The foregoing rule does not apply in international straits and waters in which the right of archipelagic sea lanes passage is exercised.**

21.1   One of the disputed provisions of Hague Convention XIII is whether the so-called 24-hour rule applies to passage through the territorial sea as well as to port stays by belligerent warships.[49] After considerable discussion on this point, the Round Table decided to adopt what it felt was the better rule, applying the 24-hour limit to passage

---

47 Hague Convention XIII, Art. 23.
48 See Smith, *The Law and Custom of the Sea*, p. 154.
49 The *Altmark* incident in the Second World War illustrates the dilemma posed by this rule.

through as well as stays in neutral waters. As noted in the second sentence of paragraph 21, however, the rule does not apply to transit passage nor to non-suspendable innocent passage through international straits nor to archipelagic sea lanes passage through archipelagic waters. This position was adopted in recognition of the fact that some straits (for example, Malacca–Singapore) are so lengthy and some archipelagic waters (for example, Indonesia) are so vast that passage through them by warships might very well take more than 24 hours. The inapplicability of the 24-hour rule to transit passage and archipelagic sea lanes passage does not, however, abrogate the general rule, stated in paragraph 30, that warships engaged in such passage are required to proceed without delay.

21.2   Since the exception does not apply to archipelagic waters generally, however, the practical effect of paragraph 21 is that warships engaged in passage through archipelagic waters for which more than 24 hours is required would be unable to exercise the right of innocent passage but would instead have to exercise their right of archipelagic sea lanes passage and remain within such sea lanes.

21.3   For an explanation of the inclusion of auxiliary vessels in the coverage of this paragraph, see paragraph 19.4.

22   Should a belligerent State be in violation of the regime of neutral waters, as set out in this document, the neutral State is under an obligation to take the measures necessary to terminate the violation. If the neutral State fails to terminate the violation of its neutral waters by a belligerent, the opposing belligerent must so notify the neutral State and give that neutral State a reasonable time to terminate the violation by the belligerent. If the violation of the neutrality of the State by the belligerent constitutes a serious and immediate threat to the security of the opposing belligerent and the violation is not terminated, then that belligerent may, in the absence of any feasible and timely alternative, use such force as is strictly necessary to respond to the threat posed by the violation.

22.1   This paragraph was the subject of perhaps the most contentious debate at the Ottawa session of the Round Table. A version proposed by the Rapporteur read as follows:

> Should a neutral State be unwilling or unable to enforce its neutral obligations with respect to hostile activities by belligerent naval forces within its neutral waters, the opposing belligerent may use such force as is necessary within such neutral waters to protect its own forces and to terminate the violation of neutral waters.

22.2   The Rapporteur's formulation reflected traditional law on this issue.[50] Both the United States[51] and Canadian[52] manuals adopt this position. The German Manual

---

50   See D. P. O'Connell, *The International Law of the Sea* (Oxford: Clarendon Press, 1982), vol. 2, p. 1117; L. Oppenheim, *International Law* (London, New York, Toronto: Longmans, Green and Co., 7th edn 1952), vol. II, *War, Disputes and Neutrality* (ed. H. Lauterpacht), p. 695.
51   NWP9A, *The Commander's Handbook*, para. 7.4.3.2.
52   Canadian Manual, para. 1504(2).

states that a neutral State is required 'to employ all means at its disposal' to prevent the fitting out or arming of belligerent vessels within its jurisdiction, and 'to prevent, within the means at its disposal, any violation of the rules of neutrality within its waters', but is silent with respect to the consequences of its failure to live up to its obligations.[53]

22.3   The debate on this issue was largely doctrinal, revolving around the question of the use of force in self-defence. Those who were opposed to the traditional formulation took the position that taking armed defensive measures in neutral waters amounted to a use of force against the territorial integrity of a neutral State, and it could only be justified by a belligerent if it was under an armed attack from that neutral State or an immediate threat of such an attack. Those favouring the traditional rule argued that at this stage the use of armed force is governed by the law of armed conflict, the issue of the justification of self-defence having been resolved at an earlier stage. They also argued that the measures taken in neutral waters were not a use of force against the territorial integrity of the neutral State but against the opposing belligerent and could be justified under a number of doctrines, including necessity and self-defence.

22.4   The first group also argued that since a neutral State's obligation under Hague Convention XIII was only 'to exercise such surveillance *as the means at its disposal allow* to prevent any violation of the provisions' of that Convention, it was too harsh a price to exact to permit immediate resort to force within neutral waters by an injured belligerent force if the neutral was unable to prevent unlawful acts within it neutral waters. In particular, it was suggested that a belligerent should be allowed to respond with force only if the violation by the opposing belligerent posed a serious and immediate threat and after the neutral State had been given notice of the violation and a reasonable opportunity to terminate the threat. A number of formulations were proposed, and the final wording, as adopted by the Round Table, reflected the views of a large majority.

22.5   Several members would have preferred permitting a more immediate response, particularly in cases in which the neutral State was 'unwilling' but not necessarily 'unable' to prevent unlawful actions within its waters. A few thought the paragraph, as finally adopted, was still too harsh in the case of a neutral State which did not have the means to terminate a belligerent's unlawful use of neutral waters.

Section II International straits and archipelagic sea lanes

General rules

23   **Belligerent warships and auxiliary vessels and military and auxiliary aircraft may exercise the rights of passage through, under or over neutral international straits and of archipelagic sea lanes passage provided by general international law.**

23.1   The Rapporteur proposed a provision which read as follows:

---

53   German Manual, paras. 1125 and 1136.

Belligerent warships and military aircraft may exercise the right of transit passage through neutral international straits and archipelagic sea lanes passage through neutral archipelagic waters. While within neutral waters comprising an international strait or an archipelagic sea lane, belligerent naval forces are forbidden to carry out any hostile act.

While the members of the Round Table did not disagree with the idea expressed in the Rapporteur's formulation, a number felt that the principles stated in the provision needed to be spelled out in more detail. Accordingly, the Round Table directed the drafting group to break down the principles reflected in the Rapporteur's proposal and to elaborate each in a separate paragraph. Paragraphs 24–30 reflect the results of this effort on the part of the drafting group.

23.2   The purpose of paragraph 23 is to reaffirm that the rights of passage that belligerent warships, auxiliary vessels and military aircraft may exercise through international straits and archipelagic sea lanes in time of peace are also exercisable in periods of armed conflict at sea. These rights for straits include both the right of transit passage through international straits joining one part of the high seas or an exclusive economic zone with another part of the high seas or exclusive economic zone (Article 38 of the LOS Convention) and the right of non-suspendable innocent passage through those straits not governed by the right of transit passage (Article 45 of the LOS Convention). Unstated but implied by the paragraph is that the status of straits formed by the mainland and an island of the same State as exceptions to the right of transit passage (Article 38(1) of the LOS Convention) is not affected by paragraph 23. Also unstated but implied by the paragraph is that the status of international straits that are governed by existing multilateral treaties (for example, the Turkish Straits) is unaffected by this provision.

23.3   For an explanation of the inclusion of auxiliary vessels in this paragraph, see paragraph 19.4. Since auxiliary aircraft occupy essentially the same relationship to military aircraft as auxiliary vessels do to warships, the Round Table considered that they should be equated to military aircraft for the purpose of this paragraph.

23.4   Paragraph 23 was adopted by the Round Table without significant dissent.

24   The neutrality of a State bordering an international strait is not jeopardised by the transit passage of belligerent warships, auxiliary vessels, or military or auxiliary aircraft, nor by the innocent passage of belligerent warships or auxiliary vessels through that strait.

24.1   Article 10 of Hague Convention XIII provides that: 'The neutrality of a Power is not affected by the mere passage through its territorial waters of warships or prizes belonging to belligerents.' Paragraph 24 adopts the principle of this Article and extends it to transit passage or innocent passage of warships, auxiliary vessels and military and auxiliary aircraft through straits. Since it has already been stated that belligerent warships, auxiliary vessels and military and auxiliary aircraft exercise transit passage as a matter of right and warships and auxiliary vessels the right of non-suspendable innocent passage, neither of which can be denied by the neutral State (paragraph 23), it must necessarily follow that a neutral State's neutrality cannot be jeopardised by such passage. The Round Table accepted this formulation of the principle without significant dissent.

24.2   For explanations for including auxiliary vessels and auxiliary aircraft within the coverage of this paragraph, see paragraphs 19.4 and 23.3 respectively.

25   **The neutrality of an archipelagic State is not jeopardised by the exercise of archipelagic sea lanes passage by belligerent warships, auxiliary vessels, or military or auxiliary aircraft.**

25.1   The commentary to paragraph 24 applies *mutatis mutandis* to this paragraph.

26   **Neutral warships, auxiliary vessels, and military and auxiliary aircraft may exercise the rights of passage provided by general international law through, under and over belligerent international straits and archipelagic waters. The neutral State should, as a precautionary measure, give timely notice of its exercise of the rights of passage to the belligerent State.**

26.1   During the Round Table's discussion it was noted that the Rapporteur's draft provisions did not include any provision concerning the right of neutral warships, auxiliary vessels and military and auxiliary aircraft to continue to exercise their rights of passage through international straits and archipelagic waters of belligerent States. This was felt to be a significant omission and accordingly paragraph 26 was adopted to fill this void.

26.2   Paragraph 26 makes it clear that the warships, auxiliary vessels and military and auxiliary aircraft of neutral States retain during times of armed conflict peacetime rights of transit passage and innocent passage through international straits and archipelagic sea lanes passage and innocent passage through archipelagic waters that are under the control of belligerent States. Although such passage by neutral warships and military aircraft is a matter of right, the Round Table felt that as a matter of prudence neutral States should give timely notice of the passage of their warships and military aircraft to avoid the possibility of mistakes in recognition that might occur in time of armed conflict. It accordingly framed the second sentence of paragraph 26 in hortatory rather than mandatory terms.

26.3   The Round Table also discussed briefly the question of the right of neutral warships to exercise innocent passage through those parts of the territorial sea of a belligerent State not forming part of a strait or an archipelagic sea lane, but it did not formulate a text on this issue. It was felt that since a coastal State may temporarily close parts of its territorial sea in time of peace,[54] *a fortiori*, it could do so in time of armed conflict.

26.4   For an explanation of including auxiliary vessels and auxiliary aircraft within the coverage of this paragraph, see paragraphs 19.4 and 23.3 respectively.

---

54   LOS Convention, Art. 25, para. 3.

Transit passage and archipelagic sea lanes passage

27   **The rights of transit passage and archipelagic sea lanes passage applicable to international straits and archipelagic waters in peacetime continue to apply in times of armed conflict. The laws and regulations of States bordering straits and archipelagic States relating to transit passage and archipelagic sea lanes passage adopted in accordance with general international law remain applicable.**

27.1   The first sentence of paragraph 27 reaffirms that the rights of transit passage and archipelagic sea lanes passage continue in time of armed conflict as well as in time of peace. In this respect it is somewhat repetitive of paragraphs 23 and 26. The second sentence, on the other hand, reaffirms that States bordering straits and archipelagic States continue to retain the powers vested in them by general international law (that is, the peacetime law of the sea) to adopt laws and regulations governing transit passage and archipelagic sea lanes passage permitted under general international law.

27.2   The Round Table agreed that the laws and regulations permitted to States bordering straits and archipelagic States were as set forth in the LOS Convention. These are contained in Articles 41 and 42 of the LOS Convention with respect to international straits and Article 54 with respect to archipelagic waters.

27.3   Paragraph 27 was adopted by the Round Table without significant dissent.

28   **Belligerent and neutral surface ships, submarines and aircraft have the rights of transit passage and archipelagic sea lanes passage through, under, and over all straits and archipelagic waters to which these rights generally apply.**

28.1   The Round Table was in general agreement that the right of transit passage for international straits and archipelagic sea lanes passage for archipelagic waters embraced all three modes of passage – subsurface, surface and air. This interpretation is consistent with the generally accepted interpretation of Articles 39 and 54 of the LOS Convention concerning the 'normal mode' of 'continuous and expeditious' transit through waters governed by these regimes. There was extensive discussion as to what the 'normal mode' might be in time of armed conflict when both belligerent and neutral forces would usually be in a heightened state of readiness. As a result of this discussion, the Round Table agreed to express its views on this subject in a separate paragraph – paragraph 30 below.

29   **Neutral States may not suspend, hamper, or otherwise impede the right of transit passage nor the right of archipelagic sea lanes passage.**

29.1   This paragraph also reflects the Round Table's decision to elaborate more fully on the subjects of transit passage and archipelagic sea lanes passage than was originally proposed in the Rapporteur's recommendations (see commentary to paragraph 23 above). The provisions of this paragraph paraphrase the protections that the LOS Convention, Articles 38, 42, 53 and 54 provide against restrictions imposed by States bordering straits or archipelagic States on the rights of transit passage and archipelagic sea lanes passage.

29.2   Paragraph 29 was adopted by the Round Table without significant dissent.

30   **A belligerent in transit passage through, under and over a neutral international strait, or in archipelagic sea lanes passage through, under and over neutral archipelagic waters, is required to proceed without delay, to refrain from the threat or use of force against the territorial integrity or political independence of the neutral littoral or archipelagic State, or in any other manner inconsistent with the purposes of the Charter of the United Nations, and otherwise to refrain from any hostile actions or other activities not incident to their transit. Belligerents passing through, under and over neutral straits or waters in which the right of archipelagic sea lanes passage applies are permitted to take defensive measures consistent with their security, including launching and recovery of aircraft, screen formation steaming, and acoustic and electronic surveillance. Belligerents in transit or archipelagic sea lanes passage may not, however, conduct offensive operations against enemy forces, nor use such neutral waters as a place of sanctuary nor as a base of operations.**

30.1   This paragraph was one of the most seriously debated provisions at the Ottawa meeting of the Round Table. There was general agreement among members of the Round Table that while in transit passage or archipelagic sea lanes passage a belligerent unit or force was required to behave with respect to the State bordering the strait or the archipelagic State in the manner prescribed in the first sentence of this paragraph (the rules for such behaviour being derived from Articles 38, 39, 53 and 54 of the LOS Convention). There also seemed to be general agreement that because of the danger of unlawful attack on a transiting unit by an opposing belligerent which might ignore its duty to respect the neutrality of the State bordering the strait or archipelagic State, the transiting unit should be allowed to go through in a high state of readiness and should be able to adopt the defensive measures necessary for the self-defence of the unit or force. The Round Table noted that with respect to transit passage the United States operational manual states:

> Belligerent forces in transit may ... take defensive measures consistent with their security, including the launching and recovery of aircraft, screen formation steaming, and acoustic and electronic surveillance. Belligerent forces may not use neutral straits as a place of sanctuary nor a base of operations, and belligerent warships may not exercise the belligerent right of visit and search in those waters.[55]

30.2   A number of participants of the Round Table, however, posed hypothetical scenarios which would put to the test the question of what were 'defensive measures' by a transiting force, particularly a large task force consisting of numerous ships and embarked fixed-wing or rotary-wing aircraft. Among the examples cited were:

---

55   NWP9, *The Commander's Handbook*, para. 7.3.5. The Canadian Manual, para. 1511, has a provision of similar import but of less specificity.

–   part of the task force is within the neutral waters of a strait or archipelago and the part which is outside is brought under attack by the opposing belligerent which is outside the neutral waters. Could the units within neutral waters launch a counter-attack? Would this be a permitted defensive measure?

–   the unit or force within neutral waters is brought under attack by a unit launching long-range missiles from outside neutral waters. Could the units within neutral waters launch a counter-attack? Would this be a permitted defensive measure?

–   a unit of the armed forces of the transiting force which is outside the neutral waters and not a part of the transiting force is brought under attack by an enemy unit outside neutral waters. Could the force within neutral waters send aircraft to assist the unit under attack? Would this be a permitted defensive measure?

–   a helicopter conducting anti-submarine surveillance ahead of the transiting force detects an enemy submarine lying in wait just outside neutral waters to attack the force upon its emergence. Could the helicopter attack the submarine? Would this be a permitted defensive measure?

30.3   After much discussion, the Round Table determined that it could not draft a provision that would meet all contingencies but would have to rely on more general language as adopted in paragraph 30. It believed that bringing out these difficulties in the commentary would serve to give some guidance to commanders without tying its guidance to scenario-specific situations. The key point, in the minds of most, was a fair interpretation of the prohibition against using neutral waters as a base of operations.

Innocent passage

31   In addition to the exercise of the rights of transit and archipelagic sea lanes passage, belligerent vessels and auxiliary vessels may, subject to paragraphs 19 and 21, exercise the right of innocent passage through neutral international straits and archipelagic waters in accordance with general international law.

31.1   Paragraph 31 points out that the right of innocent passage through neutral international straits and archipelagic waters continues to exist in parallel with the rights of transit passage and archipelagic sea lanes passage through straits.

31.2   This paragraph was adopted without dissent, although several participants of the Round Table wanted it noted in the commentary that some Governments maintained the position that innocent passage of warships, even in peacetime, was subject to prior authorisation or notification.

32 **Neutral vessels may likewise exercise the right of innocent passage through belligerent international straits and archipelagic waters.**

32.1   Paragraph 32 is the obverse of paragraph 31, and parallels the symmetry of paragraphs 23 and 26. It makes clear that the right of innocent passage through international straits and archipelagic waters which exists in peacetime continues to exist for neutral warships in time of armed conflict at sea even though the State bordering a strait or the archipelagic State is a belligerent.

32.2   This paragraph was adopted without dissent. Several members wanted it noted in the commentary, however, that some Governments maintained the position that innocent passage of warships, even in peacetime, was subject to prior authorisation or notification.

33 **The right of non-suspendable innocent passage ascribed to certain international straits by international law may not be suspended in time of armed conflict.**

33.1   Paragraph 33 reaffirms that the right of non-suspendable innocent passage through certain international straits, which is codified in Article 45 of the LOS Convention, may not be suspended in time of armed conflict at sea. Although this prohibition against suspension is strongly implied by paragraph 19, this paragraph makes the prohibition explicit.

33.2   This provision would not apply, of course, to those straits where passage is governed by a specific treaty regime if that regime permits suspension in time of armed conflict.

33.3   Paragraph 33 was adopted without dissent.

Section III Exclusive economic zone and continental shelf

34 **If hostile actions are conducted within the exclusive economic zone or on the continental shelf of a neutral State, belligerent States shall, in addition to observing the other applicable rules of the law of armed conflict at sea, have due regard for the rights and duties of the coastal State, *inter alia,* for the exploration and exploitation of the economic resources of the exclusive economic zone and the continental shelf and the protection and preservation of the marine environment. They shall, in particular, have due regard for artificial islands, installations, structures and safety zones established by neutral States in the exclusive economic zone and on the continental shelf.**

34.1   This paragraph is an elaboration of the duties of belligerent States set forth in more general terms in paragraph 12. It will be recalled that paragraph 12 obliges belligerents to have due regard for the legitimate rights and duties of neutral States in *all* areas of the oceans where neutrals enjoy any form of rights, whether flowing from sovereign rights, jurisdiction or general international law. Because the exclusive economic zone and continental shelf are areas in which coastal States have particularly important economic rights and duties which are vulnerable to interruption or destruction by hostile actions within them, the Round Table felt it was important to spell out in more detail the particular duties of belligerents to have due regard for these rights.

34.2   Although the belligerents' duties with respect to certain activities and installations, structures, etc., are explicitly stated, the use of the term *inter alia* makes it clear that the list is illustrative and not exhaustive. While the Round Table did not make explicit reference to Parts V and VI of the LOS Convention, which codify the customary international law of the exclusive economic zone and the continental shelf, it is obvious that the terms used come from that Convention and should be interpreted in the light of that Convention.

34.3   As in the case of paragraph 12 it was left for the final session of the Round Table to determine whether 'due regard' or 'respect' was the appropriate standard applicable to a belligerent's conduct under paragraph 34. For the reasons stated in paragraph 12.2, the 'due regard' standard was adopted.

34.4   At the Ottawa session the Round Table enclosed the phrase 'and the protection and preservation of the marine environment' in square brackets. This action was taken because the Round Table, while recognising the special responsibility of the coastal State for the protection and preservation of the marine environment,[56] had not yet had the opportunity for a full discussion of the rules that might be applicable. Such a discussion was held subsequently at the 1993 Geneva session, and, as a result of that discussion, the square brackets were removed indicating the Round Table's conclusion that if the belligerent undertook hostile actions in the exclusive economic zone or on the continental shelf, it had the same obligation with respect to the coastal State's rights and duties as to the environment as it did with respect to the other rights and duties of the coastal State in these zones.

35   **If a belligerent considers it necessary to lay mines in the exclusive economic zone or the continental shelf of a neutral State, the belligerent shall notify that State, and shall ensure, *inter alia*, that the size of the minefield and the type of mines used do not endanger artificial islands, installations and structures, nor interfere with access thereto, and shall avoid so far as practicable interference with the exploration or exploitation of the zone by the neutral State. Due regard shall also be given to the protection and preservation of the marine environment.**

35.1   The subject of mining of the exclusive economic zone and the continental shelf was of particular concern to several participants of the Round Table. A few would have been in favour of a rule that prohibited altogether the mining of the exclusive economic zone or the continental shelf of a neutral coastal State. The majority, however, were of the view that since the exclusive economic zone and the continental shelf were the equivalent of high seas in so far as the conduct of hostile activities of belligerent States were concerned, there should not be an outright prohibition of the employment of mines in such areas. All members recognised that mining caused

56   See LOS Convention, Art. 56(1)(a)(iii).

particular hazards to legitimate activities by neutral States in their own exclusive economic zones and continental shelves and accordingly agreed that if mining were undertaken, the State laying the mines was under a duty to take special precautions to ensure that the mines did not unduly interfere with the coastal State's exploration or exploitation of the economic resources of the zones.

35.2   The Round Table believed that it was particularly important that if a belligerent laid mines in the exclusive economic zone or continental shelf of a neutral State that it must in all cases notify the neutral State. In addition, it must not endanger artificial islands, installations and structures. The foregoing were absolute duties, whereas the duty to avoid interference with exploration or exploitation of the natural resources was a relative duty, that is to avoid interfering 'so far as practicable'. This latter expression indicates a balancing of interests between the right of the belligerent to take hostile actions against its enemy while at the same time having regard for the right of the coastal State to exploit the economic resources of its exclusive economic zone and continental shelf. Attention was particularly drawn to the size of the minefield and type of mines that might be used, although the use of the term *inter alia* makes it clear that other aspects of the employment of mines must also be considered. Although not stated, such other factors might include the time and duration of the employment of mines, the method of laying and sweeping, and the provision of access lanes to installations or structures in the zones.

35.3   As in the case of paragraph 34, the Ottawa session enclosed the provisions concerning protection and preservation of the marine environment in square brackets. At the Geneva session it was decided to remove the brackets for the same reason that the brackets were removed in paragraph 34.

35.4   For an explanation of the adoption of the 'due regard' standard for the belligerent's duty with respect to the protection and preservation of the marine environment, see paragraph 12.2.

Section IV High seas and sea-bed beyond national jurisdiction

36   **Hostile actions on the high seas shall be conducted with due regard for the exercise by neutral States of rights of exploration and exploitation of the natural resources of the sea-bed, and ocean floor, and the subsoil thereof, beyond national jurisdiction.**

36.1   As pointed out in the commentary to paragraph 10, the Round Table did not accept the proposition that Articles 88 and 301 of the LOS Convention excluded naval warfare on the high seas. Nevertheless, recognising that such hostile activities by belligerents beyond the exclusive economic zone and the continental shelf might endanger activities or installations of those States that may be engaging in sea-bed mining, it wished to include an explicit provision pointing out that these activities were entitled to the same protection as other legitimate activities by other States on the high seas. The concession zones in which such exploration or exploitation was permitted (whether under Part XI of the LOS Convention or some other lawful authority) were not, however, exclusion zones in so far as hostile actions were concerned. Where sea-bed exploratory or exploitation activities were being conducted by one of the belligerents, its vessels and installations used in connection therewith were subject to the rules for targeting according to whether they were legitimate military objectives as determined by the criteria contained in Part III of the Manual.

36.2   The Round Table's consensus as to the general duty of belligerents with respect to activities and installations of others in the 'Area' is set forth in paragraph 36.

36.3   For an explanation of the use of the 'due regard' standard for belligerents' hostile actions on the high seas, see paragraph 12.2.

37   Belligerents shall take care to avoid damage to cables and pipelines laid on the sea-bed which do not exclusively serve the belligerents.

37.1   Paragraph 37 reflects the Round Table's concern for protection of cables and pipelines laid on the sea-bed of all parts of the oceans. It recognises, however, that cables or pipelines exclusively serving one or more of the belligerents might be legitimate military objectives.

PART III

BASIC RULES AND TARGET DISCRIMINATION

Section I Basic rules

38   **In any armed conflict the right of the parties to the conflict to choose methods or means of warfare is not unlimited.**

38.1   There are no explicit treaty provisions at the present time which specifically state that the general principles applicable in armed conflict on land are also relevant to the conduct of hostilities at sea. However, it logically follows from the whole body of law that this general principle is firmly rooted in the law of naval armed conflict. Moreover, on 19 December 1968, the United Nations General Assembly, in Resolution 2444 (XXIII), unanimously affirmed certain principles underlying the law of armed conflict, including the requirements stated in paragraphs 38 and 39.

38.2   This basic rule obviously finds its roots in conferences and discussions which took place in the nineteenth century. The principle found its way into documents on the law of armed conflict as early as 1874 at the Brussels Conference (Article 12). The formulation was subsequently developed in the Hague Regulations of 1907 (Article 22). With regard to the wording of the paragraph, it should be noted that it is taken from Article 35(1) of Additional Protocol I. Although that Article falls outside the scope of Article 49(3), of the Protocol and therefore already applies in naval warfare, it was felt appropriate to include it in this document to emphasise the importance of the principle. Additional comments on the rule can therefore be found in existing commentaries.[57] Relevant to the effective implementation of this paragraph is also Article 36 of API regarding new weapons. The obligation to evaluate new means and methods of warfare in relation to the obligations of the party concerned under the law of armed conflict follows logically from the lack of freedom of choice as expressed in this paragraph. Hence, the Article is also deemed to be binding upon States that are not party to Protocol I. The provision is equally applicable in the choice of means and methods in naval warfare.

38.3   The Round Table agreed not to discuss issues related to the use of weapons of mass destruction, in particular of nuclear weapons, in the drafting of this Manual.

---

57   Cf. ICRC Commentary to Additional Protocol I, *Commentary on the Additional Protocols of 8 June 1977 to the Geneva Conventions of 12 August 1949* (eds.) Yves Sandoz, Christophe Swinarski, Bruno Zimmermann, 1987, pp. 390–9.

39 **Parties to the conflict shall at all times distinguish between civilians or other protected persons and combatants and between civilian or exempt objects and military objectives.**

39.1   There is no treaty provision at the present time which specifically states that the principle of distinction applies to the law of naval warfare. On the other hand, on 19 December 1968, the United Nations General Assembly, in Resolution 2444 (XXIII), unanimously affirmed certain principles underlying the law of armed conflict in general, including a requirement 'that distinction must be made at all times between persons taking part in the hostilities and members of the civilian population to the effect that the latter be spared as much as possible'. The Round Table agreed that this requirement applies to the law of naval warfare. Indeed, if a law of armed conflict purporting to regulate how naval operations are to be conducted is to exist, an essential element of that body of law, no matter how inchoate, is the principle of distinction, also referred to as the principle of identification. The existence of such a body of law is premised upon a requirement to distinguish between objects or persons who may be attacked and objects or persons who may not be attacked. Although the increasing percentage of civilian casualties relative to total casualties in some contemporary conflicts has caused some writers to suggest that the principle of distinction has become blurred in our century, no legal scholar would view this as a positive development.

39.2   Paragraph 39 is similar to but not identical with API, Article 48 because paragraph 39 also makes reference to military protected persons and exempt objects. These categories are not in Article 48 of API as this Article is in the section of API which only relates to the protection of the civilian population and civilian objects, and therefore the formulation of paragraph 39 is more complete.

40 **In so far as objects are concerned, military objectives are limited to those objects which by their nature, location, purpose or use make an effective contribution to military action and whose total or partial destruction, capture or neutralisation, in the circumstances ruling at the time, offers a definite military advantage.**

40.1   The participants focused initially upon the question of whether it was appropriate to start from a general definition of military objectives in naval warfare or from a list which comprises either categories of vessels that may be attacked or of vessels that are exempt from attack.

40.2   The 'list approach', whether based on categories of specially protected vessels or on categories of vessels liable to attack, was favoured by those who doubted the operability of a general definition in naval combat situations and who considered it important to provide naval commanders with what were labelled 'bright line rules'. Other participants either doubted the value of lists altogether or pointed out the difficulties that approach would imply. Those opposing the idea of lists believed a general definition to be sufficient, for a naval commander would attack only if he had reasons to think he was threatened. Hence, it depended on the circumstances and/or the perception of the individual naval commander as to whether there were sufficient reasons of military necessity to consider a vessel a military objective or not. That was also the case with regard to the vessels specially protected under the traditional law of naval warfare. For example, during Operation Market Time in the Vietnam conflict, small coastal fishing vessels had been considered legitimate military objectives owing to their integration into the North Vietnamese intelligence system. Those who saw difficulties in connection with the 'list approach', even though they considered such lists useful at least to illustrate a general definition, argued such lists would not provide answers for every case and doubts would remain. A comprehensive list of categories of vessels that may be attacked would, in their view, not be accepted by a number of States. A list of categories of ships exempt from attack would imply that those vessels not comprised therein could be attacked without any legal restraints. A single list of protected vessels would not take into account the different degrees of exemption accorded to different categories of ships under existing international law. An inflation of the list of protected vessels by, for example, according equal treatment to coastal fishing vessels and hospital ships, would undermine the protection currently accorded to hospital ships under GCII.

40.3   The protagonists of the 'general definition approach' advocated starting from the definition of military objectives laid down in API Article 52(2). In their view, one should not over-emphasise the practice of States during the First and the Second World Wars but should make use of the achievements and benefits of the work that has been done since 1969, in particular of the results of the Diplomatic Conference in Geneva, 1974–77. The root of the problem was not the categories of vessels liable to attack or specially protected but the circumstances ruling at the time. Since those circumstances could not be specified generally and in advance, there was a need for a general definition. If API Article 52(2) was considered appropriate also for the naval warfare context, then the presumption of innocence laid down in API Article 52(3) could be taken into account.

40.4   This position, however, did not remain undisputed either. For one group, the definition in API Article 52(2) was characterised as too vague. In this context the need for 'bright line rules' was emphasised once again. A commander on the bridge of a ship needed simple instructions operable in combat situations and enabling him to take a decision immediately on whether to engage a target or not. Others, while not totally opposing the definition approach, criticised any presumption of innocence as ineffective and inoperable in a modern naval warfare context, in particular in an escalating situation. Some argued that the naval commander would in any event confine himself to the definition and would simply consider any means of transportation at sea a military objective. Being thus rendered meaningless in a combat situation, any inclusion of a presumption of innocence would be contrary to the principle of effectiveness.

40.5   With regard to the allegedly vague wording of API Article 52(2), those participants favouring a general definition made clear that they did not intend to provide naval commanders with that definition exclusively. Rather, it was the duty of the respective governments to formulate appropriate rules of engagement or other instructions for a given situation that were in accordance with the general definition.

40.6   The arguments put forward against an inclusion of the presumption of innocence were dealt with to a considerable extent. It was admitted that in an escalating situation involving military aircraft the presumption of innocence might be inoperable or even counter-productive with regard to the safety of the warship concerned. That, however, was believed not to be the case in the majority of circumstances under which the principle of presumed innocence could be very useful. If that principle had been part of the law and had been functioning during the First World War, the *Lusitania* would not have been sunk. In addition, some participants pointed to the systematic context of API Article 52. Paragraph 3 would only come into operation if there were no sufficient grounds to establish that an object fulfilled the requirements of paragraph 2. Others stressed that a requirement to consider cases of doubt was already built into API Article 52(2).

40.7   At the end of the discussion on the question of how to proceed, there was a tendency among the participants to agree on a combined approach, that is, to start with a general definition that was to be supplemented by a list of vessels exempt from attack. Although at this stage there was not yet a settled consensus on the contents of such a definition, the majority regarded it as a necessity in order to have a basic and comprehensive provision that would apply to every case. Many of the participants were inclined to make use of API Article 52(2). It was understood that in that regard the principle of distinction was of considerable importance and that in the light of that principle any attempt to make use of API required an extensive analysis with a view to seeing whether the wording could be adapted to or adopted in naval warfare. Consequently, it was left to the drafting group to suggest a text. The adoption of a list of categories of protected vessels was considered useful as a means for specifying the definition and because of reasons of legal clarity, for such a list would enable naval commanders to establish whether a given vessel was liable to attack or not. With regard to the different degrees of exemption already accorded to different categories of vessels, it remained unsettled whether this problem was to be solved either by applying the principle of presumed innocence or by taking the different degrees of protection into consideration when formulating the results.

40.8   Another issue, which to a large extent was being dealt with simultaneously, arose after some participants had distinguished between general and limited war situations because they believed that in the latter case more legal restrictions had to be applied than in the former. Eventually it was agreed that the legal rules should remain the same in both general and limited war situations but that the application of these rules to the facts should result in a more restrictive approach to targeting in limited conflicts.

40.9   The Round Table eventually adopted the text of API Article 52(2) as paragraph 40 and applied it to naval warfare, although it was agreed that location would often be of less significance in a naval conflict because virtually every military objective would be mobile. It should be noted that paragraph 40 refers to objects only. Combatants also constitute military objectives.

40.10   Paragraph 40 imposes a two-pronged test. Military objectives are those objects which by their nature, location, purpose or use:

(a)   make an effective contribution to military action; *and*

(b)   whose total or partial destruction, capture or neutralisation, in the circumstances ruling at the time, offers a definite military advantage.

40.11   The objects classified as military objectives under this definition include much more than strictly military objects such as warships, military vehicles, weapons, munitions, stores of fuel and fortifications. Provided the objects meet the two-pronged test, under the circumstances ruling at the time (not at some hypothetical future time), military objectives include activities providing administrative and logistical support to military operations such as transportation and communications systems, railroads, airfields and port facilities and industries of fundamental importance for the conduct of the armed conflict.

40.12   Military objectives must make an 'effective contribution to military action'. This does not require a direct connection with combat operations. Thus a civilian object may become a military objective and thereby lose its immunity from deliberate attack through use which is only indirectly related to combat action, but which nevertheless provides an effective contribution to the military part of a party's overall war-fighting capability. The Round Table considered whether or not it should include the expression 'military action' or some alternative expression such as 'war effort' or 'war-sustaining effort' and eventually decided that these alternative expressions were too broad. See the discussions related to paragraphs 59, 60, 62, 63, 67 and 70.

41   **Attacks shall be limited strictly to military objectives. Merchant vessels and civilian aircraft are civilian objects unless they are military objectives in accordance with the principles and rules set forth in this document.**

41.1   The terms 'attack', 'merchant vessel' and 'civil aircraft' are defined in paragraph 13. 'Military objective' is defined in paragraph 40. An attack is an act of violence. Attacks must be directed against or aimed at military objectives and against a limited group of neutral ships and aircraft which are described in paragraphs 67 and 70 and are engaged in tasks which are functionally indistinguishable from those performed by enemy ships or aircraft which are military objectives. If an attack directed against a military objective causes collateral injury or damage to other persons or objects either because it misses the military objective or because it hits a military objective but the effect of the hit extends beyond the military objective, the law is not automatically violated. No method or means of warfare functions with 100 per cent accuracy. In general, the percentage of projectiles which actually hit the objective aimed at is quite small. The possibility of collateral damage does not as such render an attack unlawful.

42   **In addition to any specific prohibitions binding upon the parties to a conflict, it is forbidden to employ methods or means of warfare which:**

(a)   **are of a nature to cause superfluous injury or unnecessary suffering;** *or*

(b)   **are indiscriminate, in that:**

(i)   **they are not, or cannot be, directed against a specific military objective;** *or*

(ii)   **their effects cannot be limited as required by international law as reflected in this document.**

42.1   The rules contained in paragraph 42 reflect the general applicability of basic principles regarding unnecessary suffering/superfluous injury and discrimination. The lead-in sentence specifies that prohibitions such as those in the 1868 St Petersburg Declaration, the 1899 Hague Declaration on expanding bullets, the 1925 Geneva Protocol, and the prohibition of the use of weapons which primarily injure with non-detectable fragments as contained in Protocol I to the 1980 Certain Conventional Weapons Convention, apply equally in naval warfare. Moreover, the sentence also reflects the possibility that additional specific prohibitions might be agreed upon in the future.

42.2   Paragraph 42(a) reflects the long-standing rule regarding the prohibition against using means and methods of a nature to cause superfluous injury or unnecessary suffering. Its wording stems mainly from Article 35(2) of Additional Protocol I, but was already laid down in earlier provisions, such as the preamble to the St Petersburg Declaration and Article 23(a) of the Hague Regulations of 1907. Like paragraph 38, this provision of API is applicable in naval warfare. Generally, this principle is of relatively minor value in naval warfare as methods and means of warfare are predominantly directed at objects. Participants, however, deemed inclusion of the principle in this document useful in order not to preclude any future discussions on the basis of the principle.

42.3   Paragraph 42(b) is the naval equivalent of Article 51(4) of Additional Protocol I. In contrast to paragraph 38 and 42(a), this Article of API is not applicable in naval warfare. Insertion of the paragraph in this document logically follows from the applicability of the principle of distinction. Reference is therefore made to the commentary on paragraphs 39–41. Both the principle of distinction and the prohibition on indiscriminate attacks are developed in Part IV of the Manual containing rules with regard to specific means and methods of warfare.

43   **It is prohibited to order that there shall be no survivors, to threaten an adversary therewith or to conduct hostilities on this basis.**

43.1   The provision regarding quarter is identical to Article 40 in Additional Protocol I. As is the case with paragraphs 38 and 41(a), the effect of inclusion in this document is merely an affirmation that the provision concerned is already applicable to naval warfare.

43.2   The provision has had a long historical development, although it is only in the nineteenth century that a definite stand was taken against the declaration that no quarter be given. The present text is a further development of Article 23(d) of the 1907 Hague Regulations and is obviously closely linked to the respect and care for wounded, sick and shipwrecked at sea. In fact, it could be argued that in the light of the remarks made earlier with regard to the unnecessary-suffering rule, it should be seen more as a part of the obligation to protect wounded, sick and shipwrecked than a principle which would apply directly to the conduct of naval operations, which by their nature principally affect objects rather than combatants. This approach is reflected in the 1913 Oxford Manual of Naval War, where the prohibition against denying quarter is mentioned in Article 17 which also covers the prohibition of killing or wounding enemies who have surrendered.

43.3   The continued validity of the rule in naval hostilities has been confirmed over and over again in several famous court cases arising out of the Second World War.[58]

44   Methods and means of warfare should be employed with due regard for the natural environment taking into account the relevant rules of international law. Damage to or destruction of the natural environment not justified by military necessity and carried out wantonly is prohibited.

44.1   The Round Table of Experts at its preliminary session (San Remo, Italy, from 15–17 June 1987) noted that the 'new technologies and methods of naval warfare, new developments in the law of armed conflict and the law of the sea and the increased possibilities of grave harm to the environment as a result of armed conflict at sea ...' warranted study, *inter alia*, of armed conflict at sea adversely affecting the environment.

44.2   However, the Madrid Plan of Action for the study of the law of armed conflicts at sea did not list the protection of the environment as one of the topics to be addressed. Nevertheless, the draft text resulting from the Toulon session of the Round Table in 1989 contained a paragraph 37 between square brackets dealing with the subject. That paragraph stated: 'As far as military requirements permit, methods or means of warfare should be employed with due regard to protection of the natural environment.'

44.3   The subject-matter of protection of the environment in the law of naval warfare was introduced as an agreed agenda topic for the 1993 session of the Round Table in Geneva following preliminary discussions during the Bergen meeting in 1991 and the Ottawa meeting of 1992.

44.4   During the Geneva meeting the Special Rapporteur on the protection of the environment in armed conflict reached the conclusion that there does exist a duty upon States during peacetime not to harm the marine environment. But the application of this obligation in armed conflict, beyond the threshold indicated in the 1977 United Nations Convention on the Prohibition of Military or Any Other Hostile Use of Environmental Modification Techniques (Enmod Convention) and in Articles 35(3) and 55 of Additional Protocol I, is still ambiguous and uncertain. On the other hand the Special Rapporteur underlined that the experience of the Gulf War (1991) showed very clearly that there was at least an emerging rule forbidding the use of the marine environment as an instrument of warfare or making it an object of attack during an armed conflict at sea. Therefore he suggested *inter alia*:

(i)   that the square brackets around paragraph 37 of the draft text be removed; *and*

(ii)   that a new paragraph be added to the text which reflects the new tendency outlawing the use of the marine environment as an instrument of warfare or as a direct target or object during an armed conflict at sea.

---

58   Cf. *inter alia* the references to the Dönitz, Raeder and Von Ruchteschell trials in W. J. Fenrick, Introductory Report, published in Wolff Heintschel v. Heinegg (ed.) *The Military Objective and the Principle of Distinction in the Law of Naval Warfare*, pp. 11–17.

44.5   As a result of substantial discussion at the Geneva session it was agreed to remove the square brackets around the old paragraph and to complete it by a new sentence stating that: 'Damage to or destruction of the natural environment not justified by military necessity and carried out wantonly is prohibited.' The latter addition was meant to satisfy the suggestion made by the Special Rapporteur in this regard, and in response to the concern expressed by a number of participants, that within the limits of the principle of military necessity, the draft should outlaw the use of the marine environment as an instrument of warfare or as a direct target or object of attack during an armed conflict at sea.

44.6   During the Geneva session there was considerable discussion as to whether the operative standard for the parties to an armed conflict at sea, in carrying out their duties with regard to the protection of the marine environment, should be 'due regard' or 'respect' for marine environment. The formula of 'due regard' was originally accepted by the participants since it was already accepted in the general law of the sea and reflected the balance that should exist between the rights of the parties to an armed conflict at sea to conduct hostile activities in the maritime areas and their duty to protect and preserve the marine environment.

44.7   In fact, the 'due regard' formula came into the picture at the Toulon session in 1989, and it was a reflection of the concern for the environment that has found extensive expression in the LOS Convention as one of the important innovations the Convention brought, and which since 1989 has increased in importance in relation to the law of armed conflict at sea.

44.8   The discussion leader for the session at which environmental issues were addressed sought to go beyond the formula of 'due regard' by stating that 'there is little "hard" law dealing with the problem of environmental protection during armed conflicts at sea. Nevertheless, what little law there is should have priority over any "due regard" formula.'[59] Then he proposed an amendment to the old paragraph 37 of the draft text as follows:

> States engaged in armed conflict at sea shall have due regard to the natural environment. They shall comply with all rules of international law protecting the natural environment, whether in a treaty or other source, that specifically apply to armed conflict situations at sea.

From the point of view of the author of this proposal: 'The advantage of this approach should be its durability. As new rules emerge the "due regard" formula will automatically give way to the specific rules of, for example, a treaty on the subject.' There was no consensus in favour of this proposal.

44.9   A new formula emerged during the discussion to replace the formula of 'due regard' by the formula of 'respect for'. A number of participants felt that a higher

---

59   For a general overview of international humanitarian law that helps protect the environment, see, for example, International Committee of the Red Cross, *Protection of the Environment in Time of Armed Conflict: Report Submitted by the International Committee of the Red Cross to the Forty-Eighth Session of the United Nations General Assembly (1993)*.

burden should be placed on the parties to any armed conflict at sea and that 'respect' more adequately conveyed this meaning. Adherents of the 'due regard' formulation felt that 'due regard', a relative term, was more appropriate, especially since it was the standard already established by the LOS Convention and more appropriately expressed the balance that must exist between the right of States involved in naval conflict at sea to use lawful methods and means of warfare on the one hand, and the duty of such States to protect the marine environment on the other.

44.10   At the final session in Livorno the matter was again thoroughly discussed. Some participants proposed the following rewording of the first sentence of this paragraph:

> Methods and means of warfare shall be employed complying with all rules of international law on the protection and preservation of the natural environment which apply to a situation of armed conflict at sea, whatever their source.

In the eyes of these participants this proposal was clearer and more straightforward. Above all, it left an opening for future development of the law applicable to the protection of the environment in armed conflict. Other participants, however, felt that the reference in the paragraph to 'taking into account the relevant rules of international law' adequately provided that such rules as are applicable in armed conflict have to be respected, and that additionally retaining the due regard standard would contribute to a more effective protection. This was because the rules presently directly referring to the environment in armed conflict are very limited and that the 'due regard' formula left flexibility for an assessment of the conflicting interests in each particular case. See also the commentary on paragraph 12 on the use of the term 'due regard'.

45   Surface ships, submarines and aircraft are bound by the same principles and rules.

45.1   Concerns with respect to adherence to the principles and rules of the law of armed conflict have been expressed since the advent of submarines and aircraft in naval war. Traditional rules regarding visit and search could only be enforced to a limited extent by submarines and not at all by fixed-wing aircraft. Moreover, it was difficult for submarines, and nearly impossible for aircraft, to ensure compliance with the obligation to provide safety for crew and passengers of ships if the vessel had been or was to be sunk. In particular, the United Kingdom had endeavoured to prohibit the use of submarines in naval warfare on several occasions prior to the Second World War.

45.2   Existing treaty provisions only refer to the obligation for submarines to conform to rules governing the behaviour of surface combatants. Article 1(1) of the 1922 Washington Treaty refers to the customary law rule that merchant vessels may not be attacked, unless they actively resist visit and search or do not proceed as directed after capture. At any rate, the long-standing rule expressed in earlier instruments that crew and passengers of the vessel concerned were to be put in a place of safety, should be abided by. The Article follows on to state in paragraph 2 of the same Article that submarines are also bound by such rules and that if they cannot, under the specific circumstances, conform to them, the merchant vessel should be left unharmed. These rules were subsequently included in Article 22 of the 1930 London Treaty and, upon the expiration of this Treaty, in the 1936 London Procès-Verbal.

45.3   Both the First and the Second World Wars saw extensive submarine warfare which did not meet the requirements of the existing law. At Nuremberg, the legitimacy of the practice was reviewed. In the light of the specific circumstances in the war, in particular the role that British merchant shipping had been obliged to perform and the fact that they were armed, in effect turning them into military objectives, the International Military Tribunal did not find Admirals Dönitz and Raeder guilty of violation of the prohibition against attacking enemy merchant shipping. The Tribunal did, however, conclude that unrestricted warfare with regard to neutral merchant shipping was unlawful and that the obligation to provide a place of safety for passengers and crew had been violated. Therefore, the Tribunal found that the ineffectiveness of the relevant provisions in the specific conflict did not affect the continued validity of the rules as such and upheld the basic rules of the 1936 Procès-Verbal.

45.4   Concerns that have traditionally been raised against submitting surface ships and submarines to the same rules have been met by the development of provisions regarding the conditions under which merchant vessels and civil aircraft are liable to attack (paragraphs 60, 63, 67 and 70). The paragraph as it stands for the first time applies the rules to aircraft as well. Participants felt that this development logically follows from the increasingly important role aircraft play in armed conflict at sea.

Section II Precautions in attack

46   **With respect to attacks, the following precautions shall be taken:**

(a) **those who plan, decide upon or execute an attack must take all feasible measures to gather information which will assist in determining whether or not objects which are not military objectives are present in an area of attack;**

(b) **in the light of the information available to them, those who plan, decide upon or execute an attack shall do everything feasible to ensure that attacks are limited to military objectives;**

(c) **they shall furthermore take all feasible precautions in the choice of methods and means in order to avoid or minimise collateral casualties or damage; *and***

(d) **an attack shall not be launched if it may be expected to cause collateral casualties or damage which would be excessive in relation to the concrete and direct military advantage anticipated from the attack as a whole; an attack shall be cancelled or suspended as soon as it becomes apparent that the collateral casualties or damage would be excessive.**

Section VI of this Part provides additional precautions regarding civil aircraft.

46.1   The wording of this paragraph reflects the obligations of Article 57(2) of Additional Protocol I with regard to land and air warfare, albeit in a simpler form. After the adoption at the Bochum Round Table of a basic provision regarding precautions in attack, participants felt that analysis of possible further precautions in the light of means and methods of warfare would be appropriate. The formula agreed on at Bochum, namely, 'Those who plan or decide upon an attack shall ensure that all feasible precautions are taken to avoid losses of civilian lives and the lives of other protected persons and damage to civilian objects' was a more correct formulation of the intent of the rule laid down in Article 57(4) of API.[60] The amplifications as developed at the Toulon Round Table, however, will enhance the protection of civilians, other protected persons and civilian and exempt objects at sea. The Rapporteur on methods and means of combat in naval warfare mentioned in his report to the Toulon session the fact that precautions in attack closely relate to the general principles of necessity and proportionality which are also reflected in the military 'economy of force' doctrine. At the outset it should also be noted that an attack on military objectives on land is governed by the relevant provisions of API and that therefore precautions, both in attack and in defence, relating to naval bombardment for instance, are governed by Articles 57 and 58 of Additional Protocol I.

46.2   The basic rules with regard to precautions in attack obviously relate to the basic principle of distinction and the obligation to engage military objectives only. These obligations can only be fulfilled if target identification is effected. The relevance of these obligations in modern naval warfare must not be underestimated. Shooting on sight and the practice of free-fire zones have unfortunately been extensive in major naval conflicts. The advent of modern technology, such as the use of missiles, which is readily available to most countries in the world, only emphasises the need for the formulation of rules applicable to naval warfare.

46.3   In order to stay as closely as possible to existing texts, this paragraph uses the term 'feasible' which, in accordance with several declarations of understanding made by States upon ratification of the 1977 Additional Protocols and the 1980 Certain Conventional Weapons Convention, should be understood as 'that which is practicable or practically possible, taking into account all circumstances ruling at the time, including humanitarian and military considerations'. The obligation to limit attacks to military objectives 'in the light of the information available to them' corrects one the deficiencies of the text of API which also attracted statements of understanding by several States which are normally referred to as the 'hindsight rule'. The introductory sentence makes it clear that a violation of the rule cannot be established if planners and commanders took a decision in good faith on the basis of such information which under the factual circumstances reasonably could be assumed to have been available to them at the moment of decision-making. Introduction of an equivalent to the requirement of advance warning in land warfare was not deemed appropriate in the light of the specificities of naval warfare already alluded to earlier.

---

60   Cf. ICRC Commentary to Additional Protocol I, *Commentary on the Additional Protocols of 8 June 1977 to the Geneva Conventions of 12 August 1949*, pp. 687–9.

46.4   Participants were quite in agreement with the statement in the Rapporteur's report that in contrast to the provisions of the API relating to precautions in attack, those with regard to precautions in defence as formulated for land warfare ('precautions against the effects of attacks') and listed in Article 58 of the API were not readily applicable in the naval environment. The precautions against the effects of attacks applicable in land and air warfare concentrate on the physical separation between military objectives and the civilian population, individual civilians and civilian objects in order to enhance the protection of the latter. The economic character of naval warfare and the extensive use of merchant shipping and civil aircraft in support of the military effort, however, warrant a different approach. Consequently the results arrived at at the Bochum session and the restrictive approach adopted with regard to exemption from attack and the loss of protection as spelled out in the paragraphs below, as well as the development of criteria for the use of zones as listed in paragraphs 105–108, was considered more useful. Consequently, no paragraph has been drafted in this document with regard to precautions in defence.

46.5   Paragraph 46(d) states the principle of proportionality and applies it to the law of naval warfare. The expressions 'collateral casualties' or 'collateral damage' are defined in paragraph 13(c) as meaning the loss of life of, or injury to civilians or other protected persons, and damage to or the destruction of the natural environment or objects that are not in themselves military objectives. In accordance with paragraph 40, an attack on a military objective must offer a 'definite' military advantage. The term 'definite' in paragraph 40 is probably synonymous with 'concrete' in the present subparagraph. The expression 'direct' in paragraph 40 is a further qualification to the assessment of military advantage. 'Direct' means 'without intervening condition or agency'. A remote advantage to be gained at some time in the future is not to be included in the proportionality equation. The expression 'excessive' is somewhat subjective, at least in marginal cases. An attack which, when all the relevant factors are taken into account, is actually conducted to cause collateral damage rather than to cause damage to a military objective is clearly prohibited. With the benefit of hindsight, it is suggested that the German sinking of the *Lusitania* in 1915, resulting in the death of 1,198 passengers and crew was clearly disproportionate although the *Lusitania* was also apparently carrying a cargo which included 4,200,000 rifle cartridges, 1,250 cases of empty shrapnel shells, and 18 cases of non-explosive fuses.

46.6   The last sentence in this paragraph was introduced at the final session in Livorno in the light of the phraseology used in Section VI, paragraph 77, on precautions regarding civil aircraft. It was proposed to introduce in that paragraph a phrase indicating that the paragraph did not imply that military forces should necessarily take all the actions described in that paragraph on a 24-hours-a-day basis while they were not in any way endangering civil aviation by their behaviour. It was felt, however, that retention of paragraph 77 in its present form was preferable to inclusion of terminology that military forces should take the actions 'before launching an attack'. In order to indicate, however, that the rules in paragraph 77 only apply to activities by forces which could pose a danger to civil aviation, the sentence was added to paragraph 46.

Section III Enemy vessels and aircraft exempt from attack

Preliminary remarks

This Section lists classes of vessels and aircraft that may not be attacked unless they breach certain conditions that they need to comply with. However, even in the case of non-respect of all the conditions, the vessels or aircraft concerned cannot necessarily be immediately and automatically attacked. This Section therefore indicates not only the vessels or aircraft that fall into this exempt category, but also the conditions of this exemption and finally the procedure to be followed and the factors to be taken into account before proceeding to an attack.

The vessels and aircraft listed are those that are protected from attack by virtue of treaty or customary law, or by way of progressive development in order to give greater protection to certain humanitarian or environmental missions. However, the fact that a vessel or aircraft does not appear on this list does not mean that it may be attacked, for only vessels or aircraft that fall within the definition of a military objective may be made the object of an attack, and even then, only after the principle of proportionality has been taken into account.[61]

Classes of vessels exempt from attack

47   The following classes of enemy vessels are exempt from attack:

(a)   hospital ships;

(b)   small craft used for coastal rescue operations and other medical transports;

(c)   vessels granted safe conduct by agreement between the belligerent parties including:

    (i)   cartel vessels, e.g., vessels designated for and engaged in the transport of prisoners of war;

    (ii)   vessels engaged in humanitarian missions, including vessels carrying supplies indispensable to the survival of the civilian population, and vessels engaged in relief actions and rescue operations;

(d)   vessels engaged in transporting cultural property under special protection;

(e)   passenger vessels when engaged only in carrying civilian passengers;

---

61   See paras. 38–42 and 46 the commentary thereto.

(f) vessels charged with religious, non-military scientific or philanthropic missions; vessels collecting scientific data of likely military applications are not protected;

(g) small coastal fishing vessels and small boats engaged in local coastal trade, but they are subject to the regulations of a belligerent naval commander operating in the area and to inspection;

(h) vessels designed or adapted exclusively for responding to pollution incidents in the marine environment;

(i) vessels which have surrendered;

(j) life rafts and life boats.

47.1 **(a) hospital ships**
The vessels that fall into this category are indicated in the commentary to paragraph 13(e).

47.2 Hospital ships are not only exempt from attack by virtue of GCII Article 22, but also benefit from other protections:

– they may not be captured;[62]

– should a hospital ship be in a port that falls into the hands of the enemy, it shall be authorised to leave the port;[63]

– they are not classed as warships as regards their stay in port;[64]

– reprisals against them are prohibited.[65]

47.3 It should be noted that in order to benefit from this protection, the hospital ship must notify its name and description to the parties to the conflict at least ten days before these ships are employed.[66] For further detail on this point, see paragraph 169 of the Manual and the commentary thereto.

47.4 A hospital ship is expected to help the wounded, sick and shipwrecked without distinction as to nationality,[67] and it should also be noted that merchant ships belonging to the parties to the conflict which have been transformed into hospital ships cannot be put to any other use throughout the duration of hostilities.[68]

---

62 GCII Art. 22; see para. 136 of the Manual and the commentary thereto.
63 GCII Art. 29.
64 GCII Art. 32.
65 GCII Art. 47.
66 GCII Art. 22.
67 GCII Art. 30.
68 GCII Art. 33.

47.5   GCII Article 26 recommends that hospital ships be at least 2,000 tons gross, but this is not a compulsory requirement.

47.6   Finally, hospital ships are required, by virtue of GCII Article 47, to be marked as follows:

–   all exterior surfaces are to be white with large dark red crosses painted in such a way as to provide maximum visibility. A white flag with a red cross is also to be flown on the mainmast as high as possible

–   their national flag is to be flown, and, in the case of a hospital ship belonging to a neutral State, the flag of the party to the conflict whose direction they have accepted.

References to the red cross also apply to the red crescent.

It is not clear whether the non-observance of this requirement alone results in the ship not being legally entitled to be protected as a hospital ship, or rather whether it is a requirement for practical identification purposes. Opinions among the participants differed, but it is clear that a ship that is not marked will have difficulty in receiving recognition both as a matter of principle and from the point of view of identification.

47.7   Annex I to API has introduced additional methods of identification that are optional but which help the identification of hospital ships in today's conditions. For further detail on this, see paragraph 172 and the commentary thereto.

47.8   Conditions for the hospital ship's protection from attack that are linked to its innocent employment are dealt with in the commentary to paragraph 48.

47.9   **(b)   Small craft used for coastal rescue operations and other medical transports**
The vessels that fall into this category are listed in the commentary to paragraph 13(e).

47.10   Small craft used for coastal rescue operations are in principle exempt from attack[69] by virtue of Article 27 of the Second Geneva Convention which states that they shall:

be respected and protected as far as operational requirements permit.

This wording was used in order to take into account the inevitable risks that these craft face because of their small size and the fact that they are in a zone of military operations. However, if they have been recognised as a rescue craft by a belligerent, it may not deliberately attack them. Article 47 of GCII prohibits attacks against these vessels by way of reprisals.

47.11   These craft must be provided with certificates from the responsible authorities stating that the craft have been under their control while fitting out and on departure.[70]

---

69   They are also in principle exempt from capture; see para. 136(a).
70   GCII Arts. 27 and 24.

47.12   Article 43 of the Second Geneva Convention requires rescue craft to be marked in the same way as hospital ships.[71] It should be noted that in peacetime rescue craft are frequently painted all over in a bright colour, such as orange, for maximum visibility. Most lifeboat associations have recognised, however, the need for complying with the terms of GCII in time of armed conflict and have provided for painting the boats white with a red cross or red crescent. However, some have compromised by having the boats painted a bright colour but with part of the surface white with the red cross or red crescent painted on it and their governments have indicated that this is acceptable. Rescue craft may also benefit from the use of modern means of identification provided for by Annex I to API.[72]

47.13   The vessels that fall into the category of other medical transports are indicated in the commentary to paragraph 13(e).

47.14   The life boats of hospital ships are exempt from attack or capture under Article 26 of the Second Geneva Convention and Article 47 prohibits reprisals against them.

47.15   Ships chartered to transport medical equipment are exempt from attack and capture under Article 38 of GCII and from reprisals under Article 47 of GCII. In order to benefit from this protection, they need to have notified the particulars of their voyage to the adverse power and received its approval. However, this requirement for approval only relates to the particulars of the voyage, that is, factors such as the course to be followed, date etc.[73] The adverse party cannot contest the existence of the voyage. Conditions relating to the innocent nature of the voyage will be considered in the commentary to paragraph 48.

47.16   'Other medical ships and craft' are protected against attack by virtue of Article 23 of API and against reprisals by virtue of Article 20 of API. These vessels do not need to be notified or marked in any particular way, although they are encouraged to take these precautions under API Article 23, paragraphs 4 and 1 respectively. These vessels may be captured, subject to certain restrictions.[74]

47.17   Neutral vessels that have charitably taken on board the wounded, sick or shipwrecked or collected the dead, either as a result of a request by one of the parties to the conflict or on their own initiative, are protected from attack, capture or reprisals under Articles 21 and 47 of GCII. Article 21 provides that they are to enjoy special protection and facilities to carry out this work. This could take the form of a safe-conduct to enable them to continue their journey but they may not use the red cross or red crescent emblem nor the identification provided for in Annex I to Additional Protocol I. The protection only lasts for as long as they are carrying out this task and thereafter the normal rules applicable to neutral vessels apply.

---

71   As described above.
72   See para. 172 and commentary thereto.
73   See ICRC *Commentary on Geneva Convention II for the Amelioration of the Condition of Wounded, Sick and Shipwrecked Members of Armed Forces at Sea* (ed. J. Pictet, 1960), p. 214.
74   See para. 136(b) and the commentary thereto.

47.18   (c)   vessels granted safe conduct by agreement between the belligerent parties including:

(i)   cartel vessels, e.g., vessels designated for and engaged in the transport of prisoners of war;

(ii)   vessels engaged in humanitarian missions, including vessels carrying supplies indispensable to the survival of the civilian population, and vessels engaged in relief actions and rescue operations

A safe conduct is a written permission given by a belligerent to enemy subjects or others allowing them to proceed to a particular place for a specified purpose. The safe conduct renders the vessel concerned exempt from attack or capture as long as the receiver of the safe conduct complies with the conditions imposed and as long as the safe conduct is the result of an arrangement between the belligerents or between the belligerents and neutral powers.[75]

47.19   Cartel vessels are traditionally defined as vessels of belligerents that are commissioned for the carriage by sea of exchanged prisoners of war from the enemy country to their own country, or for the carriage of official communications to and from the enemy.[76]

47.20   The notion of a cartel vessel is that of a vessel used for any type of inter-belligerent communication or official transport and therefore does not need to be limited to prisoners of war and correspondence, although this has tended to be the usual use.

47.21   In these days of modern communications, the carriage of official communications is of less relevance,[77] although it is clear that cartel vessels could still be used for this purpose.[78] As far as prisoners of war are concerned, the terminology has been changed in this paragraph from the traditional 'exchange of prisoners of war' to 'transport of prisoners of war', because the law now requires the return of all prisoners of war at the end of active hostilities[79] and does not depend on a peace treaty or any other arrangement. Further, the Third Geneva Convention of 1949 provides for the repatriation or transport to neutral States of certain categories of wounded and sick prisoners of war[80] and a belligerent vessel commissioned for this purpose would also be a cartel ship.

75   See NWP9A, *The Commander's Handbook*, para. 8.2.3, the German Manual ZDv 15/2, para. 1043, and the Canadian Draft Manual, section 718.1.d, pp. 7–24.
76   See, for example, Oppenheim, *International Law*, vol. II, *War, Disputes and Neutrality*, para. 225.
77   NWP9A *The Commander's Handbook*, only mentions the exchange of POWs (para. 8.2.3) and the same is true for the Canadian Draft Manual (para. 718.1.a, pp. 7–24)
78   The German Manual still refers to this use, paras. 1034–5.
79   1949 Third Geneva Convention, Art. 118.
80   *Ibid.*, Arts. 109–117.

47.22 Cartel vessels are exempt from capture and attack, not only when they are carrying the prisoners of war or communications, but also on the journeys to collect the prisoners or communications and on their way back after having transported them.

47.23 In order to benefit from this protection, cartel vessels must be furnished with a document stating that they are commissioned as cartel vessels, they must not engage in any trade, or carry any cargo or other dispatches, and finally, they must not carry weapons. Although the participants of the Round Table did not specifically address the issue, it would seem unlikely that cartel vessels would lose their protection for carrying purely defensive weaponry, such as a deflective system (for example, chaff) for the vessel, and individual light weapons for the defence of the crew.

47.24 The Rapporteur on the protection of victims of armed conflicts at sea had suggested that vessels engaged in humanitarian missions do not need safe-conducts in order to be exempt from attack as only military objectives may be attacked and *bona fide* carriage of relief supplies or rescue operations could not render the vessels concerned military objectives. The Rapporteur suggested that notification should be given in order to ensure, from a practical point of view, better protection. The same would be true for enemy vessels belonging to humanitarian organisations. The Rapporteur indicated, however, that in order to pass a blockade cordon, vessels would have to seek prior permission, although the result of attempting to breach a blockade would normally be capture and not attack.

47.25 However, the Round Table was of the opinion that in order to benefit from protected status, enemy merchant vessels engaged in humanitarian missions should seek the agreement of the parties in advance and be furnished with a safe conduct. The principal reason for this decision was that the parties would need to be satisfied that the shipment in question was indeed one of goods that are necessary for the civilian population.

47.26 It was recognised that, in principle, permission for the passage of relief goods should be allowed, both generally and through a blockade, as the starvation of the civilian population as a method of warfare is generally considered to be unlawful.[81] The term 'objects indispensable to the survival of the civilian population', as found in Article 54 of API refers to absolutely essential items which may not lawfully be removed. On the other hand, relief, as indicated in Article 70 of API, refers to supplies with which the civilian population is inadequately provided, and which should be granted passage, but with the agreement of the parties concerned. The participants did not make a distinction between these categories as far as the need for agreement is necessary to render the vessels concerned protected from attack, but it is likely that it would be unlawful to withhold agreement in the case of shipments of objects indispensable for the survival of the population.

47.27 In any event, a clear distinction should be maintained between the attack and capture of such vessels. Although the capture of enemy vessels which are not exempt from capture is clearly lawful, it is not the case that enemy vessels that are not exempt

---

81 API Art. 54, and see also NWP9A, *The Commander's Handbook*, footnote 15 to para. 8.1.2, which states that the prohibition of starvation as a means of warfare 'should be observed and in due course recognised as customary law'. See also para. 7.7.3.

from attack can be automatically attacked. Rather, the list of vessels exempt from attack indicates the absolute protection of these vessels from attack as long as they comply with their conditions of protection. With regard to other enemy merchant vessels, they may only be attacked if they are military objectives as defined in paragraph 40. If, therefore, a party to the conflict is aware that an enemy merchant vessel is undertaking a *bona fide* humanitarian action, which therefore does not contribute to the military action of the enemy, it may not attack it even if the vessel is sailing without the safe-conduct unless it violates the rules applicable to its status (for example, refuses to stop for visit and search).

47.28   Humanitarian missions that are protected from attack are not only those delivering food supplies, but could also involve vessels engaged in a variety of humanitarian tasks such as water purification programmes, the transport of relief workers, the removal of besieged populations, etc. It should be noted, however, that a passenger vessel used for the transport of refugees or rescuing besieged civilians is exempt from attack without the need for a safe-conduct as it falls into the category of 'passenger vessels when engaged only in carrying civilian passengers'.

47.29   Another type of shipment that falls into this category is that of correspondence and official papers relating to prisoners of war and civilian internees and packages for them, as provided for in Articles 70–77 of the Third Geneva Convention and Articles 107–113 of the Fourth Geneva Convention. These Articles specify that these prisoners shall be entitled to write to their families and receive correspondence and packages and that these should not be stopped. Article 75 of the Third Geneva Convention and Article 111 of the Fourth Geneva Convention provides for the possibility of these shipments being undertaken by Protecting Powers, the International Committee of the Red Cross or any other organisation duly approved by the parties, and that in such a case it is recommended that safe-conducts for these shipments be granted.

47.30   **(d)   vessels engaged in transporting cultural property under special protection**
The 1954 Hague Convention for the Protection of Cultural Property in the Event of Armed Conflict provides for the protection of transport that is exclusively engaged in the transfer of cultural property. Article 12(3) of this Convention prohibits the attack or capture of these transports.

47.31   The procedure to be followed to obtain this special protection is provided in Articles 17–19 of the Regulations for the Execution of the Convention. A party to the conflict should address a request for such transfer of cultural property under special protection, together with details of the proposed transfer, to the Commissioner-General for Cultural Property. If the Commissioner-General, after appropriate consultations including the Protecting Powers, considers that the transfer is justified, he will appoint one or more inspectors who will accompany the property to its destination. Article 12(2) provides that these transports shall display the distinctive emblem provided for in Article 16 of the Convention.[82] It is not indicated whether the displaying of this emblem is a condition of protection or whether it is rather an aid to identification only.

---

82   A shield consisting of a royal-blue square, one of the angles of which forms the point of the shield, and of a royal-blue triangle above the square, the space on either side being taken up by a white triangle.

47.32   If the transfer of cultural property is urgently needed and there is insufficient time to follow the procedure described above, notification should be made to the opposing parties, and, if the property is not being taken to another country, the transport may display the distinctive emblem.[83] In this case, the Convention provides that parties 'shall take, so far as possible, the necessary precautions to avoid acts of hostility directed against the transport'. [84]

47.33   (e)   **passenger vessels when engaged only in carrying civilian passengers**
This is a category of vessels that has been recognised as being exempt from attack in both the NWP9A, *The Commander's Handbook*, and the German Manual ZDv 15/2. Under traditional customary law they were not given any special exemption as all merchant vessels could not be attacked on sight.

47.34   There are different points of view as to the reasons for this exemption. NWP9A, *The Commander's Handbook* indicates that passenger vessels would normally be military objectives as they form part of the enemy's lines of communication, but that the deaths of the civilians in such an attack would be clearly disproportionate to whatever military advantage may be expected from such an attack.[85]

47.35   A number of participants agreed with this point of view, pointing out that passenger vessels are frequently requisitioned for military purposes. However, other participants pointed out that the definition of a military objective requires that the destruction of the object offers a definite military advantage in the circumstances ruling at the time. They were of the opinion that an unrequisitioned civilian vehicle, being exclusively used for the transport of civilians, could not satisfy the definition of a military objective, merely on the premise that it may subsequently be requisitioned for military purposes.

47.36   However, whatever the reasoning adopted, the status of these vessels as exempt from attack is clear and was considered by all the participants as being an expression of customary law.

47.37   (f)   **vessels charged with religious, non-military scientific or philanthropic missions; vessels collecting scientific data of likely military applications are not protected**
The immunity of these vessels from capture was first introduced in treaty law in Hague Convention XI of 1907. As with all merchant vessels, they could not be attacked on sight under traditional customary law in any event.

47.38   The practice of granting safe-conducts to vessels on voyages of scientific discovery was well established in custom by 1907,[86] but this does not appear to have been the case with the other categories and therefore their immunity from capture was introduced by the Hague Convention.

---

83   Art. 13 of the Convention.
84   Art. 13(2).
85   NWP9A, *The Commander's Handbook*, pp. 8–20, footnote 61.
86   See the examples cited by Oppenheim, *International Law*, 2nd edn 1912, vol. II at pp. 232–3.

47.39   The wording of the treaty appears to give an absolute immunity from capture (and *a fortiori* attack) to these vessels without their having to ask for a safe conduct. The original proposal[87] was that vessels engaged in scientific, religious and philanthropic missions must notify the opposing State and the latter must then grant safe conducts indicating the conditions of exemption.

47.40   State practice seems to have followed more closely the original proposal than the letter of the treaty in that States have generally given a very narrow interpretation of the categories of vessels automatically entitled to immunity and have required an agreement and subsequent granting of a safe conduct.[88]

47.41   In the light of this practice, the question remains whether States are obliged to grant safe conducts to all vessels that fall into this category and if so, precisely which vessels are included.

47.42   The Round Table decided to exclude from this immunity scientific vessels on missions of likely military applications. This is in keeping with custom and the fact that the purpose of the treaty rule was not to protect military scientific research but exploratory voyages. A modern equivalent cited by some participants was the work of Jacques Cousteau.

47.43   It was also suggested to remove the reference to 'philanthropic' missions as this essentially means the same as 'humanitarian'. However, the decision was made to keep it, although it was recognised that it does not have an essentially different meaning, as the treaty rule appears to give a more absolute protection to 'philanthropic' missions than the customary rule applicable to 'humanitarian missions'[89] and that the possibility of benefitting from the more generous rule should not be eliminated. Mention was made of the possibility of vessels used by recognised philanthropic societies benefitting from this rule, especially if they were not delivering supplies to a belligerent territory.

47.44   There was also some discussion on the meaning of 'religious missions', but the lack of State practice interpreting this rule creates difficulty. It presumably covers voyages undertaken for missionary work and perhaps humanitarian work organised by religious orders, but would certainly not give immunity to missions which are using or are advocating the use of force for religious ends.

47.45   **(g)   small coastal fishing vessels and small boats engaged in local coastal trade, but they are subject to the regulations of a belligerent naval commander operating in the area and to inspection**
These vessels were first protected in treaty law from capture in Hague Convention XI of 1907. As with all merchant vessels, traditional customary law prohibited their attack on sight.

---

87   The Italian delegation was the origin of the proposal to grant these vessels immunity from capture in the Hague Convention.
88   Tucker, *The Law of War and Neutrality at Sea*, pp. 96–7. See also NWP9A, *The Commander's Handbook*, para. 8.2.3, pp. 8–19.
89   See commentary to para. 47(c)(ii).

47.46   The protection of coastal fishing vessels from capture was established in customary law prior to 1907. The reason for this was not the protection of the fishing industry as such, but the protection of the people that are engaged in local fishing and the population that depends on it. The prohibition of attacking these vessels is based on the same reasoning, that is, that the disruption of this fishing would give no substantial benefit to the belligerents but would harm the population.[90]

47.47   The immunity applies to fishing vessels that are operating near the coast, which does not mean that they have to be right next to the coast but can operate several miles offshore. The distinction is made between these boats which serve a local need and deep-sea fishing vessels that are usually much larger and supply fish for a wider market.

47.48   It should be noted, however, that although deep-sea fishing vessels are not specifically exempt from attack, they cannot normally be attacked as it is unlikely that they would be military objectives if they are genuinely exclusively engaged in this activity.

47.49   The immunity from capture of small boats engaged in local trade was introduced for the first time in the Hague Convention and was not previously recognised in custom. The important criterion is whether the trade concerned is really local and not general coastal trade. As these boats are protected from capture, it is evident that they are also protected from attack. However, boats engaged in trade that do not benefit from this immunity may not be attacked unless they are military objectives.

47.50   Given the frequently large numbers of coastal fishing and trade vessels, the respect of their immunity depends in practice on their *bona fide* use. It is important to note, therefore, that Hague Convention XI specifies that parties to a conflict may not use these vessels for military purposes while preserving their peaceful appearance.[91] If these vessels are nevertheless so used, they will lose their immunity and are liable to be attacked.[92]

47.51   Another safeguard that State practice has introduced is the specification that such local vessels are to be subject to the regulations of a belligerent naval commander operating in the area and to inspection.[93] This does not mean that such local vessels have to notify the commander of their existence in order to benefit from the immunity, but rather that they should identify themselves on request, be open to inspection and obey any other regulations that the commander needs to institute. However, these regulations should be limited to what is necessary and should not in practice disrupt the activities of these vessels to such a degree that it would undermine the purpose of the rule granting immunity from attack and capture.

---

90   In particular, the local population must not have its source of sustenance removed, API Art. 54.
91   Art. 3(3).
92   For example, the Argentine fishing vessel *Narwal* was sunk by the British forces during the South Atlantic conflict in 1982 as the vessel was used to shadow the British fleet and report its location; see citation in NWP9A, *The Commander's Handbook*, pp. 8–19, footnote 60.
93   NWP9A, *The Commander's Handbook*, para. 8.2.3, pp. 8–19, and Canadian Draft Manual, para. 718, pp. 7–24.

47.52   (h)   vessels designed or adapted exclusively for responding to pollution incidents in the marine environment
This is a totally new category of protected vessel which the experts decided to include by way of progressive development of the law. None of the military manuals presently include this in their lists of protected vessels and they are not yet specifically protected in customary law. However, a civilian vessel undertaking this function could not normally be classified as contributing to the military action of the enemy and therefore could not be attacked as it would not be a military objective.

47.53   The proposal was originally made in the Round Table as this type of activity at sea was seen as being in many ways analogous to civil defence operations on land that are given special protection in API. Further, the international community is becoming increasingly aware of the importance of avoiding pollution and of cleaning up pollution as effectively and as quickly as possible for the protection of the environment and of wildlife.

47.54   The wording used is intentionally general in relation to the type and source of pollution concerned in that the pollution could originate not only from incidents at sea, but also from the land or air. The scale of the pollution is also not relevant.

47.55   The vessels could be either military or civilian, but in order to benefit from this immunity, they would need to be designed or adapted exclusively for this purpose and identifiable as such. The group thought that it was not possible to give immunity to military vessels that are only temporarily engaged in this activity. As far as civilian vessels are concerned, it was thought that they too should be specially designated for this purpose in order to benefit from the special exemption, although they are in any event not subject to attack unless they are military objectives.

47.56   (i)   vessels which have surrendered.
These vessels are protected from attack in accordance with the customary law duty to give quarter, and the purpose is to spare the lives of the crew of the ship who no longer wish to fight. This rule is applicable when the adversary is in a position to capture the ship upon surrender.

47.57. The adversary is obliged to give quarter once it is evident that the vessel wishes to surrender. There is no one agreed method of signalling a wish to surrender, but there are a number of methods that are generally recognised:[94]

–   hauling down its flag;

–   hoisting a white flag;

–   surfacing in the case of submarines;

–   stopping engines and responding to the attacker's signals;

–   taking to life boats;

–   at night, stopping the vessel and switching on its lights.

94   NWP9A, *The Commander's Handbook*, para. 8.2.1; see also the judgment of the British Military Court in Hamburg in the trial of Helmuth von Ruchteschell, LRTWC, vol. IX, p. 82.

47.58   (j)   life rafts and life boats

This category comprises the life boats and life rafts of abandoned vessels. Therefore this category does not include rescue craft.

The protection of these vessels against attack is based on the prohibition of attacking the shipwrecked which is a well-established rule of customary law.[95] The duty to protect the shipwrecked applies to all persons,[96] whether military or civilian, who are in danger at sea as a result of misfortune affecting them or the vessel or aircraft[97] carrying them.[98] It is irrelevant that the persons concerned may be fit and therefore possibly in a position to participate in hostilities again, for attacking them would be a war crime.[99] On the other hand, this protection ceases if they actually start committing hostile acts again.[100]

Conditions of exemption

48   Vessels listed in paragraph 47 are exempt from attack only if they:

(a)   are innocently employed in their normal role;

(b)   submit to identification and inspection when required; *and*

(c)   do not intentionally hamper the movement of combatants and obey orders to stop or move out of the way when required.

48.1   Vessels only keep their special status of being exempt from attack if they conform to all three of these conditions. Therefore if a vessel breaches one or more of these conditions, it loses its special status. However, this does not mean that it may automatically be attacked, but rather that it becomes like any other merchant vessel which may be attacked if it is evaluated that it is a military objective and that such an attack would not violate the rule of proportionality. The procedures to be followed before one may attack vessels which have lost their exempt status are indicated in paragraphs 49–52.

48.2   (a) are innocently employed in their normal role

Being employed in their normal role means behaving in a way which is normal for the type of voyage. For example, 'passenger vessels when engaged only in carrying civilian passengers' would normally also carry the personal luggage of those

---

95   See the judgments in: *The Llandovery Castle (German Reichsgericht)* 1921, 16 AJIL 708, 1922; *The Peleus Case* LRTWC, vol. I, p. 1; the trials of Von Ruchteschell LRTWC, vol. IX, p. 82 and Moehle LRTWC, vol. XI, p. 75 (British Military Court, Hamburg, 1945–7). See also GCII Arts. 12 and 18.

96   GCII Art. 12 indicates that this rule applies to persons that are shipwrecked for any cause and includes forced landings at sea by and from aircraft.

97   The protection of persons parachuting in distress is codified in Art. 42 of API.

98   API Art. 8(b).

99   See, for example, the judgment in the case of Karl-Heinz Moehle 1946, British Military Court, Hamburg, LRTWC, vol. XI, p. 75.

100 API Art. 8(b). The commission of acts of hostility will always deprive a protected vessel of its immunity; see para. 48(a) and the commentary thereto.

passengers, equipment for the crew, catering and navigation and, in the case of ferries, the vehicles of the passengers and perhaps a small amount of non-military cargo.

48.3   In the case of vessels that are protected by virtue of being furnished with a safe-conduct, it is important that these vessels comply with the specifications agreed on, such as routes, dates, etc.

48.4   Innocent employment essentially means that these vessels must not undertake any kind of hostile action, such as attacks, carrying military material which is not purely defensive to the vessel, or gathering of intelligence.[101]

48.5   Humanitarian law frequently explicitly prohibits States from using protected vessels for military purposes, and this is certainly the case with medical transports protected under GCII[102] and small coastal fishing and trade vessels.[103] On the other hand, passenger vessels have in the past been used for military purposes which frequently led to their being attacked; for example, the passenger vessels during the Second World War which were used for intelligence purposes.[104]

48.6   The Rapporteur made the suggestion that when passenger vessels are actually being used for transporting civilian passengers, States should be prohibited from using them for military purposes during those voyages. This should be distinguished from the requisitioning of passenger vessels for military purposes which is frequently done and is quite lawful. There is no doubt, however, that the protection of the civilians being transported in passenger vessels can only be assured if they are not at the same time being used for military purposes and States should refrain from endangering civilians in this fashion.

48.7   **(b) submit to identification and inspection when required**
This condition is applicable to the vessels listed in subparagraphs (a)–(h) of paragraph 47.

48.8   This is a precautionary measure that enables belligerents to assure themselves that the vessels are indeed being used in their normal role. It is also a measure that can be taken if the vessel has for some reason excited the suspicion of a belligerent.

48.9   The duty to submit to identification when required means that a vessel must identify itself when it is asked to do so.

---

101 GCII lists in Art. 35 activities that should not be seen as hostile and therefore which cannot lead to the loss of exempt status of hospital ships or rescue craft; in particular: the fact that they are armed for the maintenance of order, for their own defence or that of the patients; the presence of apparatus used to facilitate navigation or communication; the existence of portable arms and ammunition taken from the patients and not yet handed to the proper authorities.
102 GCII Art. 30(2)
103 Hague Convention XI, 1907, Art. 3(3)
104 Dönitz was acquitted from the charge of carrying out attacks against British merchant vessels because the court found that they had been ordered to ram U-boats if possible and to send position reports when sighting submarines; *Judgment of the International Military Tribunal for the Trial of German War Criminals*, 108–9.

48.10   The duty to submit to inspection means that these vessels must allow one or more inspectors to board and search the vessel. This is a general rule applicable to these vessels, although two treaties have specific procedures:

–   the Hague Convention for the Protection of Cultural Property in the Event of Armed Conflict indicates a special procedure for the appointment of inspectors to sail with vessels that are carrying property under special protection.[105]

–   the Second Geneva Convention specifies that parties to the conflict may put on board hospital ships and rescue craft *neutral* observers, either unilaterally or by particular agreements. Thus inspectors from neutral countries or belonging to humanitarian organisations, such as the ICRC, can be put on board these vessels at the invitation of the party to which the vessel belongs.[106] In addition to this possibility, inspectors *belonging to the adverse party* may make a thorough search of the vessel, examine its equipment and supplies, verify lists of patients, check the identity of the crew, etc.[107] However, they may not put an inspector permanently on board, but only temporarily in order to carry out the search, or to check that certain orders, such as taking a certain course, are carried out.[108]

48.11   The inspection of the vessels listed in paragraph 47(a)–(h) can take place at any time, but parties should attempt, if possible, to undertake the inspection before sailing and limit as far as possible the disruption of the task of the vessel that will be caused by the search.

48.12   **(c)   do not intentionally hamper the movement of combatants and obey orders to stop or move out of the way when required**
The purpose of this rule is to prevent these vessels causing major problems to the military actions of the belligerents.

48.13   The duty not to intentionally hamper the movement of combatants is well established and is linked to the condition that the vessel must be innocently employed in its normal role.[109] The word 'intentionally' is used to make it clear that these vessels do not lose their protection because they may sometimes in practice hamper the movements of combatants whilst carrying out their work. This is bound inadvertently to happen sometimes and the exempt vessel should not be penalised for it.

48.14   The duty to stop or move out of the way when required is a condition that ensures that belligerents are able to carry out their military actions when needed.[110] The implementation in good faith of this provision means that belligerents should only give such orders when they are genuinely necessary, and therefore should try to avoid interfering with the work of these vessels as far as possible.

---

105   See commentary to para. 47(d).
106   GCII Art. 31(4).
107   GCII Art. 31(1) and ICRC *Commentary on Geneva Convention II for the Amelioration of the Condition of Wounded, Sick and Shipwrecked Members of Armed Forces at Sea*, p. 182.
108   GCII Art. 31(1) and (2).
109   See, for example, GCII Art. 30 which indicates this rule in para. 3, just after providing in para. 2 that States undertake not to use hospital ships and rescue craft for any military purpose.
110   GCII Art. 31(1), API Art. 23, paras. 2 and 3.

Loss of exemption

Preliminary remarks

Paragraphs 49–52 indicate the procedure to follow should a vessel exempt from attack lose its protection because it has breached one of its conditions of protection, as described in paragraph 48. The loss of protection does not automatically mean that the vessel concerned may be attacked. Paragraphs 49–51 state the procedures and criteria that must be fulfilled before a hospital ship may be captured or attacked. The criteria for other classes of exempt vessels are in paragraph 52.

Hospital ships

49   The exemption from attack of a hospital ship may cease only by reason of a breach of a condition of exemption in paragraph 48 and, in such a case, only after due warning has been given naming in all appropriate cases a reasonable time limit to discharge itself of the cause endangering its exemption, and after such warning has remained unheeded.

49.1   This procedure is required by Article 34 of GCII. The purpose of the warning is to give the crew of the hospital ship the chance to rectify the situation or to explain itself if it believes that it has not violated a condition of protection. The time limit is not specified other than it must be 'reasonable'. Given the purpose of the warning, this must mean that sufficient time must be given to allow the cessation of the incorrect behaviour. However, it is evident that in the case of a direct attack by the hospital ship, it would not be appropriate to give a time limit as fire would be returned immediately.[111]

50   If after due warning a hospital ship persists in breaking a condition of its exemption, it renders itself liable to capture or other necessary measures to enforce compliance.

50.1   Other than in the case of a direct attack by a hospital ship, the adverse party should aim at taking less drastic measures than an attack in order to put a stop to the unacceptable behaviour. In any event, the adverse party must, as far as possible, take appropriate measures for the safety of the wounded on board before taking any extreme action.[112]

---

111 ICRC *Commentary on Geneva Convention II for the Amelioration of the Condition of Wounded, Sick and Shipwrecked Members of Armed Forces at Sea*, pp. 191–2.

112 *Ibid.*, p. 192.

51   **A hospital ship may only be attacked as a last resort if:**

     (a)   **diversion or capture is not feasible;**

     (b)   **no other method is available for exercising military control;**

     (c)   **the circumstances of non-compliance are sufficiently grave that the hospital ship has become, or may be reasonably assumed to be, a military objective; *and***

     (d)   **the collateral casualties or damage will not be disproportionate to the military advantage gained or expected.**

51.1   This list of conditions is cumulative so that if one of these conditions is not fulfilled, the adversary is not allowed to attack a hospital ship that has lost its exempt status. This is in addition to the conditions in paragraphs 49 and 50. The severe restraints that are put on any attack on a hospital ship is an expression of the particular respect that is to be accorded to the wounded, sick and shipwrecked.

51.2   **(a)**   **diversion or capture is not feasible**
A party to the conflict may not attack a hospital ship that has lost its protected status and which has not positively responded to the warning[113] if it is at all feasible to capture the ship or simply to divert it.[114]

51.3   **(b)**   **no other method is available for exercising military control**
Belligerent military forces must exhaust all available means to exercise control of a hospital ship. Such means may include, among others, repeated attempts to provide directions visually and on distress radio frequencies, firing the traditional warning shot across the bow, escorting the ship out of harm's way, and actually boarding the hospital ship to take control. If all measures short of attack fail to establish control, the belligerent forces may, in this exceptional circumstance, attack the hospital ship in an attempt to disable it, but not to sink it. In a rare case, failing all attempts to establish control, the belligerent forces may be justified in sinking the ship provided that all other criteria in paragraph 51 are met.

51.4   **(c)**   **the circumstances of non-compliance are sufficiently grave that the hospital ship has become, or may be reasonably assumed to be, a military objective**
This stipulation is in keeping with the basic principle that only military objectives may be attacked. Therefore the non-compliance by the hospital ship of the conditions of exemption listed in paragraph 48 has to be such that the hospital ship is, or may be reasonably assumed to be, contributing to the military action of the enemy and that its destruction would give the attacker a definite military advantage in those particular circumstances.[115]

---

113 See para. 49 of the Manual and the commentary thereto.
114 The method of capture or diversion will be similar to that applicable to the capture or diversion of merchant vessels: see paras. 119 and 138–140, and the commentary thereto. In the case of the capture of hospital ships, it is evident that the ship cannot be destroyed at sea after capture for this would almost certainly be fatal for the patients on board. Therefore the same rule would apply as for passenger vessels captured at sea, namely, that the ship must be taken to a port where the persons on board can be safely disembarked.
115 See commentary to para. 40.

51.5   (d)   the collateral casualties or damage will not be disproportionate to the military advantage gained or expected

It is evident that there are likely to be numerous casualties in the event of an attack as hospital ships are usually large and cater for many patients. It is virtually inevitable that all the patients would perish as they would not be able to survive such an attack or being exposed to the elements in life boats or life rafts. The military advantage in attacking a hospital ship that has lost its exempt status would therefore have to be a very major one in order not to fall foul of this rule of proportionality.

All other categories of vessels exempt from attack:

52   If any other class of vessel exempt from attack breaches any of the conditions of its exemption in paragraph 48, it may be attacked only if:

(a)   diversion or capture is not feasible;

(b)   no other method is available for exercising military control;

(c)   the circumstances of non-compliance are sufficiently grave that the vessel has become, or may be reasonably assumed to be, a military objective; *and*

(d)   the collateral casualties or damage will not be disproportionate to the military advantage gained or expected.

52.1   It will be noticed that in the case of other vessels that have lost their exemption from attack, the adverse party does not need to follow the procedure applicable to hospital ships that is indicated in paragraph 49. This is because there is no customary or treaty rule requiring this. However, an adverse party could certainly use a warning with a reasonable time limit as one means of establishing whether the criteria listed in subparagraphs (a)–(c) are fulfilled. Otherwise the same remarks contained in the commentary to paragraph 51 are applicable (*mutatis mutandis*) to this paragraph.

52.2   As far as subparagraph (d) is concerned, whether the collateral casualties are disproportionate to the military advantage gained will depend on the nature of the violation of the conditions of exemption, on the one hand, and the likely number of casualties, on the other. For example, in the case of passenger vessels, NWP9A, *The Commander's Handbook*, gives 'transporting troops or military cargo' as an example of how they could lose their protection.[116] This would clearly in virtually all cases render the vessel a military objective, but the adverse party would have to consider the implications of the rule of proportionality very carefully before attacking. For example, the sinking of the passenger vessel *Lusitania* during the First World War was considered shocking, even though it was carrying military cargo, because it caused the death of over a thousand civilians.[117]

---

116 NWP9A, *The Commander's Handbook*, para. 8.2.3, subpara. 6, pp. 8–20.
117 See Oppenheim, *International Law*, vol. II, p. 308.

Classes of aircraft exempt from attack

53   The following classes of enemy aircraft are exempt from attack:

    (a)   medical aircraft;

    (b)   aircraft granted safe conduct by agreement between the parties to the conflict; *and*

    (c)   civil airliners.

53.1   The general rule, as reflected in the 1949 Geneva Conventions, API and military manuals, is that medical aircraft may not be the object of attack. The rule stems from the 1923 Hague Rules of Aerial Warfare which gave flying ambulances the same protection from attack as that accorded to hospital ships in Hague Convention X and mobile sanitary formations in the 1906 Geneva Convention for the Amelioration of the Condition of the Wounded and Sick in Armies in the Field.[118]

53.2   Aircraft granted safe conduct by agreement between the belligerents are normally exempt from attack. Otherwise this provision would be meaningless.

53.3   Enemy civil airliners are normally exempt from attack on the same basis as enemy passenger vessels when engaged only in carrying civilian passengers (paragraph 47(e)). Innocent civilian passengers in a civil airliner are even more at risk than those in a passenger vessel since the aircraft can be destroyed or rendered out of control by most air-to-air and surface-to-air weapons. It is noted that the 1984 Protocol to the Chicago Convention inserts, after Article 3, a new Article 3 bis which provides in subparagraph (a):

> The contracting States recognise that every State must refrain from resorting to the use of weapons against civil aircraft in flight and that, in case of interception, the lives of persons on board and the safety of aircraft must not be endangered. This provision shall not be interpreted as modifying in any way the rights and obligations of States as set forth in the Charter of the United Nations.

Although the Chicago Convention is not applicable to military (State) aircraft (Article 3) and provides 'in case of war, the provisions of this Convention shall not affect the freedom of any of the contracting States affected, whether as belligerents or as neutrals' (Article 89), it is recognised that there is a grey area with regard to the application in armed conflict of law developed for peacetime. Therefore, this humanitarian law document attempts to effect a sensible and realistic marriage between the rules applicable during peacetime and those applicable during armed conflict.

118 HRAW, Art. 17.

Conditions of exemption for medical aircraft

54   **Medical aircraft are exempt from attack only if they:**

   (a)   **have been recognised as such;**

   (b)   **are acting in compliance with an agreement as specified in paragraph 177;**

   (c)   **fly in areas under the control of own or friendly forces;** *or*

   (d)   **fly outside the area of armed conflict.**

   In other instances, medical aircraft operate at their own risk.

54.1   The 1949 Geneva Conventions provided that medical aircraft may not be the object of attack, but shall be respected by the belligerents while flying at heights, at times and on routes specifically agreed upon between the belligerents.[119] In order to reflect the practice of belligerents, accord greater protection to medical aircraft, and allow more flexibility for quick-reaction medical missions using medical helicopters, API relaxed the rules for medical aircraft. Specifically, agreement between the belligerents is not required (but is still encouraged) in all situations to ensure protection for medical aircraft and, in the absence of agreement, medical aircraft, once recognised as such, shall be protected.[120] Paragraph 54 formulates the exemption from attack in the light of the Geneva Conventions, Additional Protocol I, and the realities of armed conflict at sea. Further rules relating to medical aircraft are found in paragraphs 174–183.

54.2   In subparagraph (a), recognition provides protection in all cases.[121]

54.3   In subparagraph (b), agreement between the belligerents in accordance with paragraph 177 also affords an exemption.[122]

54.4   In subparagraph (c), agreement between the belligerents is not required for an exemption from attack if the medical aircraft fly in areas where military control by own or friendly forces is clearly established.[123] If, in an area of hostilities at sea, military control is in doubt, is only partially assured, or is clearly established by the opposing belligerent, medical aircraft can only be assured protection by agreement between the belligerents.[124] For example, in an area of actual hostilities, a belligerent may control the airspace above 20,000 feet against opposing aircraft but may not control the airspace below 20,000 feet against opposing missiles. A medical aircraft would be at risk flying in the missile threat zone without an agreement between the belligerents.

---

119 GCII Art. 39.
120 API Arts. 24–31.
121 This is specified in API Arts. 26–27.
122 GCII Art. 39; API Arts. 26–27.
123 API Art. 25.
124 API Arts. 26–27.

54.5   Subparagraph (d) provides protection from attack for medical aircraft flying outside the area of armed conflict. For example, a medical aircraft transporting the sick and wounded or medical supplies to and from a distant base and flying over international waters outside the area of actual hostilities would be protected.

54.6   In instances other than those set forth in this paragraph, medical aircraft operate at their own risk, but as stated above they shall be respected after they have been recognised as such. As a practical matter, it is very difficult to ensure the safety of medical aircraft no matter how clearly they are marked in accordance with paragraph 175. However, belligerents should ensure that the medical mission is performed in such places and in such a manner as to minimise the risk that the conduct of hostilities by combatants will imperil the safety of medical aircraft.

Conditions of exemption for aircraft granted safe conduct

55   Aircraft granted safe conduct are exempt from attack only if they:

    (a)   are innocently employed in their agreed role;

    (b)   do not intentionally hamper the movements of combatants; *and*

    (c)   comply with the details of the agreement, including availability for inspection.

55.1   Belligerents would expect that aircraft granted safe conduct would comply with the conditions in this paragraph. There is no limitation on what the agreed role could be. Aircraft granted safe conduct could be *inter alia* transporting prisoners of war, conducting relief missions, transporting cultural property, or protecting the environment. They must be innocently employed, that is, not as a subterfuge to provide a military advantage. They must not intentionally hamper the movements of the combatants and therefore must comply with the orders of belligerent forces. Aircraft granted safe conduct may be subject to inspection to verify adherence to the agreement, preferably at an airfield before beginning the flight. With regard to the identification of such aircraft, aircraft chartered by the ICRC have the same status as medical aircraft and may use the same methods of identification (paragraph 175). Other safe conduct aircraft may not use medical aircraft identification, but at present must rely on filing a detailed flight plan (paragraph 76) and using Secondary Surveillance Radar (SSR) modes and codes for civil aircraft.

Conditions of exemption for civil airliners

56   **Civil airliners are exempt from attack only if they:**

  (a)   are innocently employed in their normal role; *and*

  (b)   do not intentionally hamper the movements of combatants.

56.1   To maintain their exemption from attack, enemy civil airliners must be clearly marked and engaged in carrying civilian passengers in scheduled and non-scheduled flights along air traffic routes, namely, employed in their normal role. This employment must be innocent, that is, not as a subterfuge to gain a military advantage. Further, a civil airliner must not *intentionally* hamper the movements of the combatants. Implicit also in the conditions for exemption is the customary requirement that civil aircraft obey the orders of belligerent forces in the immediate vicinity of naval operations (paragraph 73). The precautions regarding civil aircraft in paragraphs 72–77 apply to civil airliners.

Loss of exemption

57   **If aircraft exempt from attack breach any of the applicable conditions of their exemption as set forth in paragraphs 54–56, they may be attacked only if:**

  (a)   diversion for landing, visit and search, and possible capture, is not feasible;

  (b)   no other method is available for exercising military control;

  (c)   the circumstances of non-compliance are sufficiently grave that the aircraft has become, or may be reasonably assumed to be, a military objective; *and*

  (d)   the collateral casualties or damage will not be disproportionate to the military advantage gained or anticipated.

57.1   This paragraph corresponds to paragraphs 49–52 pertaining to attacking enemy vessels normally exempt from attack. The enemy medical aircraft, aircraft granted safe conduct and the civil airliner must first be in violation of the respective conditions of exemption in paragraphs 54–56. An attack can then only be ordered if *all* the conditions in subparagraphs (a)–(d) are met.

57.2   As to subparagraph (a), the rules for interception, visit and search of civil aircraft are contained in paragraphs 125–134. The rules for the capture of an enemy civil airliner are in paragraphs 141–145. Medical aircraft and aircraft granted safe conduct are exempt from capture, but may be ordered to land for inspection.

57.3   Regarding subparagraph (b), belligerent military forces must exhaust all available means to exercise control of the enemy aircraft. This means giving the aircraft time to comply with orders to land, divert or otherwise refrain from violating their conditions of exemption.

57.4   Subparagraph (c) prescribes that the breach of conditions of exemption from attack must be extraordinarily harmful to belligerent forces *and* must meet the basic rule on military objectives in paragraph 40.

57.5   Subparagraph (d) is another way to state the basic rule on collateral casualties or damage in paragraph 46(d). In the case of an enemy civil airliner with innocent passengers, only an immediate and imperative military requirement would appear to tip the proportionality scale and justify an attack.

58   In case of doubt whether a vessel or aircraft exempt from attack is being used to make an effective contribution to military action, it shall be presumed not to be so used.

58.1   If a vessel or aircraft does not make an effective contribution to military action, then it does not constitute a military objective and may not be attacked. A presumption that a vessel or aircraft which appears to be entitled to exemption from attack is in fact entitled to such an exemption unless the contrary is established enhances the protection of civilian objects. The presumption is only applicable in case of doubt and is rebuttable. If a party to the conflict is able to establish on a balance of probabilities that the vessel or aircraft is making an effective contribution to military action, it may act accordingly. This rule, the so-called rule of doubt, imposes an obligation on a party to the conflict to gather and assess relevant information before commencing an attack.

Section IV Other enemy vessels and aircraft

Enemy merchant vessels

59   Enemy merchant vessels may only be attacked if they meet the definition of a military objective in paragraph 40.

59.1   If enemy merchant vessels are not legitimate military objectives, they are exempt from attack although they may be captured under certain circumstances (see paragraphs 135–140). Although they may not be the object of attack, they may, in certain circumstances, incur collateral damage as a result of attacks directed against military objectives.

60   The following activities may render enemy merchant vessels military objectives:

    (a)   engaging in belligerent acts on behalf of the enemy, e.g., laying mines, minesweeping, cutting undersea cables and pipelines, engaging in visit and search of neutral merchant vessels or attacking other merchant vessels;

    (b)   acting as an auxiliary to an enemy's armed forces, e.g., carrying troops or replenishing warships;

(c) **being incorporated into or assisting the enemy's intelligence gathering system, e.g., engaging in reconnaissance, early warning, surveillance, or command, control and communications missions;**

(d) **sailing under convoy of enemy warships or military aircraft;**

(e) **refusing an order to stop or actively resisting visit, search or capture;**

(f) **being armed to an extent that they could inflict damage to a warship; this excludes light individual weapons for the defence of personnel, e.g., against pirates, and purely deflective systems such as 'chaff';** *or*

(g) **otherwise making an effective contribution to military action, e.g., carrying military materials.**

60.1   As indicated in the discussion concerning paragraph 40, the Round Table eventually agreed that the best approach to the military objective issue was a combination of a general definition and an illustrative list. The Rapporteur on the Military Objective and the Principle of Distinction initially suggested the following list:

(a)   engagement in acts of war on behalf of the enemy;

(b)   acting as a *de facto* auxiliary to the enemy's armed forces;

(c)   incorporation into, or assistance to the intelligence system of the enemy's armed forces;

(d)   being armed;

(e)   active resistance to visit, search and capture;

(f)   refusing to stop upon being duly summoned;

(g)   sailing under convoy of enemy warships or military aircraft; *and*

(h)   integration into the enemy's war-fighting or war-sustaining effort.

60.2   According to the written comments submitted by participants, some of those categories were widely accepted. Others, however, especially categories (b), (c), (d), and (h) needed to be discussed thoroughly. In this context the discussion leader noted that there was obviously some tendency among the participants to exempt enemy merchant vessels from attack, at least if they had no direct connection to the armed conflict.

60.3   At its first stage the discussion concentrated on the definition of enemy merchant vessels. With regard to the term 'merchant vessel' the participants quickly agreed that it comprised all vessels that fell neither into the category of warships, nor auxiliary vessels, nor into the category of specially protected vessels. However, as regards the nationality or enemy character of merchant vessels there were two opposing positions. One group pointed at the fact that many ships flying a neutral flag, especially a flag of convenience, were controlled by nationals or even governments of another State. Very often there were economic or financial aspects involved that could not be ascertained easily, at least not by the commander on the bridge. If such vessels were controlled by the enemy government and were operating for the benefit of the enemy's economy they were probably also integrated into the enemy's war-sustaining effort.

60.4   A second group was not inclined, for various reasons, to take those aspects into consideration when establishing the enemy character of merchant vessels. First, they felt that the issue of flags of convenience was part of the law of neutrality and the status of neutral merchant vessels. Secondly, they did not want to complicate the question of a ship's nationality. In law, the difference between enemy and neutral merchant vessels was that the former were liable to capture. Economic or financial interests that might cause doubt on the neutral status could be verified by a prize court. A commander on the bridge would neither look at registration nor at economic or financial interests. Hence, *prima facie* the flag was decisive and the commander would then rely on intelligence material in order to establish whether there were sufficient reasons for suspicion. See also paragraphs 112–117.

60.5   In view of the task to formulate 'bright line rules' that latter position seemingly prevailed. Thus, in the further course of the working session the participants turned to the criteria rendering an enemy merchant vessel liable to attack.

60.6   At the beginning of that part of the discussion reference was made to the different reasons rendering enemy merchant vessels liable to attack. Either, by their nature or function, they were military objectives, or, by their behaviour in the concrete case, they could be attacked without being a military objective *strict sensu*. The latter was true especially in the case of vessels resisting visit, search and capture.

60.7   Then, after it had been stated that in many cases the cargo was the proper objective if it contributed to the war-sustaining effort, the central issue became category (h) (integration into the enemy's war-fighting or war-sustaining effort). In this context some participants proposed to classify generally enemy merchant vessels as legitimate military objectives and then to formulate criteria exempting some of them from attack. The reasons put forward in support of this proposal, however, differed to a considerable extent. While some believed that the status of protected vessels would thus be improved, others invoked primarily military reasons. For example, if enemy merchant vessels were generally classified as military objectives, rules of engagement could be drafted much more easily. A third group sponsoring that proposal considered category (h) to be the main category in the light of the definition of military objective. Even though the wording of category (h) was rather broad it was realistic since in practice, as in the recent Iran–Iraq War, enemy merchant vessels were indeed integrated into the war-sustaining efforts. Hence, in spite of the need to define precisely this category, State practice was supporting the presumption that enemy merchant vessels were military objectives. Others opposed this line of reasoning by referring to the arguments put forward with regard to the protection of the civilian population during the Geneva Diplomatic Conference that led to the adoption of the Additional Protocols of 1977. On the one hand, there were specially protected persons and, on the other hand, the civilian population was protected as such. The difference lay in the extent of protection. This could be accepted for the various kinds of vessels as well. Moreover, if enemy merchant vessels were *per se* military objectives, the burden of proof for exempt status would be imposed upon those vessels.

60.8   In view of the two opposing standpoints it was considered necessary to elaborate on the questions whether enemy merchant vessels falling into category (h) were in fact military objectives and what was to be understood by 'integration into the enemy's war-sustaining effort' as proposed by the Rapporteur. Those opposing the proposal argued that during the World Wars the practice had been justified by way of reprisals. Hence, the belligerent States themselves had considered attacks on enemy merchant vessels illegal. The Iran–Iraq conflict could not be relied upon since the parties to that conflict obviously had not taken any legal aspects into consideration. In the Falklands conflict the parties had not attacked enemy merchant shipping even though they had had the capacity to do so. Therefore, category (h) had not become part of customary international law. In any event, State practice of the past should not be decisive since the task of the Round Table was to formulate rules for future conflicts. Moreover, if integration into the war-sustaining effort was considered a sufficient reason to justify attack on sight, the standards achieved by API would be jeopardised. Thus, the *opinio juris* of States would develop in a dangerous way. Therefore, category (h) should be replaced by the wording of API Article 52(2). If that could be accepted, it would depend on each single case whether an enemy merchant ship was a legitimate military objective. Finally, practical considerations like the facilitation of the drafting of rules of engagement were of secondary importance. The rule of law had to be first established. Then, it would be the duty of the respective governments to formulate simple rules of engagement enabling the commander on the bridge to comply with the law.

60.9   Those supporting the proposal considered it necessary to agree on a provision that was acceptable for States. In order to establish whether that was the case and whether a rule of law constituted a reasonable balance between humanitarian and military standards, it was indispensable to scrutinise State practice. For example, the failure of the 1936 London Protocol had been caused by the fact that the drafters of that agreement had ignored the different capabilities of the belligerents in the Second World War. While Great Britain had been able to exercise the right of capture effectively, Germany, due to the inferiority of its surface fleet, had been forced to take other measures to infringe upon the enemy's economy. In modern armed conflicts, attacks on an enemy's merchant shipping that is regularly integrated into the war-sustaining effort would be militarily advantageous and, hence, of legal significance. However, two situations had to be kept apart. The crux of category (h) was not, for example, oil tankers sailing to enemy or enemy-controlled territory and supplying his armed forces with fuel. Such ships would not differ from vessels carrying troops. Therefore, they were military objectives and liable to attack. Rather, especially in long-lasting conflicts, category (h) could apply to merchant vessels contributing to the enemy's export economy. If, due to the wording of category (h), doubts remained, those could be met by inserting the term 'effective'. According to an intermediate position the term 'war-sustaining effort' was either to be qualified by 'circumstances prevailing at the time' or to be defined on a case-by-case basis. If the latter was accepted there should be a clarification to the effect that in all other cases enemy merchant vessels would only be liable to capture.

60.10. The current manual of the United States Navy suggests that enemy merchant ships may be attacked and destroyed without warning if they are integrated into the enemy's 'war-fighting/war-sustaining effort' and compliance with the 1936 London Protocol would subject the attacking force to imminent danger or otherwise preclude mission accomplishment.[125] The annotation to this provision states: 'Although the term "war-sustaining" is not subject to precise definition, "effort" that indirectly but effectively supports and sustains the belligerent's war-fighting capability properly falls within the scope of the term.'[126] Another annotation provides as examples 'imports of raw materials used for the production of armaments and exports of products the proceeds of which are used by the belligerent to purchase arms and armaments'.[127]

60.11. After intense discussion, however, the Round Table accepted the view that the descriptive phrase 'integration into the enemy's war-fighting/war-sustaining effort' was too broad to use for the residual category. The phrase chosen to describe the residual category of merchant vessels which were legitimate military objectives was merchant vessels which make an effective contribution to military action by, for example carrying military materials. This wording is the same as the wording used in paragraph 40 as part of the definition of military objective. It must be noted that the categories of enemy merchant vessels liable to attack is narrower than the categories of enemy merchant vessels liable to capture. All enemy merchant vessels may be captured. Only some may be attacked.

60.12. At the end of the discussion on war-fighting/war-sustaining/military action, a further proposal was made to abolish the distinction between merchant and other vessels and between enemy and neutral vessels. When discussing attack, the reasons for the employment of weapons had to be taken into consideration. Those were twofold: either the warship was threatened or attack was indispensable for mission accomplishment (sea denial/sea control). Neither the category of vessel nor its nationality was of relevance but whether the vessel concerned was a military objective or not. Hence, in accordance with this proposal, it would suffice to agree on the following categories of vessels: (a) ships liable to attack in any case; (b) ships liable to attack under certain circumstances only; and (c) ships not liable to attack. Such a procedure would also facilitate the drafting of adequate rules of engagement. This proposal was not followed up.

60.13. The remaining time was devoted to category (d) concerning the arming of enemy merchant vessels. The only controversial issue was whether the traditional rule according to which merchant vessels could be armed defensively without rendering them liable to attack was to be maintained. In the beginning some participants considered it necessary to allow armament of a purely defensive character. The majority, however, rejected that view since in modern warfare conditions it was impossible to distinguish between offensive and defensive weapons. After it had been clarified that small arms necessary for the maintenance of order on board or for defence

---

125 NWP9A, *The Commander's Handbook*, para. 8.2.2.2.
126 *Ibid.*, pp. 8–12, footnote 52.
127 *Ibid.*, pp. 7–23, footnote 90.

against pirate attacks were not to be included into that category, the question whether, for example, anti-missile systems belonged to it was discussed. While there was agreement that chaff was not to be considered armament in the sense of category (d), some doubts remained with regard to those systems that could not be directed against ships but only against missiles and projectiles.

60.14   In the final result, the Round Table adopted what is now paragraph 60. Paragraph 60(a)–(e) essentially restates the traditional law. Under the traditional law, however, enemy merchant vessels could be equipped with defensive weapons but were subject to attack on sight if they were equipped with offensive weapons. Paragraph 60(f) changes the traditional law because in light of modern weapons, it is impossible to determine, if it ever was possible, whether the armament on merchant ships is to be used offensively or merely defensively. It is unrealistic to expect enemy forces to be able to make that determination. Enemy merchant vessels which are armed to the extent that they could damage any warship, including a submarine, may be attacked on sight. In this context, the ship's bow, which could be used to ram a submarine, is not considered to be a weapon. The ship's crew may be armed with personal weapons such as rifles or pistols, particularly in waters where piracy is prevalent, and the ship may be equipped with deflective systems such as 'chaff' without the vessel being classified as armed.

61   Any attack on these vessels is subject to the basic rules set out in paragraphs 38–46.

61.1   See commentary on paragraphs 38–46. These basic rules must be followed when any targeting decision is made.

Enemy civil aircraft

62   Enemy civil aircraft may only be attacked if they meet the definition of a military objective in paragraph 40.

62.1   This paragraph, like that pertaining to enemy merchant vessels in paragraph 59, places a general limitation on attacks on enemy civil aircraft. In addition to engaging in a specific military-related activity, the enemy civil aircraft by its nature, location, purpose or use must be making an effective contribution to military action. Its total or partial destruction, capture or neutralisation, in the circumstances ruling at the time, must also offer a definite military advantage. The definition of military objective in paragraph 40 is identical to Article 52(2) of API.

62.2   Civil aircraft, whether enemy or neutral, are broadly defined in paragraph 13(l) as aircraft other than military, auxiliary, or other State aircraft such as customs and police aircraft, that are engaged in commercial or private service. The enemy civil aircraft addressed in paragraphs 62–64 are civil aircraft other than medical aircraft, aircraft granted safe conduct and civil airliners which are exempt from attack.

63   **The following activities may render enemy civil aircraft military objectives:**

(a) engaging in acts of war on behalf of the enemy, e.g., laying mines, minesweeping, laying or monitoring acoustic sensors, engaging in electronic warfare, intercepting or attacking other civil aircraft, or providing targeting information to enemy forces;

(b) acting as an auxiliary aircraft to an enemy's armed forces, e.g., transporting troops or military cargo, or refuelling military aircraft;

(c) being incorporated into or assisting the enemy's intelligence-gathering system, e.g., engaging in reconnaissance, early warning, surveillance, or command, control and communications missions;

(d) flying under the protection of accompanying enemy warships or military aircraft;

(e) refusing an order to identify itself, divert from its track, or proceed for visit and search to a belligerent airfield that is safe for the type of aircraft involved and reasonably accessible, or operating fire control equipment that could reasonably be construed to be part of an aircraft weapon system, or on being intercepted clearly manoeuvring to attack the intercepting belligerent military aircraft;

(f) being armed with air-to-air or air-to-surface weapons; *or*

(g) otherwise making an effective contribution to military action.

63.1   Advances in propulsion and materials technologies have dramatically changed the role of aircraft in armed conflict at sea since the First World War. Speed, endurance, lift, manoeuvrability and capacity have enabled aircraft to perform a variety of missions in addition to launching weapons. Aircraft are regularly employed at sea in surveillance, targeting, electronic warfare, command, control, communications, visit and search, refuelling, search and rescue, transporting troops and military supplies, and medical support. Aircraft can be fixed or rotary wing, sea or land based, manned or unmanned. Weapons carried can be missiles, rockets, guns and bombs. A number of weapon systems are portable and can be quickly installed in small, fixed-wing aircraft or helicopters.

63.2   Subparagraphs (a)–(c) are examples of military-related activities that may render an enemy civil aircraft a military objective. Some of these activities would require extensive modification to a civil aircraft. Others, such as providing targeting information, gathering intelligence, relaying vital communications or transporting troops and military cargo, can be performed without changing the visible characteristics of a civil aircraft.

63.3   Subparagraph (d) is similar to paragraph 60(d) which includes sailing under convoy of enemy warships or military aircraft, an activity that may render an enemy merchant vessel a military objective. An enemy civil aircraft that flies under the protection of accompanying enemy warships or military aircraft places itself at risk in the immediate area of hostilities since the enemy warships or military aircraft are military objectives. Belligerent forces might assume that the protected enemy civil aircraft is acting as an auxiliary aircraft to the enemy's armed forces, or, in pressing an attack, belligerent forces may misidentify the enemy civil aircraft. The 1990 International Civil Aviation Organisation (ICAO) *Manual Concerning Safety Measures Relating to Military Activities Potentially Hazardous to Civil Aircraft Operations* states that normally civil aircraft should not operate in an area of hazardous military operations.[128]

63.4   Subparagraph (e) addresses the tactical situation in which belligerent forces encounter an enemy civil aircraft that may not be engaging in a military-related activity. The enemy civil aircraft is obliged to identify itself when so ordered. It can also be ordered to divert from its track or to proceed to a belligerent airfield for visit and search. Refusal to comply with these orders may render the enemy civil aircraft a military objective. The rules governing interception, diversion, and visit and search of civil aircraft are indicated in paragraphs 125–134 of this Manual.

63.5   Under the rules of engagement practised by most belligerents, warships and military aircraft are not obliged to wait until actually being fired upon before acting in self-defence if there are clear and unmistakable hostile actions indicating that they are about to be attacked. An enemy civil aircraft that illuminates a warship or military aircraft with fire control sensors indicates that a missile could immediately be fired. Similarly, an enemy civil aircraft that manoeuvres to take a firing position on an intercepting military aircraft indicates an intention to immediately attack. The usual procedures for intercepting civil aircraft advise civil aircraft to maintain heading, speed and altitude on being intercepted by a military aircraft. Committing either of these hostile acts may render the enemy civil aircraft a military objective and result in immediate defence measures by belligerent forces.

63.6   Subparagraph (f) is a prohibition against arming an enemy civil aircraft with weapons that could be used to attack warships or military aircraft. This excludes light individual weapons for defence of the crew, and equipment that deflects an attacking weapon or warns of an attack. Technology has enabled air-to-air and air-to-surface weapons to be compact, accurate and lethal. It is important that belligerent forces be reasonably assured that such weapons are not carried on enemy civil aircraft. In this regard, the 1923 Hague Rules of Aerial Warfare state the customary rule that no private aircraft, when outside the jurisdiction of its own country, shall be armed in time of war.

63.7   Subparagraph (g) covers other military-related activities by enemy civil aircraft that make an effective contribution to enemy military action and thus may render the enemy civil aircraft a military objective. In this regard, the 1923 Hague Rules of Aerial Warfare state the customary rule that no aircraft other than a belligerent military aircraft shall engage in hostilities in any form.

---

128 ICAO Doc. 9554-AN/932, 1990.

64   Any attack on these aircraft is subject to the basic rules set out in paragraphs 38–46.

64.1   This paragraph, like paragraph 61 pertaining to enemy merchant vessels, specifies that any attack on enemy civil aircraft is subject to the basic rules on distinction, military objectives and collateral damage in paragraphs 38–46.

Enemy warships and military aircraft

65   Unless they are exempt from attack under paragraphs 47 or 53, enemy warships and military aircraft and enemy auxiliary vessels and aircraft are military objectives within the meaning of paragraph 40.

65.1   Paragraph 47 lists classes of enemy vessels which are exempt from attack and paragraph 53 lists classes of enemy aircraft which are exempt from attack. Paragraph 13 defines warship, auxiliary vessel, military aircraft and auxiliary aircraft. The classes of military enemy aircraft exempt from attack are few and, it is hoped, easily identifiable: medical aircraft and aircraft granted safe conduct by agreement. The classes of enemy vessels exempt from attack are somewhat broader, to some extent because vessels move much more slowly than aircraft and therefore more time is available to assess the nature of the threat they pose. Further, there has historically been a *prima facie* assumption that an approaching aircraft constitutes a threat. In general, enemy warships and auxiliary vessels are exempt from attack if they have been granted safe conduct, if they have surrendered, or if they fall into certain easily recognisable categories such as hospital ships, medical transports or vessels designed or adapted exclusively for responding to marine pollution incidents. The mere fact that warships are engaged in humanitarian missions such as rescuing the survivors of torpedoed vessels does not render them exempt from attack.

66   They may be attacked, subject to the basic rules in paragraphs 38–46.

66.1   See commentary on paragraphs 38–46. These basic rules must be followed when any targeting decision is made.

Section V Neutral merchant vessels and civil aircraft

Neutral merchant vessels

67   Merchant vessels flying the flag of neutral States may not be attacked unless they:

   (a)   are believed on reasonable grounds to be carrying contraband or breaching a blockade, and after prior warning they intentionally and clearly refuse to stop, or intentionally and clearly resist visit, search or capture;

(b) engage in belligerent acts on behalf of the enemy;

(c) act as auxiliaries to the enemy's armed forces;

(d) are incorporated into or assist the enemy's intelligence system;

(e) sail under convoy of enemy warships or military aircraft; *or*

(f) otherwise make an effective contribution to the enemy's military action, e.g., by carrying military materials and it is not feasible for the attacking forces to first place passengers and crew in a place of safety. Unless circumstances do not permit, they are to be given a warning, so that they can re-route, off-load, or take other precautions.

67.1   The discussion leader formulated possible bases for discussion on the status of neutral merchant vessels – the topic of the Round Table that by many was considered the most important. He preferred not to elaborate on the establishment of enemy or neutral character but instead to concentrate on the circumstances under which neutral or non-belligerent vessels were liable to attack. For this purpose, the list of cases possibly justifying attack that had been presented by the Rapporteur and other participants was taken as a basis for discussion.

According to the list proposed by the discussion leader, neutral merchant vessels are liable to attack:

(a)   after prior warning, when they wilfully and persistently resist visit, search or capture;

(b)   after prior warning, when they wilfully and persistently refuse to stop after being duly summoned to do so;

(c)   without warning, when they engage in acts of war on behalf of the enemy;

(d)   without warning, when they act as *de facto* auxiliaries to the enemy's armed forces;

(e)   without warning, when they are incorporated into, or assist, the enemy's intelligence system;

(f)   without warning, when they sail under convoy of enemy warships or military aircraft;

(g)   without warning, when they are integrated into the enemy's war-fighting effort and it is not a feasible option for the attacking ship to first place passengers and crew in a place of safety; and

(h)   without warning, when they are integrated into the enemy's war-sustaining effort and it is not a feasible option for the attacking ship to first place passengers and crew in a place of safety.

67.2   The discussion leader opposed the view that in practice neutral merchant vessels would play a minor role. For example, in geographically limited armed conflicts such as the Iran–Iraq War neutral merchant vessels were affected by belligerent measures. As regards the different categories in the list he believed item (h) to be the most controversial. In that context he suggested taking into consideration the idea of a code of conduct for neutral merchant vessels in times of armed conflict. In view of the provisions of API, he conceded that the protection of civilian objects was a major issue. However, the participants also had to take into account the other interests involved. Concluding, he proposed to start from the presumption that neutral merchant vessels were not liable to attack and to proceed by discussing the exceptions laid down in the aforementioned list.

67.3   Despite the discussion leader's proposal not to deal with it extensively, the distinction between the enemy or neutral character of merchant vessels became a major point of controversy. One group supporting maintenance of the distinction argued that under the UN Charter the protected status of neutral merchant vessels had increased in comparison to the traditional law. Whereas neutral merchant vessels could still be stopped, visited and searched, they could be attacked only if the attack was justified by Article 51 of the UN Charter. That did not mean that the law of naval warfare as such was being modified by the Charter. However, due regard had to be paid to the undeniable fact that, with the outbreak of an international armed conflict, the Charter would not cease to be in force especially in the relationship between belligerents and neutrals. It could even be argued that, in view of the practice of neutral States during the Iran–Iraq War, this fact had to be taken into consideration to the same extent as the practice of the belligerents. In particular, with the British Government referring to Article 51 of the UN Charter, there already was a trend towards a restriction of the right of visit and search in the exercise of the right of self-defence.

67.4   As in former instances, this position was rejected by those who pointed out the different scopes of application of the UN Charter on the one hand and of the laws of war and neutrality on the other hand. They argued that in times of armed conflict the former played no role with regard to the legality of the belligerents' conduct. Moreover, the practice of neutral States was not to be over-emphasised. In the Iran–Iraq conflict they had had the capability, and had made use of it, to demonstrate that they were not willing to tolerate any interference with their economic interests. That had been an exceptional case that could not be generalised.

67.5   A second, though smaller, group proposed to go even further and to differentiate between States not parties to the conflict on the one hand and those subscribing to a status of permanent neutrality on the other hand. Merchant vessels flying the flag of a State of the latter category were to be accorded a higher degree of protection. These States had a special interest in having their vessels not involved and would act accordingly, for example, by a stricter supervision of their respective merchant vessels. It would, they added, be unbearable if in the Iran–Iraq conflict Kuwaiti and Swiss or Swedish merchant vessels had been treated equally. Most of the participants, however, were not inclined to agree to a further distinction depending on the difference of the type of neutrality of flag States. That, they believed, was not feasible in practice. Moreover, even States subscribing to a status of permanent or strict neutrality were not obliged to prohibit commercial intercourse between their nationals and the parties to an armed conflict.

67.6   In view of the diversity of practical and legal problems involved, another group among the participants suggested the abolition of the distinction between neutral and enemy merchant vessels altogether. They wondered whether it was necessary to maintain two sets of rules if, in the light of the definition of military objectives, the legal status of merchant vessels, be they neutral or enemy, depended on their cargo and their function in the circumstances ruling at the time. Hence, vessels flying the enemy's flag operating in sea areas remote from the theatre of war could not be considered military objectives. In contrast, neutral ships transporting important goods to the enemy could be considered military objectives. Therefore, the presumption of innocence applied to all merchant vessels irrespective of the flag they were flying. Only if they qualified as military objectives and only if all precautions in attack were observed were they liable to attack.

67.7   The majority view was, however, that the distinction between neutral and enemy merchant vessels was to be maintained for three reasons. First, the definition of military objectives did not apply to the legal relationship between belligerent and neutrals. Secondly, there was a decisive difference in so far as all enemy merchant vessels were liable to capture and condemnation. Third, as a matter of practical politics, neutrals were not involved in the conflict.

67.8   The participants then discussed the general status of neutral merchant vessels. It was submitted that if belligerents did not have the capacity to exercise the right of visit and search they were never allowed to proceed to attack but were obliged to let all neutral vessels pass unmolested. That view was rejected by others who doubted its feasibility. Because of the lack of means of enforcement in international law, States could not be expected to accept rules that would force them to lose the war. There were certain limits that had to be taken into account. The same was true with regard to developments in weapons technology and with regard to economic relationships.

67.9   After it had been clarified that not the definition of military objectives as such but only the criteria included in that definition were to be applied to neutrals, the view, obviously shared by the majority, crystallised that neutral merchant vessels were liable to attack under exceptional circumstances only. Hence, they were liable to attack if they effectively contributed to military action of the enemy and if their destruction offered a definite military advantage. Those preconditions as well as direct or indirect economic contribution had to be established clearly. Further, neutral merchant vessels departing from an enemy port and those carrying export cargoes such as oil were not to be treated as military objectives. In this context, some participants suggested reformulating the rules on unneutral service and to adapt them to the criteria laid down in the definition of a military objective.

67.10   The participants then turned to the list proposed by the discussion leader. While categories (a)–(f) did not give rise to major objections, categories (g) (integration into the war-fighting effort) and (h) (integration into the war-sustaining effort) were controversial. Some doubted whether any distinction between those categories could be drawn. Therefore, they suggested either replacing them by the definition of military objective or deleting them altogether. Others wanted to maintain categories (g) and (h) because they considered it indispensable to have a complete list of exceptional cases justifying attack. They conceded, however, that those categories still needed to be elaborated upon in detail.

67.11   Since it was felt necessary to arrive at a concluding statement with regard to the status of neutral merchant vessels, a discussion leader was appointed whose task was to submit proposals that would help structure the discussion. The discussion leader stated that there was general agreement on the validity of the principle of distinction, the definition of military objective and the principle of proportionality. However, it had remained unclear to what extent they had an impact on the categories of the list. That problem, the discussion leader believed, could only be solved if agreement on the specific elements of the law of naval warfare was reached. Hence, the participants still had to deal with a number of issues that had been addressed. Those were *inter alia* the distinction, if any, between neutrality and non-belligerency[129] and the definition of unneutral service. With regard to the latter issue the discussion leader, without elaborating on the possible consequences, identified six categories that could be made use of in specifying that term. Accordingly, a neutral merchant vessel was to be considered rendering unneutral service when:

(a)   engaged in acts of war on behalf of the enemy;

(b)   acting as a *de facto* auxiliary;

(c)   incorporated into, or assisting, the enemy's intelligence system;

(d)   integrated into the enemy's war-fighting effort;

(e)   integrated into the enemy's war-sustaining effort; *or*

(f)   sailing under convoy of enemy warships or military aircraft.

67.12   Those categories still needed to be dealt with extensively, especially category (e). With regard to 'integration into the enemy's war-sustaining effort' the participants also had to take into consideration that in most cases the flag States were unaware of the conduct of vessels flying their respective flags. Such an enumeration of acts of unneutral service alone, the discussion leader added, would not suffice to mitigate the effects of war on merchant shipping. Hence, it was indispensable to agree on two further sets of rules.

67.13   The first set of rules would be a code of conduct for neutral merchant ships. In that context the definition of unneutral service was to be taken as a starting point. Accordingly, neutral merchant vessels would not be allowed to sail under enemy convoy, to engage in acts of war on behalf of the enemy, etc. Additionally, the code had to include the fact that they were obliged to stop when duly summoned and that they were not allowed to resist visit and search. However, the discussion leader saw no reason justifying a prohibition of arming neutral merchant vessels.

67.14   The second set would be rules of behaviour for the parties to an armed conflict in their relation to all merchant vessels, whether enemy or neutral. According to these rules of behaviour, belligerents were to be accorded the right:

---

129 It was decided in the Geneva session not to recognise a distinction between 'neutrals' and 'non-belligerents' in the final document, but to name all States not party to the conflict as 'neutral'. See commentary to para. 13(d).

(a)   to issue zonal restrictions;

(b)   to request all merchant vessels to stop;

(c)   to visit and search all merchant vessels;

(d)   under certain conditions, to capture merchant vessels; *and*

(e)   with or without prior warning, to attack merchant vessels.

67.15   The discussion leader did not want to elaborate on zonal restrictions because that topic was to be dealt with extensively at a future session of the Round Table. With regard to his category (d) he submitted that neutral merchant vessels were liable to capture when they were military objectives or when engaged in unneutral service. They could be attacked after prior warning if they actively resisted visit, search and capture. He felt, however, unable to establish whether integration into the enemy's war-fighting and war-sustaining efforts justified attack without prior warning.

67.16   That statement by the discussion leader, which was intended to suggest a broader approach to the issue of neutral merchant vessels, gave rise to a discussion on basic questions of how the Round Table was to proceed. The majority, while welcoming the discussion leader's detailed proposals, considered them to be outside the scope of the meeting. Rather, the question to be dealt with was whether the definition of military objective was of legal relevance for the status of neutral merchant vessels. That was the basic question and everything else depended on it. Details could only be worked on if a consensus was achieved on the validity of the general definition. For these reasons, the wording of the definition was quite wide.

67.17   In contrast to the majority, some participants felt unable to start from the general definition and from general principles because they believed that the definition could only be the result of detailed findings. They therefore suggested taking the discussion leader's proposals as a basis for further discussion. During the discussion that followed two aspects of the discussion leader's proposals were dealt with to a considerable extent: the definition of unneutral service and the code of conduct for neutral merchant vessels.

67.18   In the context of unneutral service the different wording of the authentic French and of the English translation of Articles 45 ff. of the 1909 London Declaration was referred to. It was argued that the French term 'assistance hostile' implied more than violations of the duty of impartiality. There were two kinds of 'assistance hostile', a direct and an indirect one. While the latter comprised, for example, the transport of troops, the former referred to acceptance of orders by a belligerent and to similar acts. Hence, according to the 1909 London Declaration, unneutral service did not mean engagement in economic and trade relations but exclusively assistance in acts of war. That was to be taken into account by the participants.

67.19   Others, opposing this position, considered the London Declaration to be of limited value for the purpose of discussion since it was confined to condemnation and since it was to be addressed in an international prize court. In 1909, it reflected the then existing customary law and in those days acts of unneutral service did not render neutral merchant vessels liable to attack. However, already in the First World War the practice, and presumably the law, had changed. Therefore, they argued, the question to be considered was the extent to which the concept of unneutral service, as developed by post-1909 State practice, could be made use of in the context of attacks on neutral merchant vessels.

67.20   In the further course of the discussion it was suggested that the original categories (g) and (h) be replaced by 'effective/direct contribution to war-like activities'. Initially, there was a certain sympathy for that proposal because the original categories (g) and (h) were considered inadequate for justifying attacks on neutral merchant vessels. Shortly afterwards, however, the wording was criticised. The term 'direct' was opposed because this could exclude neutral ships supplying the respective enemy with important goods. Such an act would be considered as only an indirect contribution even though it could be most effective. Moreover, the big naval powers would only accept a wording that applied in general as well as in limited armed conflicts. Hence, it was agreed to maintain the term 'effective'. The term 'war-like activities' was also rejected. The majority preferred to replace it by 'military action' because there would be thus a congruence to the wording of API. Finally, it was agreed to replace the original categories (g) and (h) by 'effective contribution to military action'.

67.21   Then the participants concentrated on examples that would be comprised by that new category. The most controversial issue was whether economic support, especially the export of important goods, was to be characterised an 'effective contribution'. In that context some participants pointed to the practice of the Gulf War between Iran and Iraq when neutral oil tankers that had been integrated into the shuttle service to and from Kharg island had been attacked by Iraqi forces. However, it was soon agreed that the practice of the Gulf War should not be generalised.

67.22   After the participants had agreed to delete from the original categories (a) and (b) the requirement of prior warning, they turned to the proposal of a code of conduct for neutral merchant vessels. While many considered it useful to have such a code, the majority was not inclined to deal with that question for various reasons. First, they argued, it lay outside the scope of the Bochum meeting. Rather, national chambers of shipping, as in the Gulf War, had to publish recommendations for each conflict. Secondly, such a code of conduct could raise the question of international responsibility of the flag State for acts committed by individual merchant vessels flying their respective flags. Finally, a code of conduct was not legally obligatory. Hence, an infringement of such a code could not lead to legal consequences on the international level. For these reasons it was agreed to propose that other institutions, such as the International Maritime Organisation, take up that question.

67.23   Finally, the Round Table adopted the text of the present paragraph 67. Ships in the categories referred to in subparagraphs 67(a)–(e) have normally been regarded as subject to attack. Concerning subparagraph 67(a), there must be a substantial basis for a belief that the vessel is carrying contraband or breaching a blockade. A vessel may breach a blockade by travelling to or from a blockaded area. Contraband goods, however, are certain potential imports by the adverse party, not potential exports. The categories referred to in subparagraphs 67(a) and 67(e) are normally considered together because vessels which sail under convoy of enemy warships or military aircraft are deemed to be resisting visit, search and capture. Because they are so deemed, there is no need to warn them before conducting an attack.

67.24   Concerning subparagraph 67(b), acts of war include: laying of mines, minesweeping, cutting undersea cables, and attacking friendly merchant ships.

67.25   Concerning subparagraph 67(c), merchant vessels act as auxiliaries to the enemy's armed forces when they carry troops, carry supplies of any sort for the replenishment of warships or amphibious task groups, or accompany warships or amphibious task groups on military operations. The British STUFT (ships taken up from trade) which accompanied the British forces which retook the Falklands/Malvinas Islands in 1982 would be acting as auxiliary vessels within the meaning of subparagraph 67(c).

67.26   Subparagraph 67(d) must be interpreted strictly. In most conflicts merchant vessels do not become military objectives subject to attack on sight merely because they have instructions to report the sighting of vessels or aircraft of the adverse party which they come across while engaged in normal commercial operations. Merchant vessels may, however, become subject to attack on sight if they are employed primarily for intelligence-gathering purposes and have special communications or detection equipment and personnel on board. For example, during the Falklands conflict, British forces attacked and sank the Argentine fishing trawler *Narwal* which was repeatedly engaged in reporting the location of British warships and which had an Argentine naval detachment on board. In the Nuremberg Judgment, the fact that British armed merchant vessels were given standing orders to report the sighting of enemy vessels or aircraft was only one of the factors which led the Tribunal to decide that the German forces were not prohibited from attacking them on sight.

67.27   The residual category in subparagraph 62(f) would include most imports which could be used for military operations or for the production of military equipment but it would not include exports by the adverse party which might be vital for financing the war effort because the connection between the exports and military action would be too remote.

68   Any attack on these vessels is subject to the basic rules in paragraphs 38–46.

68.1   See commentary on paragraphs 38–46. These basic rules must be followed when any targeting decision is made.

69   The mere fact that a neutral merchant vessel is armed provides no grounds for attacking it.

69.1   Piracy remains a genuine threat in some areas of the world. Further, under traditional law, neutral merchant vessels may be armed, at times quite heavily, for self-defence.

Neutral civil aircraft

70   Civil aircraft bearing the marks of neutral States may not be attacked unless they:

    (a)   are believed on reasonable grounds to be carrying contraband, and, after prior warning or interception, they intentionally and clearly refuse to divert from their destination, or intentionally and clearly refuse to proceed for visit and search to a belligerent airfield that is safe for the type of aircraft involved and reasonably accessible;

    (b)   engage in belligerent acts on behalf of the enemy;

    (c)   act as auxiliaries to the enemy's armed forces;

    (d)   are incorporated into or assist the enemy's intelligence system; *or*

    (e)   otherwise make an effective contribution to the enemy's military action, e.g., by carrying military materials, and, after prior warning or interception, they intentionally and clearly refuse to divert from their destination, or intentionally and clearly refuse to proceed for visit and search to a belligerent airfield that is safe for the type of aircraft involved and reasonably accessible.

70.1   This paragraph parallels paragraph 67 pertaining to attacks on neutral merchant vessels and the commentary thereto generally applies. Neutral civil aircraft may not be attacked unless they engage in specific activities as listed. Even then paragraph 71 governs. The neutral civil aircraft addressed in paragraphs 70 and 71 are civil aircraft other than medical aircraft, aircraft granted safe conduct and civil airliners which are exempt from attack.

70.2   Subparagraph (a) addresses the situation in which belligerent forces have reasonable grounds to believe that a neutral civil aircraft is carrying contraband (paragraphs 148–150 contain the rules regarding contraband, the publication of contraband lists and 'free goods'). If the suspected neutral civil aircraft, after being warned or intercepted by belligerent forces, refuses to divert from its destination or refuses to proceed for visit and search to a safe and accessible belligerent airfield, the aircraft risks being attacked. In addition to the reasonable grounds and the prior warning or interception by belligerent forces, the neutral civil aircraft must *intentionally* and *clearly* refuse to divert or to proceed for visit and search. The rules governing interception, diversion, and visit and search are in paragraphs 125–134. In this regard, the 1923 Hague Rules of Aerial Warfare provided that refusal, after warning, to obey the orders of belligerent military aircraft to alight or proceed to a suitable locality reasonably accessible for visit and search, exposed the private aircraft to the risk of being fired upon.

70.3   Subparagraphs (b)–(d) parallel the provisions in subparagraphs 67(b)–(d) regarding neutral merchant vessels. Such actions by a neutral civil aircraft would constitute unneutral service and would place the aircraft at risk of being attacked.

70.4   Subparagraph (e) covers the situations in which a neutral civil aircraft makes an effective contribution to the enemy's military action. The conditions of prior warning or interception, and intentionally and clearly refusing to obey belligerent orders in this subparagraph apply. It is noted that the 1923 Hague Rules of Aerial Warfare provided for the right of belligerent forces to control neutral civil aircraft in the immediate vicinity of its forces.

71   Any attack on these aircraft is subject to the basic rules in paragraphs 38–46.

71.1   This paragraph like paragraph 68 pertaining to neutral merchant vessels specifies that any attack on neutral civil aircraft is subject to the basic rules on distinction, military objectives and collateral damage in paragraphs 38–46.

Section VI Precautions regarding civil aircraft

Preliminary remarks

Paragraphs 72–77 contain provisions regarding the safety of civil aircraft, enemy and neutral, that apply to both belligerents and neutrals. The paragraphs are interrelated and should be read as a whole. The provisions represent a consolidation of the various customary rules and practices, the procedures promulgated by military forces and by the International Civil Aviation Organisation (ICAO), and the lessons learned from various incidents. The paragraphs provide for advance notice of naval operations and civil aircraft routes by belligerents and neutrals, including authorities providing air traffic services. Communication and identification procedures are stressed. A maximum exchange of information between commanders of warships and military aircraft, captains of civil aircraft and air traffic service authorities is directed in order to verify status, clarify intentions, resolve ambiguities and cope with unforeseen circumstances. Adherence to the rules in paragraphs 72–77 by belligerents and neutrals will minimise the chances of misunderstanding and confusion at the operational level. Under these rules, belligerents have an obligation to take all possible measures to prevent a civil aircraft engaged in commercial or private service from being fired upon inadvertently. See also paragraph 46 of the Manual and the commentary thereto. Neutrals have an obligation to take all possible measures to prevent the civil aircraft from placing itself at risk of being fired upon. The lives of the persons on board civil aircraft and the safety of the aircraft must not be endangered.

72   Civil aircraft should avoid areas of potentially hazardous military activity.

72.1   Paragraph 72 places an obligation on all States, air traffic services and civil aircraft captains to take action so that civil aircraft will avoid areas of potentially hazardous military activity. Both the 1923 Hague Rules of Aerial Warfare and the 1990

ICAO *Manual Concerning Safety Measures Relating to Military Activities Potentially Hazardous to Civil Aircraft Operations*[130] contain a similar admonition. In the event of armed conflict at sea, civil aircraft should fly on courses and at altitudes well clear of the area of actual hostilities. Air traffic service authorities should modify normal routes accordingly.

73   **In the immediate vicinity of naval operations, civil aircraft shall comply with instructions from the belligerents regarding their heading and altitude.**

73.1   This paragraph states the customary rule that belligerents have the right to control civil aircraft in the immediate vicinity of naval operations. Paragraph 77 describes how this control is to be exercised.

74   **Belligerents and neutral States concerned, and authorities providing air traffic services, should establish procedures whereby commanders of warships and military aircraft are aware on a continuous basis of designated routes assigned to or flight plans filed by civil aircraft in the area of military operations, including information on communication channels, identification modes and codes, destination, passengers and cargo.**

74.1   This paragraph requires all parties to keep themselves informed at all times of routes assigned and flight plans filed by civil aircraft (paragraph 76) in the area of military operations. Belligerent and neutral military forces must then ensure that commanders of warships and military aircraft are aware on a continuous basis of the routes, flight plans and air traffic service procedures in their area of operations.[131]

75   **Belligerent and neutral States should ensure that a Notice to Airmen (NOTAM) is issued providing information on military activities in areas potentially hazardous to civil aircraft, including activation of danger areas or temporary airspace restrictions. This NOTAM should include information on:**

    (a)   **frequencies upon which the aircraft should maintain a continuous listening watch;**

    (b)   **continuous operation of civil weather-avoidance radar and identification modes and codes;**

    (c)   **altitude, course and speed restrictions;**

    (d)   **procedures to respond to radio contact by the military forces and to establish two-way communication;** *and*

    (e)   **possible action by the military forces if the NOTAM is not complied with and the civil aircraft is perceived by those military forces to be a threat.**

---

130 ICAO Doc. 9554-AN/932, 1990.
131 *Ibid.*

75.1   This paragraph obliges belligerents and neutrals to issue a Notice to Airmen (NOTAM) providing detailed information on military activities in areas potentially hazardous to civil aircraft. These activities could include training exercises, practice firings or testing of weapons in addition to armed conflict at sea. This NOTAM procedure follows the long-standing practice by the military forces of belligerents and neutrals. The NOTAM issued during naval operations in the Adriatic Sea and the Gulf are recent examples. NOTAMs are also prescribed in the ICAO procedures for planning and co-ordinating military activities potentially hazardous to civil aircraft.[132] Subparagraph (e) warns civil aircraft that if the NOTAMs are not adhered to *and* the civil aircraft flies in a manner perceived to be threatening by naval forces, such as flying an attack profile, the civil aircraft could be fired upon in self-defence by the naval forces.

76   Civil aircraft should file the required flight plan with the cognisant Air Traffic Service, complete with information as to registration, destination, passengers, cargo, emergency communication channels, identification modes and codes, updates en route and carry certificates as to registration, airworthiness, passengers and cargo. They should not deviate from a designated Air Traffic Service route or flight plan without Air Traffic Control clearance unless unforeseen conditions arise, e.g., safety or distress, in which case appropriate notification should be made immediately.

76.1   This paragraph sets forth the requirements to be fulfilled by civil aircraft engaged in international navigation as prescribed by the Chicago Convention[133] and in ICAO standards and procedures. It is particularly important that advance information on civil aircraft flight plans, emergency communication channels and the identification modes and codes associated with the Secondary Surveillance Radar (SSR) system (Annex 10, Chicago Convention) be made available to military forces by the cognisant Air Traffic Service authority. States providing air traffic services in their flight information region have a special responsibility for the safety of civil aircraft.

77   If a civil aircraft enters an area of potentially hazardous military activity, it should comply with relevant NOTAMs. Military forces should use all available means to identify and warn the civil aircraft, by using, *inter alia*, secondary surveillance radar modes and codes, communications, correlation with flight plan information, interception by military aircraft, and, when possible, contacting the appropriate Air Traffic Control facility.

77.1   This paragraph places an obligation on both the civil aircraft and the military forces involved if a civil aircraft enters an area of potentially hazardous military activity. The civil aircraft should comply with all provisions in the NOTAM, particularly maintaining a continuous listening watch on specified radio frequencies and operating continuously its radar and identification modes and codes. The naval forces must use all available means to identify and warn the civil aircraft, including where possible, direct communication with the appropriate air traffic service to exchange real-time flight-progress information, delays and information on non-

---

132 *Ibid.*
133 Chicago Convention, Chapters V and VI.

scheduled flights. If feasible, naval forces should be equipped to monitor appropriate air traffic control frequencies for correlating and identifying radar contacts. In some cases, naval forces may be required to intercept and visually identify civil aircraft in the vicinity of naval operations. The procedures for interception are addressed in paragraph 128 and the commentary thereto.

PART IV

METHODS AND MEANS OF
WARFARE AT SEA

Section I Means of warfare

Missiles and other projectiles

78   **Missiles and projectiles, including those with over-the-horizon capabilities, shall be used in conformity with the principles of target discrimination as set out in paragraphs 38–46.**

78.1   The formulation of this paragraph gave rise to severe controversy between those who believed that specific rules should be developed with regard to weapons with over-the-horizon (OTH) and beyond-visual-range (BVR) capabilities and those who believed that such specific rules were not necessary in the light of the general principles applicable to naval warfare, in particular, existing provisions regarding precautions in attacks. The controversy centred around the question whether the use of such missiles and other projectiles should be restricted specifically within the framework of this document, *inter alia*, by formulating obligations with regard to technical target acquisition systems and with regard to self-destruct mechanisms. Lengthy discussions were held regarding the technical aspects of the use of such weapon systems and whether appropriate formulae could be found to establish the obligation to conform to the general and detailed rules regarding target discrimination. In terms of the technology used it was argued that ideally spatial separation between military objectives and objects exempt from attack would effectively ensure the protection of the latter. This aspect, however, is dealt with under paragraphs 105–108 below.

78.2   The absence of a paragraph regarding a mandatory self-destruct device on missiles or a prohibition of means normally characterised as fire-and-forget weapons follows from the fact that participants felt that the speed at which these weapons travel does not allow for reconsideration of a decision by a commanding officer once the launch is executed. Fears were also expressed with regard to the fact that missiles having missed their intended target might independently engage other vessels in the area which would not necessarily be military objectives. Consequently, participants attached great importance to a crystal-clear formulation of the obligations relating to the principles of distinction and to precautions in attack. Moreover, it was noted that most weapons in this category would either explode upon impact on the surface of the sea or sink after impact, thereby becoming harmless in much the same way as torpedoes which have run their course.

78.3   Lengthy discussions were also devoted to the question whether the formulation used in NWP9 regarding weapons with OTH and BVR capabilities[134] would be adequate for inclusion in the text. This formulation appears to base lawfulness of the missiles and projectiles on whether or not they are dependent on OTH or BVR guidance systems. Since a determination of what is BVR or OTH depends on many factors at the time of attack, the participants felt that a broader criterion linked to the principles of target discrimination would be more appropriate. The criterion of lawfulness should apply to all missiles and projectiles irrespective of whether or not they have BVR or OTH guidance systems which are equipped with sensors or employed in conjunction with external sources of targeting.

78.4   The solution chosen makes it abundantly clear that commanders should, when faced with a decision to launch any missile or projectile, including those with OTH or BVR capabilities, give special emphasis to basic principles of target discrimination and precautions in attack, including the weighing of considerations of collateral damage.

Torpedoes

79   It is prohibited to use torpedoes which do not sink or otherwise become harmless when they have completed their run.

79.1   This paragraph is a mere reiteration of the provision on torpedoes found in Hague Convention VIII of 1907.[135] Restatement of the rule was considered to be uncontroversial and useful in order to remind those involved with the further developments of torpedoes that the rule is still valid, although automatic sinking to the bottom is the normal way in which this obligation is met.

79.2   The origins of this specific provision lie in the assumption that, in the absence of such a requirement, as soon as a torpedo would have run its course, it might lie dead in the water in much the same way as a free-floating mine. Such a torpedo would then quickly become a hazard to vessels exempt from attack. Consequently it stands out as an Article of Hague Convention VIII that remains timely and worthy of reaffirmation in this document.

Mines

Preliminary remarks

Mine warfare is addressed in Hague Convention VIII Relative to the Laying of Automatic Submarine Contact Mines. At the time the Convention was drafted, it was deplored that no absolute prohibition could be agreed upon. The fact that restrictions as

---

134 'Missiles and projectiles dependent upon over-the-horizon or beyond-visual-range guidance systems are lawful, provided that they are equipped with sensors, or employed in conjunction with external sources of targeting data, that are sufficient to ensure target discrimination', NWP9, *The Commander's Handbook*, para. 9.7.

135 Art. 1(3).

formulated in the Convention only apply to one specific category of mines (automatic contact mines) is commonly considered to be a major defect, although practice by belligerents in the first Gulf War showed that the provisions of the Convention have continued validity in modern naval warfare. Consequently participants considered that, building upon the basis of customary law and the adoption of Protocol II to the Convention on Certain Conventional Weapons in 1980 regarding prohibitions and restrictions on mine warfare on land, major improvement of the existing rules would be possible. The necessity for the improvement of the rules also logically followed from the importance participants attached to the further development of the principle of distinction and of the applicability of the general rules regarding precautions in attack. The Rapporteur on means and methods of warfare proposed relying mainly upon the introduction of the already-agreed rules regarding military objectives in naval warfare, upon close relationship with the practices and regulation by maritime nations and upon a Swedish proposal for a Protocol on naval mines which had been submitted to the United Nations.[136] The Round Table felt, however, that a different approach should be taken. Preference was expressed for the development of concise and clear rules. These rules are reflected in paragraphs 80–92 of this document.

For the purposes of the document, the following definition of a mine is used:

> A mine is an explosive device laid in the water, on the sea-bed or in
> the subsoil thereof, with the intention of damaging or sinking ships
> or of deterring ships from entering an area.

The definition excludes explosive devices which may be attached to ships and shore installations by frogmen. Also participants noted that devices, such as encapsulated torpedoes (CAPTOR), which are technically called mines, may, depending on how they are employed also be subject to the requirements listed in paragraphs 78 and 79.

80   Mines may only be used for legitimate military purposes including the denial of sea areas to the enemy.

80.1   The obligation to use mines for legitimate military purposes logically flows from the rules of international humanitarian law. Participants deemed reaffirmation of the rule in specific relation to naval mining to be useful in order to establish unequivocally that indiscriminate mining practices on the high seas are unlawful. Paragraph 87 is a clear example of implication of this paragraph.

80.2   The inclusion of an explicit reference to the legitimacy of the use of mines for area denial purposes was deemed useful. Mines are the preferred means to deny an enemy the use of a certain area. Such denial can be achieved in different ways, including either disinformation to the enemy to the effect that areas are mined when they are not or the notification of the presence of an actual field. Military doctrine generally distinguishes the following uses:

---

136 The report drew on the working paper originally submitted on 8 May 1990 (UN Doc. A/CN.10/141). Following further discussions among experts, Sweden submitted a revised version to the First Committee of the General Assembly on 4 November 1991 (UN Doc. A/C.1/46/15 of 6 November 1991).

–   defensive mining: the mines are generally used to deny access by the enemy to the territory of a belligerent (coastal waters, beaches, roadsteads, etc.);

–   protective mining: the mines are generally used to protect shipping routes, thereby especially denying enemy submarines or surface craft the use of certain waters outside the coastal waters of a belligerent;

–   offensive mining: the mining of waters under the control of the enemy or of roadsteads essential to its maritime lines of communication.

The requirement stated in this paragraph merely emphasises that indiscriminate mining is unlawful. This is in keeping with traditional military doctrine.

80.3   Mining to deny sea areas to the enemy is not unlawful provided that paragraphs 81–92 are adhered to. These paragraphs establish the criteria for target discrimination since most mines are not constructed in such a way as to guarantee that only legitimate military targets are engaged.

80.4.   This paragraph deals with relations between belligerents. The relations between belligerents and neutrals are covered by paragraph 88.

81   Without prejudice to the rules set out in paragraph 82, the parties to the conflict shall not lay mines unless effective neutralisation occurs when they have become detached or control over them is otherwise lost.

81.1   The wording of this paragraph reflects the language used in Article 1(2) of Hague Convention VIII with regard to automatic contact mines. Participants saw no difficulties in extending the scope of the prohibition to cover all sorts of mines. It should be noted that the proposed regime is much stricter than the regulatory regime currently contained in Protocol II regarding mine warfare on land. The paragraph in its original form required that an effective neutralising mechanism be fitted to each mine in order to ensure that it would become harmless when the conditions listed in the paragraph were fulfilled. This formulation was in line with the proposal contained in Article 5 of the draft Protocol on naval mines, submitted by Sweden on 16 May 1994, to the Group of Government Experts to Prepare the Review Conference of the 1980 Convention on Certain Conventional Weapons.[137] The participants felt, however, that the requirements of this paragraph would also be met if the mine became inactive. Hence, the formulation 'effective neutralisation' was chosen.

81.2   The word 'detached' is used because mines lying on the sea-bed and in the subsoil are also covered by the paragraph while they need not necessarily be moored. Originally, the question was also raised whether controlled mines should not be treated differently from other mines. That idea was dropped mainly because of the uncertainty whether technological means of control could effectively guarantee that mines would

---

137 Document CCW/CONF.I/GE/CRP.4 of 16 May 1994. The full title of this convention is 'Convention on Prohibitions or Restrictions on the Use of Certain Conventional Weapons Which May be Deemed to be Excessively Injurious or to Have Indiscriminate Effects'.

not form a danger to shipping exempt from attack during the conflict or to peaceful shipping in general.

81.3   The loss of control referred to in this paragraph covers the rules already laid down in Hague Convention VIII with regard to control. By the use of the word 'otherwise' the present wording also absorbs the notion of surveillance as expressed in Article 3 of the same Convention. The notion that an actual presence was necessary for surveillance was deemed to have become obsolete in the light of technological developments on the one hand and stricter regulation of mines forming a hazard to navigation on the other.

81.4   During the final session, extensive discussion was devoted to the exact meaning of the term 'control' as used in this paragraph. While some participants interpreted it in the sense that belligerents would physically have to control the mines at all times, others considered knowledge of the location and the status of the mine sufficient in order to conform to the restrictions considered appropriate. One of the examples given was that of a bottom mine which could be left unattended for a prolonged period of time. While it still would not necessarily pose a threat to the safety of navigation, it might at the same time, due to the influence of currents, have moved away from the position where it was laid. Clarification of the restrictions imposed on such mines could have been effected by introducing into the paragraph an approach which would focus on the protection of peaceful shipping. A proposed amendment therefore required the mine to become harmless as soon as the risks involved could no longer be effectively controlled. Participants, however, felt that the text already reflected the understanding described above and by a slight majority decided to keep the text as it stood.

82   It is forbidden to use free-floating mines unless:

(a)   they are directed against a military objective; *and*

(b)   they become harmless within an hour after loss of control over them.

82.1   This paragraph is a development of Article 1(1), of Hague Convention VIII. The term 'free-floating' is used because the Round Table felt that no other adequate wording could be found to describe the mines which should be covered by this paragraph. The term 'independent' was not retained because it had a connotation of activity to it. The term 'drifting' is not used because it was argued that all categories of mines should be covered. The phrase 'loss of control' in this paragraph means the moment they have been dropped.

82.2   Some participants would have preferred to prohibit this category altogether. They argued that these mines form an extreme danger to shipping exempt from attack. The majority, however, felt that military necessity still required the use of these mines, for instance in the case of immediate pursuit by opposing forces. In order to clarify that use of the mines should be in conformity with the general principles, the obligation to use these mines solely against military objectives was included.

83 **The laying of armed mines or the arming of pre-laid mines must be notified unless the mines can only detonate against vessels which are military objectives.**

83.1   The principle of notification of dangers to peaceful shipping is mandatory in peacetime. Extension of this obligation to armed conflict was, albeit with restrictions, already provided for in Articles 3 and 4 of Hague Convention VIII with regard to automatic contact mines. The present wording reflects the general wish of participants to extend the notification requirement to all types of mines, while at the same time taking into consideration the fact that technology has evolved so that not all mines form a danger to navigation at all times. Therefore, the requirement is limited to the laying of armed mines and the arming of pre-laid mines.

83.2   For the purpose of this paragraph, the obligation to notify will normally be fulfilled by notification through the usual channels established for international shipping, that is, publication in 'Notice to Mariners' and communication to the International Maritime Organisation. These publications are considered an effective modern means of conveying the information necessary. Notification through diplomatic channels to all States may be appropriate in some circumstances.

83.3   Participants felt that retention of the provision, found in Article 3 of the 1907 Hague Convention VIII, that notification should only take place as soon as military exigencies permit, was not justified in the light of the general requirement imposed upon belligerents to limit as far as possible the effect of hostilities.

84 **Belligerents shall record the locations where they have laid mines.**

84.1   The duty to record the locations where mines have been laid, on the one hand, is a logical sequel of the obligation to notify the laying of armed mines to international shipping and, on the other hand, ensures that mines may be kept under adequate surveillance and, if necessary, can be removed at the close of hostilities (see paragraphs 90 and 91).

84.2   The paragraph does not differentiate between types of mines or refer to whether they are armed. Records need not be made public if the presence of the mines does not endanger shipping exempt from attack or other peaceful shipping.

85 **Mining operations in the internal waters, territorial sea or archipelagic waters of a belligerent State should provide, when the mining is first executed, for free exit of shipping of neutral States.**

85.1   This paragraph is new in relation to naval mining. It is, however, considered to have evolved into a customary law obligation.[138] Participants felt that it was timely to formulate a rule which would effectively protect neutral shipping in much the same way as the protection of such shipping under the rules of blockade.[139]

---

138 Cf. the US notification regarding the mining of Haiphong in 1972.
139 The corresponding rule with regard to blockade is found in Art. 9(3) of the 1909 London Declaration.

85.2   The extension of the obligation not only to ports but also to territorial and archipelagic waters is deemed to be a logical sequel to the precautions in attack which have to be respected by the belligerents.

86   Mining of neutral waters by a belligerent is prohibited.

86.1   Mining, being an act of hostility, is already prohibited in neutral waters under Article 2 of Hague Convention XIII Concerning the Rights and Duties of Neutral Powers in Naval War. Since hostile actions may not be conducted against neutrals, that specific prohibition has been superseded by the general obligation not to use armed force in international relations as laid down in Article 2(4) of the United Nations Charter.

86.2   Neutral waters are defined in paragraph 14 above. Nothing in this paragraph is intended to derogate from the right of neutrals to lay mines in their own waters in accordance with Article 4 of Hague Convention VIII. Article 25(3) of the LOS Convention, however, indicates that such mining may not have the effect of permanently closing the waters concerned to innocent passage by other neutral States or, subject to the duty of impartiality, by the belligerents.

86.3   The prohibition is equally applicable to all types of mines, regardless of whether they are armed or controlled.

87   Mining shall not have the practical effect of preventing passage between neutral waters and international waters.

87.1   This paragraph constitutes an amplification of paragraph 80. The obligation referred to in this paragraph may be inferred from the general obligation not to interfere unduly with the interests of neutral States.

88   The minelaying States shall pay due regard to the legitimate uses of the high seas by, *inter alia*, providing safe alternative routes for shipping of neutral States.

88.1   The general comments regarding paragraph 87 and, on the subject of 'due regard', paragraph 12, also refer to this paragraph.

88.2   The formulation of the 'due regard' obligation for belligerents expresses the margins of appreciation which may be exercised with regard to the measures which must be taken by belligerents in order to guarantee protection of interests of peaceful shipping, in particular neutral vessels.

88.3   The provision of alternative safe routes is only one of the ways in which belligerents may choose to protect peaceful shipping. Another effective possibility would be the provision of piloting or escort services in order to sail through the minefield unharmed. As such, the obligation contained in this paragraph also relates to the principle of distinction and precautions in attack.

89 **Transit passage through international straits and passage through waters subject to the right of archipelagic sea lanes passage shall not be impeded unless safe and convenient alternative routes are provided.**

89.1   The new regimes regarding transit and archipelagic sea lanes passage do not have the effect of rendering the mining of straits and sea lanes unlawful *per se*. In view, however, of the importance of these straits and sea lanes for international navigation, belligerents may not exercise unlimited mining rights in those waters.

89.2   Participants at the final session discussed whether the alternative route should necessarily be situated within the strait or sea lane concerned. While, from a mere factual point of view, an alternative sea lane might be easy to provide, in the case of straits such an alternative may not be available. Hence, it was found that alternatives for straits need not necessarily be within the same strait or provide identical facilities for shipping. The alternative offered should in any event ensure the safety of shipping and accommodate the interests of shipping as much as possible. Ongoing belligerent operations in the strait might therefore justify the designation of an alternative route outside the strait.

89.3   With regard to the safety of alternative routes, see the commentary to paragraph 88. The addition of the word 'convenient' was deemed necessary to rule out those cases in which either no alternative or only alternatives with unacceptable commercial consequences are offered by belligerents. An extreme example of the latter situation could be that transit passage through the Gibraltar straits would be impeded on the grounds that shipping could proceed through the Suez canal and around the Cape of Good Hope.

90 **After the cessation of active hostilities, parties to the conflict shall do their utmost to remove or render harmless the mines they have laid, each party removing its own mines. With regard to mines laid in the territorial seas of the enemy, each party shall notify their position and shall proceed with the least possible delay to remove the mines in its territorial sea or otherwise render the territorial sea safe for navigation.**

90.1   This paragraph is a modernisation and expansion of the obligations laid down in Article 5 of Hague Convention VIII. Participants felt that the State practice of developing specific provisions with regard to mine clearance in peace treaties had proven to be unsuccessful. The exact extent of the obligations of belligerents to remove their mines, however, was the subject of some controversy. Some participants argued that it may be sufficient to render them harmless, while others contended that the mines should actually be removed. Consensus was reached on the former proposal.

90.2   The phrase 'after the cessation of active hostilities' was chosen in order to restate the general principle that means and methods of warfare are also subject to the rule that no hostile acts may be undertaken once hostilities have come to an end. This phraseology is also used in Article 118 of the Third Geneva Convention of 1949 and Article 33 of Additional Protocol I of 1977. The formulation of the obligation in Hague Convention VIII ('at the close of war') or any other formal agreement to end hostilities has not been retained as such a requirement could unnecessarily prolong the period in which dangers to peaceful shipping would continue to exist. However, a mere cease-fire, which by definition is only temporary in character, would not automatically trigger the obligation under this paragraph. The importance of the term 'otherwise render them harmless' cannot be underestimated. In the case of controlled mines for instance, belligerents may choose to render such mines harmless at the earliest possible moment in order to promote speedy return to peaceful relations, without unduly jeopardising their military posture.

90.3   As in Hague Convention VIII, the present paragraph also focuses on the problem of clearance of mines in the territorial waters of the former enemy. The approach chosen reflects modern technology which would enable belligerents to take other measures short of removal in order to guarantee the safety of navigation. An example of such a measure might be the marking by buoys of minefields, as was done in the Baltic in the aftermath of the Second World War.

90.4   The obligations with regard to clearance of naval mines contrast sharply with the lesser obligations found at the time of writing in Article 9 of its counterpart in land warfare, Protocol II to the Certain Conventional Weapons Convention adopted in 1980. Participants emphasised that the rules agreed upon were without prejudice to international law on state responsibility.

91   In addition to their obligations under paragraph 90, parties to the conflict shall endeavour to reach agreement, both among themselves and, where appropriate, with other States and with international organisations, on the provision of information and technical and material assistance, including in appropriate circumstances joint operations, necessary to remove minefields or otherwise render them harmless.

91.1   Originally, two alternative formulae with regard to mine clearance and international co-operation were proposed to the participants. These formulae were as follows:

> After the cessation of active hostilities, parties should co-operate with a view to clear minefields or render them safe for shipping; *and*

> After the cessation of active hostilities, the belligerents shall take all necessary steps to remove, or render harmless, the mines which they have laid. They shall co-operate to that end.

Neither formula is retained in the present paragraph. The obligation to remove the mines or render them harmless is now included in the new paragraph 90.

91.2   The importance of obligations with regard to clearance and/or rendering harmless minefields should not be underestimated. Naval mines used during the Second World War are still routinely recovered in the North Sea, thereby endangering the exercise of legitimate peacetime rights. With regard to its counterpart in land warfare, it has become obvious that the problems of mine clearance by now seriously endanger the economic viability of nations in which armed conflict has occurred. One may wonder, however, whether belligerents will immediately after the end of hostilities agree to co-operate with others in removing or otherwise rendering harmless the mines which they may have laid only shortly before. This is the reason that this paragraph on co-operation has not yet been formulated in a compulsory fashion. It is obvious that any substantial progress made within the review process of the 1980 Certain Conventional Weapons Convention, and, in particular, the Swedish proposal on naval mines, may have an influence on this paragraph.

91.3   The phraseology used with regard to the possible avenues of co-operation with other States and international organisations stems from the development of mine clearance in land warfare. While it must be acknowledged that for the moment, these States and organisations may not have the necessary expertise to handle naval mine clearance, such a possibility should not be excluded in the future. The rise of non-governmental organisations that have gained expertise in this field should, when beneficial to the protection of international shipping, be used as a complementary resource whenever mine clearance needs to be undertaken.

92   Neutral States do not commit an act inconsistent with the laws of neutrality by clearing mines laid in violation of international law.

92.1   This paragraph reflects the right of neutrals to actively take measures to enforce their rights, without warning and possibly at the expense of one of the parties to the conflict, in case one of the belligerents violates the relevant rules of international law specifically applicable to mine warfare. As such, it is an exception to the traditional rules of impartiality and abstention. The paragraph should be considered as declaratory of international customary law.

Section II Methods of warfare

Blockade

<u>Preliminary remarks</u>

The Round Table engaged in an extensive discussion on the issue of whether the practice of blockade was, on the one hand, entirely archaic or, on the other, remained a viable method of naval warfare. Blockade is the blocking of the approach to the enemy coast, or a part of it, for the purpose of preventing ingress and egress of vessels or aircraft of all States. Although a minority believed that the traditional rules for formal blockade were in complete desuetude, a majority believed that the occurrence of a number of incidents subsequent to the Second World War, in which States engaged in actions adopting some or all of the traditional rules of blockade, indicated that the doctrine still had utility as a coercive instrument. This view was reinforced by the fact that 'blockade' was mentioned in Article 42 of the United Nations Charter as a possible mode of enforcement action and that modern naval manuals on naval operational law included blockade as a permissible form of naval warfare. It was therefore the decision of the Round Table to include provisions on blockade in its text, and, where appropriate, to modernise the provisions of the 1856 Paris Declaration Respecting Maritime Law and the 1909 London Declaration dealing with blockade. Paragraphs 93–

104 represent the fruits of this effort. It was the sense of the Round Table that the rules stated in these paragraphs were applicable to blockading actions taken by States regardless of the name given to such actions.

Although the specific rules on blockade in paragraphs 93–104 refer only to vessels, the Round Table recognised that modern naval warfare might include establishing a blockade of the air space above sea areas. In such a case, the belligerents should apply the general principles of a sea blockade as expressed in this document.

93   A blockade shall be declared and notified to all belligerents and neutral States.

93.1   This paragraph is self-explanatory. With regard to the requirement of notification, reference is made to the commentary to paragraph 83.

94   The declaration shall specify the commencement, duration, location, and extent of the blockade and the period within which vessels of neutral States may leave the blockaded coastline.

94.1   This paragraph is self-explanatory.

95   A blockade must be effective. The question whether a blockade is effective is a question of fact.

95.1   This paragraph is a mere reiteration of the principle enunciated in principle 4 of the 1856 Paris Declaration. The Declaration, however, did not specify how effectiveness should be assessed. The paragraph therefore also incorporates the wording of Article 3 of the London Declaration.

95.2   The Round Table considered whether the fact that aircraft could still land within the territory of the blockaded belligerent would affect the effectiveness of a sea blockade. This was found not to be the case, as, on the one hand, transport of cargo by air only constitutes a very small percentage of bulk traffic and, on the other hand, the fact is that transport over land could take place without affecting this criterion.

96   The force maintaining the blockade may be stationed at a distance determined by military requirements.

96.1   The manner in which belligerents traditionally have enforced blockades has been the subject of lengthy discussions in the past. While some States argued that physical presence of warships immediately off the blockaded coastline was necessary, others maintained that the force may operate at a considerable distance. The wording of the paragraph reflects the concern which the blockading power may have with respect to operations within the range of coastal armaments, aircraft or submarines of the opposing belligerent. The paragraph maintains the traditional principle that the blockade must, however, still be conducted at such a distance that there is a reasonable risk that access to the blockaded coastline and egress from those waters will be effectively prevented.

97   **A blockade may be enforced and maintained by a combination of legitimate methods and means of warfare provided this combination does not result in acts inconsistent with the rules set out in this document.**

97.1   This paragraph does not require the enforcement of a blockade by surface ships only. It does, however, prohibit the enforcement solely by weapon systems, such as mines, unless they are employed in such a manner as not to endanger legitimate sea-going commerce. The blockading power is obliged to allow ships entry into and egress from the blockaded coastline under certain circumstances. This may be the case when shipping is in distress or when permission has been given to warships to enter and leave a blockaded port[140] or when the situation described in paragraphs 102 and 103 arise. The paragraph takes into account that modern technology and the extensive use of aircraft have, for instance, significantly increased the radius in which a single warship may effectively enforce the blockade.

98   **Merchant vessels believed on reasonable grounds to be breaching a blockade may be captured. Merchant vessels which, after prior warning, clearly resist capture may be attacked.**

98.1   See the commentary to paragraphs 67(a) and 146(f).

99   **A blockade must not bar access to the ports and coasts of neutral States.**

99.1   This paragraph is a modernisation of Article 18 of the 1909 London Declaration.

100   **A blockade must be applied impartially to the vessels of all States.**

100.1   This paragraph contains the long-standing rule on impartiality, as contained in Article 5 of the 1909 London Declaration. It applies to all vessels of any nationality, including merchant ships flying the flag of the blockading power. Although neutral warships and military aircraft enjoy no positive right of access to blockaded areas, the belligerent imposing the blockade may authorise their entry and exit.

101   **The cessation, temporary lifting, re-establishment, extension or other alteration of a blockade must be declared and notified as in paragraphs 93 and 94.**

101.1.   This paragraph is self-explanatory.

---

140 Cf. the 1909 London Declaration, Arts. 7 and 8.

102   **The declaration or establishment of a blockade is prohibited if:**

    (a) it has the sole purpose of starving the civilian population or denying it other objects essential for its survival; *or*

    (b) the damage to the civilian population is, or may be expected to be, excessive in relation to the concrete and direct military advantage anticipated from the blockade.

102.1   The subject-matter of this paragraph is one of the few aspects of the law of naval warfare which has been affected by the adoption of Additional Protocol I. The prohibition regarding starvation of the civilian population is as follows: 'Starvation of civilians as a method of warfare is prohibited.'[141]

102.2   It has been argued that the prohibition of starvation has rendered naval blockade unlawful. The argument was the subject of intensive discussions among the participants. The discussions centred on the question whether the law prohibited blockades which led to starvation as a side-effect or whether the blockade had to be established with the purpose of starving the civilian population.

102.3   The wording of subparagraph (a) as it stands reflects the view of the majority of the participants that the blockade, in order to be of itself illegal, must have the sole purpose of starving the population or have a disproportionate effect as indicated in subparagraph (b). Whenever the blockade has starvation as one of its effects, the starvation effectively triggers the obligation, subject to certain limitations, to allow relief shipments to gain access to the coasts of the blockaded belligerent. This obligation is reflected in the next paragraph.

102.4   At the session in Livorno some participants argued that subparagraph (a) should be deleted as it has never been possible to prohibit methods of warfare which rely on a factual establishment of the subjective purpose of belligerents. Others argued that, as starvation of the civilian population as such was already prohibited under existing law, the word 'sole' should be deleted. The majority of the participants, however, decided on retention of the rule as originally drafted. First they felt that clear enunciation of the rule is of value even if an intention is difficult to prove. Secondly, the word 'sole' was retained because if a blockade has both the unlawful purpose of starvation together with a lawful military purpose, the provision in (b) is applicable thereby rendering the blockade unlawful if the effect on the civilian population is excessive in relation to the lawful military purpose. Subparagraph (b) therefore reflects the impact of the rules of proportionality and precautions in attack on blockade.

141 API Art. 54(1).

103   If the civilian population of the blockaded territory is inadequately provided with food and other objects essential for its survival, the blockading party must provide for free passage of such foodstuffs and other essential supplies, subject to:

    (a)   the right to prescribe the technical arrangements, including search, under which such passage is permitted; *and*

    (b)   the condition that the distribution of such supplies shall be made under the local supervision of a Protecting Power or a humanitarian organisation which offers guarantees of impartiality, such as the International Committee of the Red Cross.

103.1   The general obligation to allow passage of relief consignments in certain situations has already been addressed in the commentary to paragraph 102. Although the text of the paragraph has been drawn from the wording of Article 70 of Additional Protocol I, it contains some major differences which, in the eyes of the participants, may be considered improvements over that specific Article.

103.2   One of the improvements is that the language has been simplified. This change is in accordance with the wish of the Round Table to draft a document which can, as far as possible, be used directly by military forces. Simplification of the language has allowed the unequivocal statement that the blockading power is obliged to allow transit of relief shipments through the blockade. The issue whether such an obligation exists under the Protocol, is still heavily debated.

103.3   The conditions which the blockading power may impose are reflected in subparagraphs (a) and (b). Article 70 lists a third condition which purports to state that relief consignments may not be diverted or delayed unnecessarily. In the light of the obligatory character of the norm as reflected in this paragraph, the Round Table did not deem inclusion of that specific provision necessary. The mentioning of humanitarian organisations in subparagraph (b) reflects modern developments in the field of humanitarian aid.

104   The blockading belligerent shall allow the passage of medical supplies for the civilian population or for the wounded and sick members of armed forces, subject to the right to prescribe technical arrangements, including search, under which such passage is permitted.

104.1   See the commentary to paragraph 103.

Zones

Preliminary remarks

Parties to twentieth-century naval conflicts have on a number of occasions established different kinds of zones in and over water areas whereby they purport to interfere with the normal rights of passage or overflight by denying or restricting access to ships or aircraft of non-parties without permission. A variety of names have been given to these zones, such as exclusion zones, military areas, barred areas, war zones or operational zones. Unauthorised ships or aircraft entering the zone have done so at the risk of facing sanctions, often including being attacked by missiles, aircraft, submarines or surface warships, or of steaming into minefields. The zone issue is not addressed in treaties relevant to the law of naval warfare. Some participants were of the view that zones were simply unlawful and that the topic should not be addressed. The majority were of the view, however, that the existence of such zones was a reality and that it was desirable to develop guidelines for them.

105 **A belligerent cannot be absolved of its duties under international humanitarian law by establishing zones which might adversely affect the legitimate uses of defined areas of the sea.**

105.1   The fundamental issue addressed by the Round Table was whether or not belligerents establishing zones were entitled to be absolved from their duties under international humanitarian law or to acquire additional rights thereby. Some participants, focusing on the history of the use of zones, particularly during the two World Wars and the Iran–Iraq conflict, argued that State practice supported the view that belligerents could be absolved from their duties under international humanitarian law or acquire rights by establishing zones and that, indeed, free-fire areas could be established in carefully circumscribed areas. After an extended discussion, however, a consensus emerged that the establishment of zones did not and could not absolve belligerents from their duties or create new rights to attack ships or aircraft. Bearing in mind the factual circumstances surrounding zone creation, however, parties might be more likely to do certain things in a zone than outside of a zone, particularly if the zone were created for defensive purposes. For example, if a party established a zone in accordance with the criteria listed in paragraph 106, it might be more likely to presume that ships or aircraft in the area without permission were there for hostile purposes than it would be if no zone had been established.

106 **Should a belligerent, as an exceptional measure, establish such a zone:**

(a) **the same body of law applies both inside and outside the zone;**

(b) **the extent, location and duration of the zone and the measures imposed shall not exceed what is strictly required by military necessity and the principle of proportionality;**

(c) **due regard shall be given to the rights of neutral States to legitimate uses of the seas;**

    (d)   **necessary safe passage through the zone for neutral vessels and aircraft shall be provided:**

        (i)   **where the geographical extent of the zone significantly impedes free and safe access to the ports and coasts of a neutral State;**

        (ii) **in other cases where normal navigation routes are affected, except where military requirements do not permit;** *and*

    (e)   **the commencement, duration, location and extent of the zone, as well as the restrictions imposed, shall be publicly declared and appropriately notified.**

106.1   Bearing in mind the fact that zones have been established in a number of twentieth-century conflicts, the Round Table considered that setting out criteria for such zones would be a useful progressive development of the law. These criteria apply to all zones, irrespective of the name given to the zone. A fundamental condition for the establishment of a permissible zone is that a belligerent cannot acquire additional rights or be absolved from duties through such establishment. A belligerent may, as a matter of policy, decide, for example, not to attack certain ships or aircraft which constitute legitimate military objectives outside a zone while reserving its right to attack such ships or aircraft inside the zone. Such an approach is acceptable provided that the belligerent is merely declining to exercise rights it could exercise outside the zone.

106.2   A rule of reason prevails in determining the extent, location and duration of the zone. There must be a proportional and demonstrable nexus between the zone and the measures imposed, including both restrictive and enforcement measures, and the self-defence requirements of the State establishing the zone. For example, in the Falklands conflict, Argentina's 200-mile zone around the Falklands was probably adequate but its declaration that the entire South Atlantic was a war zone was disproportionate to its defence requirements and would affect shipping unconnected with the conflict. Zones located in isolated areas far from normal shipping routes, such as those used in the Falklands, are less likely to raise objections than zones on major shipping routes such as those in the Persian Arabian Gulf. Zones occupying relatively small areas or established for relatively brief periods are more likely than the converse to be considered acceptable.

106.3   The participants engaged in a discussion concerning the extent to which the State establishing the zone could or should be required to publicise both restrictive measures it intended to require vessels in the zone to obey, and enforcement measures it intended to apply against vessels which did not comply with the restrictive measures. One group argued that any publication of restrictive or enforcement measures enhanced the legitimacy of the zonal concept. Another group argued that publication of enforcement measures would be similar to publication of rules of engagement, which States would not accept. The participants eventually decided that publication of restrictive measures was necessary so that vessels knew what was required of them, but also that publication of both types of measures was desirable, although States need merely disclose the general range of enforcement measures and would not be required to indicate precise rules of engagement.

106.4   The rights referred to in paragraph 106(c) include rights to fish and to use pipelines and cables.

106.5   If there is a significant possibility that ships or aircraft not involved in the conflict will have to pass through the zone, special routes should be provided for them and special measures should be taken to minimise the risk of attack upon them. This approach does limit freedom of navigation but it also minimises the risk to these ships or aircraft.

106.6   The notification requirement in paragraph 106(e) should include diplomatic channels and appropriate international organisations, in particular the International Maritime Organisation and the International Civil Aviation Organisation.

107   Compliance with the measures taken by one belligerent in the zone shall not be construed as an act harmful to the opposing belligerent.

107.1   A particular problem faced by neutrals in naval conflicts is that compliance with measures taken by one belligerent, particularly with economic warfare measures such as navicert procedures, is often construed by the opposing belligerent as the commission of a harmful act. If one belligerent establishes a zone and requires compliance with certain inoffensive measures concerning the zone, such as passage through particular sea lanes, acquisition of certain certificates or use of certain signals or lighting arrangements, these shall not be considered as acts harmful to the opposing belligerent.

107.2   It is essential that the expression 'measures taken by one belligerent in the zone' be construed fairly narrowly as referring to measures which are essential for passage through the zone. If, for example, the belligerent establishing the zone were to require all shipping passing through the zone to travel in convoy with an escorting warship of that belligerent, the ships in convoy would be deemed to be resisting visit and search and therefore liable to attack on sight.

108   Nothing in this Section should be deemed to derogate from the customary belligerent right to control neutral vessels and aircraft in the immediate vicinity of naval operations.

108.1   Within the immediate area or vicinity of naval operations, a belligerent may establish special restrictions upon the activities of neutral vessels and aircraft and may prohibit altogether such vessels and aircraft from entering the area. For example, a belligerent warship may exercise control over the communications of any neutral merchant vessel or civil aircraft whose presence in the area might otherwise endanger or jeopardise naval operations. Vessels or aircraft which ignore directions concerning communications risk being fired upon or captured. The immediate area or vicinity of naval operations is that area within which hostilities are taking place or belligerent forces are actually operating.

Section III Deception, ruses of war and perfidy

<u>Preliminary remarks</u>

Deception at sea has been a most remarkable feature in naval history. Warships were entitled to disguise themselves if they so wished by, for instance, flying other colours. Only the use of a false flag during an attack was prohibited under the traditional law. Aircraft, on the other hand, have never been entitled to bear false markings.

From the outset, a number of participants were uncomfortable with this specific feature in naval warfare, in particular with regard to the feigning of neutral status. In contrast to land warfare, where combatants are generally required to distinguish themselves from the civilian population and where derogation from this rule is only possible in very specific circumstances, combatants at sea have never been subject to these rules. In the light of the acceptance by participants of the general rules regarding the engagement of military objectives only, the question logically arose whether the traditional rules on deception at sea should not be departed from. This debate has been intensified by the use of modern technology by naval combatants when taking defensive or protective measures.

The extensive practice of deception in the past has significantly affected the protection of peaceful shipping. Should one wish to establish an absolute protection, a total prohibition of deception in naval armed conflict should be pursued. Participants felt, however, that such a goal was unachievable, given the fact that the law of armed conflict in general does not prohibit belligerents to take measures such as camouflage. Even in these modern times, warships may attempt to escape detection on the high seas by various means and routinely exercise such operations. While obviously not being able to escape detection by the human eye at a certain stage, a number of other measures can be taken in order to conceal their presence. An example of such behaviour is the discontinuance of all electronic emissions emanating from the ship. The following paragraphs attempt to clearly define which behaviour is to be considered unlawful.

109 **Military and auxiliary aircraft are prohibited at all times from feigning exempt, civilian or neutral status.**

109.1 This paragraph needs no further amplification in the light of the preliminary remarks made above.

110 **Ruses of war are permitted. Warships and auxiliary vessels, however, are prohibited from launching an attack whilst flying a false flag and at all times from actively simulating the status of:**

    (a) hospital ships, small coastal rescue craft or medical transports;

    (b) vessels on humanitarian missions;

    (c) passenger vessels carrying civilian passengers;

(d)   vessels protected by the United Nations flag;

(e)   vessels guaranteed safe conduct by prior agreement between the parties, including cartel vessels;

(f)   vessels entitled to be identified by the emblem of the red cross or red crescent; *or*

(g)   vessels engaged in transporting cultural property under special protection.

110.1   This and the following paragraph have been modelled along the lines of Article 37 of Additional Protocol I. The paragraph first establishes that ruses of war are still permitted. Article 37(2) of the Protocol lists as examples of ruses of war: the use of camouflage, decoys, mock operations and misinformation.[142] The traditional right regarding the use of false flags is reflected in the present text.

110.2   The paragraph goes on to clarify a number of actions by warships which, although they might not necessarily qualify as perfidy, are prohibited under the law of armed conflict. It should be noted that in order to commit a violation, the warship must actively endeavour to establish its identity as one of the vessels mentioned under this paragraph. This qualification is necessary as warships might for instance only display electronic and acoustic characteristics which are commonly related to commercial shipping. Hence, warships are only denied the active simulation of the characteristics of such vessels. This prohibited simulation could be achieved by using means of communications and terminology reserved for the shipping concerned.

110.3   The list of vessels included in this paragraph is exhaustive and differs in some respects from the list of vessels exempt from attack and capture. At the final session, it was decided to include vessels protected by the flag of the United Nations. This formulation emanates from Article 37(1)(d) of Additional Protocol I. It has not yet been determined precisely in which circumstances flying United Nations colours would indicate protected status. It is clear that if UN forces are not taking part in the conflict in any way, they are entitled to a form of protected status. At the time of writing, negotiations are being conducted in order to draft a convention aimed at the further improvement of the protection of United Nations personnel and materiel in armed conflicts.

---

142 See further the ICRC Commentary to Additional Protocol I, *Commentary on the Additional Protocols of 8 June 1977 to the Geneva Conventions of 12 August 1949*, pp. 440 ff.

111   Perfidy is prohibited. Acts inviting the confidence of an adversary to lead it to believe that it is entitled to, or is obliged to accord, protection under the rules of international law applicable in armed conflict, with intent to betray that confidence, constitute perfidy. Perfidious acts include the launching of an attack while feigning:

   (a)   exempt, civilian, neutral or protected United Nations status;

   (b)   surrender or distress by, e.g., sending a distress signal or by the crew taking to life rafts.

111.1   The definition of perfidy follows the definition laid down in Article 37(1) of Additional Protocol I. The definition clarifies a number of issues revolving around what – under the terms of the 1907 Hague Regulations – constituted treachery.[143] The naval counterpart of that rule was indicated in Article 15 of the 1913 Oxford Manual of Naval War.

111.2   The examples provided in subparagraphs (a) and (b) are self-explanatory. The crucial element in the examples listed is that while protected status is simulated by a warship or military aircraft, an act of hostility is prepared and executed. The Round Table therefore was of the view that the former British practice of Q-ships is no longer acceptable.

---

143   See also ICRC Commentary to Additional Protocol I, *Commentary on the Additional Protocols of 8 June 1977 to the Geneva Conventions of 12 August 1949*, pp. 434 ff.

PART V

MEASURES SHORT OF ATTACK: INTERCEPTION, VISIT, SEARCH, DIVERSION AND CAPTURE

Preliminary remarks

Part V deals with what traditionally used to be the law of prize. However, the measures belligerents may take against enemy and neutral vessels and aircraft according to the subsequent paragraphs are not only those of economic warfare at sea. The title to Part V has been changed to 'measures short of attack' in order to clarify this.

According to the rules laid down in Part V, enemy as well as neutral vessels and aircraft, under certain circumstances, may be captured. That kind of capture needs to be distinguished from capture according to paragraph 40. Enemy merchant vessels and civil aircraft that are characterised as military objectives may not only be attacked but, *a fortiori*, also captured. In that case property passes as soon as capture is completed. The same holds true as regards neutral merchant vessels and aircraft that are liable to attack. In other words, objects liable to attack may in any event be captured. Property passes simultaneously with the completion of capture.

The applicability of the definition of military objectives has not superseded the rules governing economic warfare at sea that remain applicable *qua* customary international law.[144] Hence, according to the rules laid down in Part V, enemy as well as neutral merchant vessels and civil aircraft may be captured in certain cases even if they are not liable to attack. However, if they are captured and do not qualify as objects liable to attack, they are captured for adjudication as prize.

Section I Determination of enemy character of vessels and aircraft

112 **The fact that a merchant vessel is flying the flag of an enemy State or that a civil aircraft bears the marks of an enemy State is conclusive evidence of its enemy character.**

112.1 At first glance this rule may seem self-evident. However, a lengthy discussion was devoted to this point in the light of conclusions in the Rapporteur's report and the participants' comments thereto.

---

144 Cf. W. Heintschel v. Heinegg, 'Visit, Search, Diversion, and Capture in Naval Warfare: Part II, Developments since 1945', XXX *Canadian Yearbook of International Law*, pp. 89–136, pp. 131 ff. (1992).

112.2   The Rapporteur on visit, search, diversion and capture had presented the conclusion that '*prima facie*, the enemy character of a ship is determined by the flag she flies'. There were some objections to that formulation by those who pointed out that there were rules on the nationality of ships that were equally applicable in times of peace and in times of international armed conflict. The determination of enemy character was not to be confused with the nationality of merchant vessels. During the discussion and drafting of the conclusions of the Bergen session, agreement was reached that there are a number of criteria, also discussed by the Rapporteur, for establishing enemy character which, in principle, do not interfere with a ship's nationality. Hence, a ship flying the flag of, and registered in, a neutral State, may be considered enemy in character without repercussions on its nationality, for example by ownership or other criteria.

112.3   However, it was generally felt that despite the weaknesses of the flag principle, such criteria alone would not be adequate. The naval commander on the spot should not have to deal with questions of ownership etc., if the vessel encountered flies the flag of an enemy State. With regard to such vessels there is no need to change the traditional law according to which 'the flying of an enemy flag in wartime is conclusive of the nationality'[145] and thus of the enemy character of a ship.[146] This traditional law has been reaffirmed by the practice of States after 1945[147] and its validity has been approved by three recent military manuals on the law of armed conflict at sea.[148] Thus, if a merchant vessel is operating under an enemy flag, that is, if it is displaying the national emblem or other visible indications of its nationality, it possesses enemy character and is liable to capture and confiscation.[149] In that case, any other criterion, as for example ownership, is irrelevant. These other criteria, that predominantly apply in cases of doubt, are, if at all, of minor importance for the naval commander. They are dealt with in paragraph 117.

112.4   It needs to be emphasised that paragraph 112 only deals with *one*, albeit important, criterion for legitimately determining a ship's enemy character. In other words: the flag alone is conclusive evidence only if it is an enemy's flag. In all other cases, that is, when the vessel concerned is flying a flag other than the enemy's, its enemy character needs to be determined by applying other criteria.[150] This also holds

---

145 Privy Council, *The Unitas* [1950] AC 536, 552, 558. See also US Supreme Court, *Lauritzen v. Lauritzen* [1953] 345 US 571; F. Berber, *Lehrbuch des Völkerrechts*, vol. II, p. 201 (2nd edn, München, 1969); Tucker, *The Law of War and Neutrality at Sea*, p. 76 (Washington, DC, 1957).
146 This rule is also laid down in Art. 57(1) of the 1909 London Declaration, and in Art. 51(1) of the 1913 Oxford Manual.
147 Cf. Heintschel v. Heinegg, 'Visit, Search, Diversion, and Capture in Naval Warfare: Part II, Developments since 1945', pp. 89 ff.; R. Ottmüller, *Die Anwendung von Seekriegsrecht in militärischen Konflikten seit 1945*, pp. 49 ff. (Hamburg, 1978).
148 NWP9 *The Commander's Handbook*, para. 7.5: '[a]ll vessels operating under an enemy flag, and all aircraft bearing enemy markings, possess enemy character.' According to an annotation to para. 716 of the Canadian Draft Manual, and according to para. 1022 of the German Manual, the enemy character of vessels and aircraft is established by the same criteria.
149 The terms 'confiscation' and 'condemnation' can be used interchangeably and mean that the property to the object in question passes to the captor.
150 See para. 119.

true for so-called flags of convenience. In times of peace, ship owners adopt flags of convenience primarily for economic reasons.[151] Even if there is no genuine link between the ship and the flag State, the fact that a vessel is flying such a flag has no impact on its nationality. The same applies in times of armed conflict. Unless there has been an illegitimate transfer to a neutral flag,[152] the mere fact that a ship is flying a flag of convenience may not be considered as giving rise to suspicion nor, even if there in fact is no genuine link, lead to a presumption of enemy character.

113   The fact that a merchant vessel is flying the flag of a neutral State or a civil aircraft bears the marks of a neutral State is *prima facie* evidence of its neutral character.

113.1   The right to capture neutral merchant vessels and aircraft (and neutral goods) is conferred on a belligerent in certain exceptional situations only. Therefore, a distinction has to be made between enemy ships/aircraft on the one hand and neutral ships/aircraft on the other hand. Since merchantmen have always tried to evade the consequences arising from the flying of an enemy flag, paragraph 113 could not be formulated in the same way as paragraph 112. Accordingly, the fact that a merchant vessel is flying the flag of a neutral State is only *prima facie* evidence of its neutral character, and hence of its primarily protected status. This corresponds with the traditional law[153] and with modern customary law as developed by the practice of States.[154] The cases in which the neutral flag does not necessarily establish neutral character are being dealt with in paragraphs 114–116.

113.2   It needs to be emphasised that 'neutral' according to paragraph 13(d) means 'any State not party to the conflict',that is, which does not participate in ongoing hostilities by the use of armed force. At its Geneva session, the Round Table agreed that many parts of the law of maritime neutrality do not qualify for a differentiation between

---

151   According to B. A. Boczek, *Flags of Convenience: An International Legal Study* (Cambridge, Mass., 1962), p. 2: 'functionally, a 'flag of convenience' can be defined as the flag of any country allowing the registration of foreign-owned and foreign-controlled vessels under conditions which, for whatever reasons, are convenient and opportune for the persons who are registering the vessel.'

152   See Arts. 55 and 56 of the 1909 London Declaration and Art. 52 of the 1913 Oxford Manual; C. C. Hyde, *International Law*, vol. 3, p. 2079 (2nd edn, Boston, 1945), C. J. Colombos, *The International Law of the Sea*, para. 609 (5th edn, London, 1962); Berber, *Lehrbuch des Völkerrechts*, vol. II, pp. 193 ff.; Tucker, *The Law of War and Neutrality at Sea*, pp. 80 ff.

153   Cf. W. Heintschel v. Heinegg, 'Visit, Search, Diversion, and Capture in Naval Warfare: Part I, The Traditional Law', XXIX *Canadian Yearbook of International Law*, pp. 283–329, at pp. 288 ff. (1991).

154   Cf. Heintschel v. Heinegg, 'Visit, Search, Diversion, and Capture in Naval Warfare: Part II, Developments since 1945', pp. 91 ff. See also NWP9 *The Commander's Handbook*, para. 7.5: 'However, the fact that a merchant ship flies a neutral flag, or that an aircraft bears neutral markings, does not necessarily establish neutral character. Any vessel or aircraft, other than a warship or military aircraft, owned or controlled by a belligerent possesses enemy character, regardless of whether it is operating under a neutral flag or is bearing neutral markings.' To the same effect are the rules in the Canadian Draft Manual, para. 716 and in the German Manual, para. 1022.

'benevolent' and strict neutrality. Even if an intermediate status were accepted, the 'non-belligerent' position taken by the flag State would be without significance for the legal status of its ships and aircraft. The neutral character has always been established by the non-belligerent flag or marks regardless of whether the flag State has taken a 'benevolent' or strict position of neutrality.[155] After 1945 that practice has not been altered.[156]

114   **If the commander of a warship suspects that a merchant vessel flying a neutral flag in fact has enemy character, the commander is entitled to exercise the right of visit and search including the right of diversion for search under paragraph 121.**

114.1   According to paragraph 113, the fact that a merchant vessel is flying a neutral flag is *prima facie* evidence of its neutral character. Such vessel may, however, have enemy character, for example because it is owned or controlled by enemy interests.[157] If the commander of a belligerent warship has reason to suspect that that is the case, the vessel has a duty to verify its character.

---

155 Cf. Heintschel v. Heinegg, 'Visit, Search, Diversion, and Capture in Naval Warfare: Part I, The Traditional Law', pp. 288 ff. It may be added that the rules on neutral prizes have never been influenced by the attitude of the respective flag state. Only their behaviour or the character of their cargoes have been of significance. See *inter alia* Chapter 276 of the famous Consolat del Mare of the fourteenth century (printed in F. Jordá, *Das 'Consulat des Meeres' als Ursprung und Grundlage des Neutralitätsrechtes im Seekriege bis zum Jahre 1856*, pp. 16–21 [Hamburg, 1932]); see also G. Schramm, *Das Prisenrecht*, pp. 12–28 (Berlin, 1913); A. P. Rubin, 'The Concept of Neutrality in International Law', in A. T. Leonhard (ed.), *Neutrality–Changing Concepts and Practices*, pp. 9–34, at pp. 13 ff. (Lanham, 1988).

156 Cf. Ottmüller, *Die Anwendung von Seekriegsrecht in militärischen Konflikten seit 1945*, pp. 47 ff., pp. 117 ff., pp. 180 ff., pp. 219 ff., pp. 271 ff., pp. 292 ff.; Heintschel v. Heinegg, 'Visit, Search, Diversion, and Capture in Naval Warfare: Part II, Developments since 1945', pp. 89 ff.

157 The provisions of the 1909 London Declaration, which may be considered as an attempt to find a compromise between differences in State practice, did not successfully contribute to the establishment of a generally accepted rule of international law. Cf. Berber, *Lehrbuch des Völkerrechts*, vol. II, pp. 193 ff.; Tucker, *The Law of War and Neutrality at Sea*, pp. 80 ff. In the annotation to NWP9, *The Commander's Handbook*, para. 7.5 the situation is correctly described as follows: 'A neutral nation may grant a merchant vessel or aircraft the right to operate under its flag, even though the vessel or aircraft remains substantially owned or controlled by enemy interests. According to the international law of prize, such a vessel or aircraft nevertheless possesses enemy character and may be treated as an enemy by the concerned belligerent. There is no settled practice among nations regarding the conditions under which the transfer of enemy merchant vessels (and, presumably, aircraft) to a neutral flag legitimately may be made. Despite agreement that such transfers will not be recognized when fraudulently made for the purpose of evading belligerent capture, nations differ in the specific conditions that they require to be met before such transfers can be considered as bona fide. However, it is generally recognized that, at the very least, all such transfers must result in the complete divestiture of enemy ownership and control. The problem of transfer is mainly the proper concern of prize courts rather than of an operating naval commander, and the latter is entitled to seize any vessel transferred from an enemy to a neutral flag when such transfer has been made either immediately prior to, or during, hostilities.'

114.2   It does not matter whether the commander of the warship has obtained the relevant information by himself or whether it has been communicated to him by external sources. It merely is important that there are in fact reasons for suspicion. Those reasons need to be sufficiently well-founded. Hence, if there is information that the vessel concerned is, for instance, owned or controlled by enemy interests, the naval commander undoubtedly may exercise the right under paragraph 114. If, however, as already stated above, the vessel is merely flying a flag of convenience, that alone would not be considered a sufficient ground for suspicion. It may be added in this context that the limitation in paragraph 116 to cases of suspicion follows from military as well as from legal considerations. Visit and search, and to some extent diversion for that purpose, may imply considerable dangers for the intercepting warship. A naval commander would expose his ship and crew to such dangers only on well-founded grounds. As regards the legal considerations, the said limitation can be derived from the principle of proportionality. As in the case of paragraph 118 dealing with visit and search aiming at possible capture, neutral merchant shipping may not be interfered with in an unrestricted manner.[158] This is taken into account by the present provision.

114.3   Weather conditions and/or the naval environment may render visit and search at sea hazardous. Moreover, in view of the size and configuration of modern merchant vessels, for example, container ships, it is impossible in most cases to accomplish search at sea.[159] Therefore, paragraph 114 contains a reference to paragraph 121. In such situations the vessel concerned may be diverted to an appropriate sea area or port in order to verify the ship's true character by visit and search.[160]

158 Any search, diversion or detention must be of the shortest possible duration. In cases of unreasonable diversion, undue delay, or unnecessary interference with the ship's voyage compensation should be awarded by the prize court. Cf. U. Scheuner, 'Durchsuchung von Schiffen', in K. Strupp and H. J. Schlochauer (eds.), *Wörterbuch des Völkerrechts*, vol. I, p. 407 (2nd edn, Berlin, 1960); Colombos, *The International Law of the Sea*, para. 893.

159 Tucker, *The Law of War and Neutrality at Sea*, p. 340 believes that 'the substantial and compelling reason for diversion was that little or no evidence to support a case of seizure – let alone for later condemnation – could be worked up by restricting attention to the ship's papers and to the nature of the cargo carried. In the vast majority of instances where vessels were encountered bound for a neutral port, and carrying cargo to be delivered to a neutral consignee, the ship's papers themselves furnished no real assurance of the ultimate destination of the cargo. Instead, the evidence necessary to justify seizure normally could come only from external sources. Not infrequently, this information was collected prior to the act of visit. More often, however, it could be gathered only after a vessel had been diverted to a belligerent contraband control base.'

160 The practice of diversion for the purpose of visit and search developed during the World Wars is today generally acknowledged as a customary right of belligerents at sea. See *inter alia* J. Wolf, 'Ships, Diverting and Ordering into Port', in R. Bernhardt (ed.), *Encyclopedia of Public International Law*, Instalment 4, pp. 223–4 (1984); Colombos, *The International Law of the Sea*, paras. 887 ff.; Tucker, *The Law of War and Neutrality at Sea*, pp. 340 ff. Note, however, that in *The Bernisse and The Elve* (LIPC, [1920] pp. 243 ff.), the Privy Council made clear that under certain circumstances diversion could be held as unjustified. In *The Mim* (Ann. Dig. (1947), Case No. 134, pp. 311 ff.) the British Prize Court held that 'in the absence of reasonable suspicion the ship must be allowed to proceed'.

115 **If the commander of a military aircraft suspects that a civil aircraft with neutral marks in fact has enemy character, the commander is entitled to exercise the right of interception and, if circumstances require, the right to divert for the purpose of visit and search.**

115.1   Paragraph 115 is the equivalent of paragraph 114 as regards aircraft. The Chicago Convention prescribes that a civil aircraft engaged in international air navigation has the nationality of the State in which it is registered.[161] Further, the aircraft can only be registered in one State and must bear the nationality and registration marks of that State.

115.2   Since aircraft cannot be visited and searched while in flight, they have to be intercepted and diverted for the purpose of visit and search in accordance with paragraph 125. It is important to emphasise that even though there have to be reasons for suspicion they will, in general, have to be less compelling than in the case of vessels. An aircraft *per se* constitutes a considerable danger. If its character is not clearly established or establishable, the belligerent's interest in positive identification justifies interception and/or diversion.

116   **If, after visit and search, there is reasonable ground for suspicion that the merchant vessel flying a neutral flag or a civil aircraft with neutral marks has enemy character, the vessel or aircraft may be captured as prize subject to adjudication.**

116.1   Paragraph 116 deals with cases in which visit and search, especially of the vessel's or aircraft's papers, reveal or at least give reasonable ground for suspicion that the vessel is, for example, owned by enemy individuals or enemy corporations, or that it is chartered by the enemy.[162] The enemy character need not be established with certainty. It suffices if the visiting officer remains unsatisfied with the ship's papers or with the answers given by its master and crew. Another reasonable ground for suspicion would be a transfer to the neutral flag after or immediately prior to the outbreak of hostilities, namely, a transfer of flag in contemplation of the consequences of war.[163] In those cases the naval commander may treat the vessel as if it were an enemy vessel,

161 Arts. 17–20.
162 According to the traditional and contemporary law of naval operations a vessel acquires enemy character if it is owned or controlled by enemy persons. The question whether ownership is to be determined on the basis of nationality or domicile remains an unsettled issue. Cf. Heintschel v. Heinegg, 'Visit, Search, Diversion, and Capture in Naval Warfare: Part I, The Traditional Law', pp. 288 ff.; 'Visit, Search, Diversion, and Capture in Naval Warfare: Part II, Developments since 1945', pp. 105 ff. See also NWP9, *The Commander's Handbook*, para. 7.5; Canadian Draft Manual, para. 716; German Manual, para. 1022. According to NWP9, *The Commander's Handbook*, para. 7.5.2, neutral vessels and aircraft, other than warships and military aircraft, acquire enemy character and may be treated by a belligerent as enemy merchant vessels or aircraft when 'operating directly under enemy control, orders, charter, employment, or direction, [or when] resisting an attempt to establish identity, including visit and search.'
163 Colombos, *The International Law of the Sea*, para. 609; Arts. 55 ff. of the 1909 London Declaration.

that is, it may capture it regardless of the neutral flag. Of course, any prize, be it an enemy or a neutral vessel, must be adjudicated upon by a prize court.[164] The prize court may rule that the vessel concerned in fact has neutral character. This, however, would not render the act of capture illegal. It would only lead to the release of the vessel, that is, it will not be confiscated. Capture would be illegal and the ship owner entitled to compensation only if the court rules that the grounds put forward by the naval commander to justify capture are not reasonable.

117 Enemy character can be determined by registration, ownership, charter or other criteria.

117.1 Paragraph 117 addresses the naval commander only to a minor degree. In a very general way this provision lays down those criteria by which a prize court may determine the enemy character of ships and goods. Whereas 'registration' (that means registration in accordance with the laws of the flag State and, partly, with the relevant rules of international law) is self-explanatory, 'ownership' and 'other criteria' need some specification. As regards ownership, it has never been a settled matter whether the owner's enemy character is to be determined according to the principle of nationality or the principle of domicile.[165] The Round Table was not able to reach an agreement on this issue either. There are only a few 'safe' statements that can be made in this context. In view of State practice, both during and after the two World Wars, it seems to be generally accepted that a vessel owned by an enemy national residing or doing business in enemy or enemy-controlled territory may legitimately be considered to be of enemy character. As regards ships owned by corporations, the so-called control test that has been accepted by the majority of States in times of war applies.[166] Accordingly, a corporation not registered under enemy law nor doing business in enemy or enemy-controlled territory is nevertheless treated as an enemy if effectively controlled by enemies. Since, however, the person controlling the corporation must be an enemy, the differences between nationality and domicile again do not allow a final answer. States are under no particular restriction in determining the enemy character of individuals. Rather, they may apply any test they consider most suitable for their needs. Hence, the only acceptable compromise seems to be the one suggested by the Institut de Droit International in Article 51(3) of the 1913 Oxford Manual. According to that provision:

> each State must declare, not later than the outbreak of hostilities, whether the enemy or neutral character of the owner of the goods is determined by his place of residence or his nationality.

164 This obligation stems from the old rule 'toute prise doit être jugée'. Cf. P. Reuter, *Etude de la règle: 'Toute prise doit être jugée'*, pp. 14 ff. (Paris, 1933); W. Röpcke, *Das Seebeuterecht*, pp. 122 ff. (Leipzig, 1904); see also Art. 55 of the 1923 Hague Rules of Aerial Warfare.
165 Cf. Heintschel v. Heinegg, 'Visit, Search, Diversion, and Capture in Naval Warfare: Part I, The Traditional Law', pp. 288 ff.
166 Associations controlled by the enemy, even though not incorporated in an enemy territory, are deemed to be enemy if they are under the control of a person resident or carrying on business in enemy territory. *Daimler Co. v. Consolidated Tyre and Rubber Co.* [1916] 2 AC 307 (HL); Colombos, *The International Law of the Sea*, para. 631.

117.2   Registration, ownership and charter are not the only criteria belligerents may use for the purpose of determining enemy character. That is made clear by the term 'other criteria'. Some concern was expressed with regard to the vagueness of that term and some participants wished to qualify it by, for example, 'reasonable'. The majority of participants, however, felt that that was unnecessary as all such criteria would at any rate need to be relevant to the determination of enemy character.

117.3   One of the 'other criteria' is the illegitimate or fraudulent transfer to a neutral flag. However, despite some attempts, *inter alia* by the London Naval Conference of 1908–9, to formulate rules on this matter, there is no settled State practice regarding the conditions under which the transfer to a neutral flag may legitimately be made. There is agreement that, if made for the purpose of evading belligerent capture, the transfer may be ignored. Another point of agreement is that any transfer must result in the complete divestiture of enemy ownership and control. That is, it must be unconditional, complete, and in conformity with the laws of the countries concerned. Its effect must be such that neither the control of, nor the profits arising from the employment of, the vessel remain in the same hands as before the transfer. However, the conditions under which the transfer of enemy merchant vessels (and aircraft) to a neutral flag may legitimately be made, are disputed. State practice with regard to the specific conditions that are required to be met before such transfers can be considered as *bona fide* is still far from uniform.[167] However, the difficulties with regard to the transfer of flags (and the determination of enemy character) are of only minor importance to the naval commander. If visit and search justify the reasonable suspicion that there might have been a transfer from an enemy flag to a neutral flag in order to evade belligerent capture, this will regularly suffice to qualify the ship as an enemy vessel. It is not the commander's duty to establish with certainty the enemy character. The problem of transfer is mainly the concern of prize courts rather than of an operating naval commander.

117.4   In this context it may be added that acts of resisting an attempt to establish identity do not alter the neutral character of a ship. Such acts only make them liable to be treated as if they were enemy vessels. If a neutral merchant vessel resists by the use of force it may be treated as a legitimate military objective.[168]

117.5   In the present proposal there is no rule on enemy character of goods. According to the traditional law, the enemy character of goods found on board enemy merchant vessels is determined by the neutral or enemy character of the owner.[169] With regard to this old rule, which is laid down in Article 58 of the 1909 London Declaration

167 See the annotation to NWP9, *The Commander's Handbook*, para. 7.5; Heintschel v. Heinegg, 'Visit, Search, Diversion, and Capture in Naval Warfare: Part I, The Traditional Law', pp. 293 ff.
168 Neutral merchant vessels are under an obligation to submit without resistance to visit and search. If they attempt flight, the warship is entitled to employ sufficient force to stop them. Forcible resistance on the part of a neutral merchant ship to visit and search is an act of hostility and renders it liable to capture and even attack. Berber, *Lehrbuch des Völkerrechts*, vol. II, p. 195; Oppenheim, *International Law*, vol. II, p. 856; NWP9, *The Commander's Handbook*, paras. 7.6.1, 7.9; Canadian Draft Manual, paras. 717, 720.
169 Cf. Heintschel v. Heinegg 'Visit, Search, Diversion, and Capture in Naval Warfare: Part I, The Traditional Law', pp. 295 ff.

the above-stated differences between the principle of nationality and the principle of domicile become decisive. In the absence of proof, goods found on board enemy merchant vessels are presumed to be enemy goods: '*robe d'ennemi confisque robe d'ami.*' This rebuttable presumption dates back to Hugo Grotius. It is laid down in Article 59 of the 1909 London Declaration and it was applied by the prize courts during the two World Wars. Thus, it is incumbent upon the neutral claimant to establish that the cargo carried in the enemy vessel belongs to him.

117.6   In State practice the question whether or not ownership in the goods has passed is determined by the municipal laws of the parties involved or in accordance with the municipal law of the captor, if the goods were sold prior to the outbreak of, and without anticipation of, hostilities. With regard to the transfer of goods made after the outbreak of war or in contemplation of hostilities, the rule laid down in Article 60(1) of the 1909 London Declaration comes into operation. Accordingly, enemy goods on board an enemy vessel retain their enemy character until they reach their destination, notwithstanding any transfer effected after the outbreak of hostilities while the goods are being forwarded. They retain their neutral character only if, prior to capture, a former neutral owner exercises, on the bankruptcy of an existing enemy owner, a recognised legal right to recover the goods (Article 60(2) of the London Declaration).

117.7   The problems arising from these differences, however, again do not concern a naval commander. He may consider any goods found on board an enemy merchant vessel to be of enemy character. The fact that, according to the law of prize, this is merely a rebuttable presumption does not affect the rights exercised by the commander. It will, therefore, rest with the prize court to verify the true character of goods found on board enemy merchant vessels. If neutral subjects are able to prove their ownership, the prize court will release the goods concerned.

117.8   With regard to goods on board neutral merchant vessels there is no need for a rule on their enemy or neutral character. If they are contraband of war they may be captured and confiscated by decision of the prize court, regardless of their enemy or neutral character. If they have enemy character, but do not qualify as contraband, they may not be captured. This is the principle 'free ship – free goods', as laid down in the 1856 Paris Declaration which has since remained unchanged.

Section II Visit and search of merchant vessels

Basic rules

118   **In exercising their legal rights in an international armed conflict at sea, belligerent warships and military aircraft have a right to visit and search merchant vessels outside neutral waters where there are reasonable grounds for suspecting that they are subject to capture.**

118.1   The measures of surveillance and control adopted by the Coalition forces during the Iraq–Kuwait conflict have illustrated the ability of naval means to identify neutral and enemy shipping over distances far beyond radar range. Thus it may well be expected that in the near future the great sea powers at least will be able to monitor and control the world's oceans with the help of highly advanced methods and technical means. Visit and search might then become superfluous. That, however, is not the case yet. For example, despite the sophisticated equipment possessed by the Coalition, visit, search and diversion were still practised in order to enforce the embargo imposed on Iraq. During the seven months of the conflict 'more than 165 ships from 19 Coalition navies challenged more than 7,500 merchant vessels, boarded 964 ships to inspect manifests and cargo holds, and diverted 51 ships carrying more than one million tons of cargo in violation of the UNSC sanctions'.[170] Hence, for the time being, visit and search still have to be considered necessary, and generally accepted, belligerent rights. Otherwise, belligerents would be unable effectively to control and enforce the prohibition of the carriage of contraband or the institution of a blockade.

118.2   The Round Table, therefore, did not hesitate to acknowledge the right of belligerent warships to visit and search all merchant vessels, be they enemy or neutral. These rights, it may be added, are not restricted to neutral merchant vessels because not all enemy vessels are liable to capture and condemnation. Even exempt enemy vessels may be visited and searched if the intercepting warship has reasonable grounds to suspect that they have lost their exempt status according to paragraph 136.

118.3   The Round Table also wished to emphasise that the right of visit and search may not be exercised arbitrarily. An unrestricted practice of visit and search has never been considered to be in accordance with international law.[171] Hence, the exercise of visit and search is made dependent upon 'reasonable grounds for suspecting that they are subject to capture'. Again, it must be stressed that the commander of the intercepting warship need not establish with certainty whether the merchant vessel concerned is in fact liable to capture.

118.4   As regards possible further limitations of the right of visit and search, reference is made to the commentary on paragraphs 3–5. As regards the sea areas where visit and search as well as other belligerent rights may be exercised, see the commentary on paragraphs 10 and 14–37.

119   As an alternative to visit and search, a neutral merchant vessel may, with its consent, be diverted from its declared destination.

119.1   According to the traditional law and State practice the right to have neutral merchant vessels alter their declared destination or course is conferred upon belligerents in exceptional cases only.[172] Neutral merchant vessels may be ordered not

---

170 US Department of Defense, *Conduct of the Persian Gulf War*, Final Report to Congress, pp. 76 ff. (Washington, DC, April 1992)

171 Cf. Heintschel v. Heinegg, 'Search, Visit, Diversion, and Capture in Naval Warfare: Part I, The Traditional Law', pp. 297 ff.

172 Especially before its entry into the First World War the United States, then a neutral, protested against the British practice of diverting neutral vessels into port for search. See the letter of the State Department dated 7 November 1914, in 9 AJIL pp. 55 ff. (1915, Special Supplement). Tucker, *The Law of War and Neutrality at Sea*, p. 340 believes that 'the substantial and compelling reason for diversion was that little or no evidence to support a case of seizure – let alone for later condemnation – could be worked up by restricting attention to the ship's papers

to approach warships or combat areas. They may also be prohibited from entering or leaving coastal areas or ports in case of a blockade established in accordance with international law. Finally, they may be diverted to a specific sea area or port in order to be visited and searched there for the purpose of verifying whether they are liable to capture or of verifying their neutral character.

119.2. However, especially in view of the practice to this effect in the 1990–91 Gulf War, the Round Table considered it useful to suggest, as an alternative to visit and search and as a means of mitigating the effects on neutral merchant shipping, a further belligerent right to divert neutral merchant vessels from their declared destination. The rationale behind paragraph 119 is to meet both the interests of belligerents as well as of neutral merchant shipping. Visit and search, and diversion for the purpose of visit and search, are relatively time consuming and may be hazardous to both the merchant vessel and the intercepting warship. In addition, it has to be kept in mind that visit and search according to paragraph 118 serve the purpose of enabling the naval commander to decide whether or not he may capture the neutral merchant vessel. Capture is a means of economic warfare, that is, it is directed against the enemy's commerce and economic power. However, it is not necessarily in the belligerent's interest to confiscate the merchant vessel in question. There are situations in which it will suffice to keep merchant vessels out of certain areas instead of diverting them to a belligerent port or some sea area for the purpose of visit and search. Such a diversion, however, interferes with the neutral's right of freedom of navigation and, other than in the cases mentioned above, is not justified by existing international law. Moreover, with this procedure there will be no verification of carriage of contraband, of some act of unneutral service, etc. Therefore, the master of the neutral merchant vessel has to consent to the diversion. If the neutral master does not agree with the belligerent's request, the commander of the intercepting warship may either exercise his right of visit and search under paragraph 118, or divert the merchant vessel for that purpose, or let it proceed on its original course.

Merchant vessels under convoy of accompanying neutral warships

120   A neutral merchant vessel is exempt from the exercise of the right of visit and search if it meets the following conditions:

(a)   it is bound for a neutral port;

(b)   it is under the convoy of an accompanying neutral warship of the

---

and to the nature of the cargo carried. In the vast majority of instances where vessels were encountered bound for a neutral port, and carrying cargo to be delivered to a neutral consignee, the ship's papers themselves furnished no real assurance of the ultimate destination of the cargo. Instead, the evidence necessary to justify seizure normally could come only from external sources. Not infrequently, this information was collected prior to the act of visit. More often, however, it could be gathered only after a vessel had been diverted to a belligerent contraband control base.' See also J. Wolf, 'Ships, Diverting and Ordering into Port', in EPIL 4, pp. 223–4 (1982); U. Scheuner, 'Kursanweisung', in WVR II, p. 385; Colombos, *The International Law of the Sea*, para. 887. With regard to State practice during the World Wars see *ibid.*, paras. 889 ff.

same nationality or a neutral warship of a State with which the flag State of the merchant vessel has concluded an agreement providing for such convoy;

(c) the flag State of the neutral warship warrants that the neutral merchant vessel is not carrying contraband or otherwise engaged in activities inconsistent with its neutral status; *and*

(d) the commander of the neutral warship provides, if requested by the commander of an intercepting belligerent warship or military aircraft, all information as to the character of the merchant vessel and its cargo as could otherwise be obtained by visit and search.

120.1   Under traditional law neutral merchant ships travelling alone may be visited and searched in accordance with the above rules.[173] However, different rules apply if they travel under convoy.[174]

120.2   There was some debate during the Bergen meeting whether the term 'convoy' should be maintained. A number of participants suggested to use instead the more descriptive term 'vessels under the operational control of accompanying neutral warships' as, under modern warfare conditions, the warship might not be travelling in close vicinity of the merchant vessels. Hence, it was sufficient if the warship exercised 'operational control' over the accompanied merchant vessels. The term 'convoy' was finally maintained because it was understood as a term of art with a long-standing legal tradition. There was, however, general agreement that this does not imply a duty on the accompanying warship to travel in close vicinity of the merchant vessels. On the other hand, it must be kept in mind that the accompanying warship may not sail at too far a distance because, according to subparagraph (d), its commander may be obliged to provide to the commander of the intercepting warship information as to the character of the merchant vessels and their cargoes. In any event, the neutral warship must be sufficiently close to the accompanied merchant vessels that it is evident that the merchant vessels are under convoy.

120.3   Two situations have to be kept distinct. Neutral merchant vessels under the convoy of an *enemy* warship are subject to the same treatment as enemy merchant ships. Travelling under enemy convoy is held to be sufficient evidence of forcible resistance to the right of visit, search and capture which renders the vessel subject to attack without warning.[175] With regard to neutral merchant vessels under convoy of

173 In the 1913 arbitration between France and Italy in the case of *The Carthage* (Award of the Arbitral Tribunal of the Permanent Court of Arbitration at The Hague in the Case of the French Mail Steamer *Carthage*, AJIL 1913, pp. 623–9; RIAA, vol. 11, pp. 449–61), the arbitral tribunal held: '... d'après les principes universellement admis, un bâtiment de guerre belligérant a, en thèse générale et sans conditions particulières, le droit d'arrêter en pleine mer un navire de commerce neutre et de procéder à la visite pour s'assurer s'il observe les règles sur la neutralité, spécialement au point de vue de la contrebande.'
174 For a general overview see R. Stödter, *Flottengeleit im Seekrieg* (Hamburg, 1936); and R. Stödter, 'Convoy', in EPIL 3, pp. 128–30 (1982).
175 Art. 63 of the 1909 London Declaration. See also Lord Stowell in *The Maria* [1799] 1 C. Rob.

neutral warships of the same nationality the rule has developed that they are exempt from visit and search.[176] In the opinion of the Round Table this exemption is, however, dependent on the requirements laid down in subparagraphs (a)–(d). In particular, neutral States are not entitled to protect their merchant vessels by warships if the merchant vessels' destination is an enemy port.

120.4   The element of progressive development in paragraph 120 is to be seen in the right of neutral States to form multinational convoys. These are also exempt from visit and search if all the conditions in subparagraphs (a)–(d) are fulfilled. Accordingly, not every neutral merchant vessel encountered in the vicinity of a neutral warship flying a different flag is exempt from visit and search. Only if the flag State of the neutral warship has concluded an agreement with another neutral State whose flag the merchant vessel concerned is flying, will multinational convoys be regarded as exempt from visit and search. The reason for this is to be found in subparagraphs (c) and (d). The flag State of the neutral warship and the commander of the accompanying neutral warship would not be in a position *bona fide* to comply with their duties if there is no such agreement between the flag States concerned.

120.5   If the commander of the neutral warship is unwilling or unable to satisfy the request of the commander of the intercepting warship, the latter will be entitled to visit and search the merchant vessels.

Diversion for the purpose of visit and search

121   If visit and search at sea is impossible or unsafe, a belligerent warship or military aircraft may divert a merchant vessel to an appropriate area or port in order to exercise the right of visit and search.

121.1   The right of diversion according to paragraph 121 has to be distinguished from the right of diversion according to paragraph 119. The latter is permissible only if the master of the neutral merchant vessel consents to the change of course. Here, the merchant vessel concerned is being diverted in order to be visited and searched in a safe place. Therefore, in this case, the neutral merchant vessel is obliged to obey the order of diversion.[177]

340; the decision of the US–German Mixed Claims Commission, United States, *Garland Steamship Corp. and others v. Germany* (1924), RIAA, vol. 7, p. 73; *The Motano*, RIAA, vol. 7, p. 83; Berber, *Lehrbuch des Volkerrechts*, vol. II, p. 195; Stödter, *Flottengeleit im Seekrieg*, pp. 63 ff.; Canadian Draft Manual, para. 717.

176   Originally it had been an unsettled matter whether or not the right of visit and search may be exercised upon neutral merchant vessels under convoy of neutral warships of the same nationality. Today, neutral merchant vessels under convoy of neutral warships of the same nationality are exempt from visit and search. See NWP9, *The Commander's Handbook*, para. 7.6; German Manual, para. 1142.

177   The right of diversion for the purpose of visit and search was not always undisputed. See the references in note 172. In view of modern State practice, as e.g. during the Iraq–Kuwait conflict, as well as according to modern military manuals, the right of diversion for this purpose is undisputed.

Measures of supervision

122   **In order to avoid the necessity of visit and search, belligerent States may establish reasonable measures for the inspection of cargo of neutral merchant vessels and certification that a vessel is not carrying contraband.**

122.1   On the one hand, diversion and detention entail a considerable financial loss for the neutral vessel diverted from its course. On the other hand, belligerents are confronted with the choice of 'either permitting goods to enter neutral ports, part of which are certainly destined to find their way into enemy hands, or to impose rigid controls upon such commerce at the risk of interfering on occasion with what is undeniably legitimate neutral trade'.[178] This dilemma was partially resolved by Great Britain and her allies by the introduction of an alternative system, which is considered 'the most promising method by which friction between neutrals and belligerents could be avoided':[179] the system of 'navicerts'.[180] Today, the right to issue such certificates is acknowledged in NWP9, paragraph 7.4.2, in Canadian Draft Manual, paragraph 720, and in the German Manual, paragraph 1141. Such navicerts or aircerts issued by one belligerent have no effect on the visit and search rights of a belligerent of the opposing side.[181]

123   **The fact that a neutral merchant vessel has submitted to such measures of supervision as the inspection of its cargo and grant of certificates of non-contraband cargo by one belligerent is not an act of unneutral service with regard to an opposing belligerent.**

123.1   Because of doubts raised, in particular during the Second World War, with regard to the consequences of the acceptance of navicerts by a neutral merchant vessel,[182] the Round Table wished to stress that this may not be considered an act of unneutral service which would render the neutral merchant vessel liable to the same treatment as an enemy merchant vessel.

124   **In order to obviate the necessity for visit and search, neutral States are encouraged to enforce reasonable control measures and certification procedures to ensure that their merchant vessels are not carrying contraband.**

---

178   Tucker, *The Law of War and Neutrality at Sea*, p. 280.
179   Colombos, *The International Law of the Sea*, para. 898.
180   See H. Ritchie, *The 'Navicert' System during the World War* (1938); J. V. Lovitt, 'The Allied Blockade', Department of State Bulletin, vol. 11 (1944), pp. 597 ff.; G. G. Fitzmaurice, 'Some Aspects of Modern Contraband Control and the Law of Prize', XXII BYIL, pp. 73–95, at pp. 83 ff. (1945); D. Steinicke, *Kriegsbedingte Risiken der neutralen Seeschiffahrt* (Hamburg, 1968); D. Steinicke, *Das Navicertsystem* (Hamburg, 1966).
181   NWP9, *The Commander's Handbook*, para. 7.4.2.
182   At the beginning of the Second World War, neutral governments such as those of Switzerland, Sweden, The Netherlands and Belgium, opposed the reintroduction of the certificate system and prohibited their subjects from submitting to investigation by foreign authorities.

124.1   According to the traditional law as laid down in Article 7 of Hague Convention XIII, 'a neutral Power is not bound to prevent the export or transit, for the use of either belligerent, of arms, ammunition, or, in general, of anything which could be of use to an army or fleet'. Neutral States have never been under an obligation to issue certificates covering cargoes on board vessels of their nationality.[183] Moreover, the carriage of contraband has never been prohibited by international law. Rather, it is a neutral merchantman's right that merely conflicts with the belligerent's right to contraband control.[184] However, in view of the inconveniences and even financial losses brought about by visit and search, the Round Table considered it appropriate to encourage neutral States to ensure that their merchant vessels do not engage in the carriage of contraband.

Section III Interception, visit and search of civil aircraft

Basic rules

125   **In exercising their legal rights in an international armed conflict at sea, belligerent military aircraft have a right to intercept civil aircraft outside neutral airspace where there are reasonable grounds for suspecting they are subject to capture. If, after interception, reasonable grounds for suspecting that a civil aircraft is subject to capture still exist, belligerent military aircraft have the right to order the civil aircraft to proceed for visit and search to a belligerent airfield that is safe for the type of aircraft involved and reasonably accessible. If there is no belligerent airfield that is safe and reasonably accessible for visit and search, a civil aircraft may be diverted from its declared destination.**

125.1   The 1923 Hague Rules of Aerial Warfare state the customary rule that private aircraft are liable to visit and search and to capture by belligerent military aircraft. This paragraph describes how the right of visit and search is to be exercised. First, the belligerent military forces must have reasonable grounds to suspect that the civil aircraft is subject to capture in accordance with paragraphs 141–145 and 153–158.

---

183 See Colombos, *The International Law of the Sea*, para. 899 referring *inter alia* to the Havana Convention of 20 February 1928 on Maritime Neutrality, LNTS, vol. 135, pp. 188–216.

184 The right of a belligerent to capture and condemn contraband goods and vessels carrying such goods does not correspond with a legal duty on behalf of neutral merchantmen to refrain from such an activity. It is simply a case of two conflicting rights with the belligerent right of capture prevailing over the neutral's right of carrying contraband: 'It is no transgression of the limits of a neutral's duty, but merely the exercise of a hazardous right, in the course of which he may come into conflict with the rights of the belligerent and be worsted': *The Kronprinsessin Margareta* [1921] 1 AC 754. Lord Summer in *The Prins der Nederlande* [1921] 1 AC 760 put it as follows: 'Neutrals who carry contraband do not break the law of nations; they run a risk for adequate gain, and, if they are caught, take the consequences. If they know what they are doing, those consequences may be very serious; if they do not, they may get off merely with some inconvenience or delay; this must suffice them.'

Secondly, the belligerent military aircraft must intercept the civil aircraft in accordance with paragraph 128. Thirdly, the military aircraft must attempt to communicate with the civil aircraft to obtain information as to registration, destination, passengers, cargo and other relevant information (paragraph 129) and to resolve any ambiguities. Further, after exchanging information (or failing to do so), the belligerent military forces must still have reasonable grounds to suspect that the civil aircraft is subject to capture. In this event, the military aircraft can order the civil aircraft to proceed for visit and search to a belligerent airfield that is safe for the type of civil aircraft involved and reasonably accessible. If there is no belligerent airfield that is safe and reasonably accessible for visit and search, the civil aircraft may be diverted from its declared destination. For example, if the only belligerent airfield reasonably accessible is the flight deck of an aircraft carrier, the safety criteria would not be met and diversion could be ordered.

125.2   Obviously, diversion as mentioned in the last sentence of this paragraph is prohibited if it would result in jeopardising the safety of the aircraft concerned. This would, for example, be the case if the aircraft is in distress or short on fuel.

126   **As an alternative to visit and search:**

    (a)   **an enemy civil aircraft may be diverted from its declared destination;**

    (b)   **a neutral civil aircraft may be diverted from its declared destination with its consent.**

126.1   This alternative is similar to that for merchant vessels in paragraph 119. In some situations, the belligerent military forces, after interception and an exchange of information, may prefer to divert the suspected civil aircraft from its declared destination instead of exercising the right of visit and search. Similarly, a civil aircraft may prefer to proceed to a new destination instead of proceeding to a belligerent airfield, landing and undergoing visit and search. This paragraph provides such an alternative which, in the case of a neutral civil aircraft, requires its consent. Consent is not required to divert an enemy civil aircraft from its declared destination.

Civil aircraft under the operational control of an accompanying neutral military aircraft or warship

127   **A neutral civil aircraft is exempt from the exercise of the right of visit and search if it meets the following conditions:**

    (a)   **it is bound for a neutral airfield;**

    (b)   **it is under the operational control of an accompanying:**

        (i)   **neutral military aircraft or warship of the same nationality; or**

> (ii) **neutral military aircraft or warship of a State with which the flag State of the civil aircraft has concluded an agreement providing for such control;**
>
> (c) **the flag State of the neutral military aircraft or warship warrants that the neutral civil aircraft is not carrying contraband or otherwise engaged in activities inconsistent with its neutral status;** *and*
>
> (d) **the commander of the neutral military aircraft or warship provides, if requested by the commander of an intercepting belligerent military aircraft, all information as to the character of the civil aircraft and its cargo as could otherwise be obtained by visit and search.**

127.1   This paragraph provides the same exemption for a neutral civil aircraft under the operational control of accompanying neutral military aircraft or warship that is provided for a neutral merchant vessel under neutral military convoy in paragraph 120. Although there is no customary rule or long-standing practice applicable to neutral civil aircraft in these circumstances, there have been instances of neutral civil aircraft being escorted by neutral military forces in areas of hostilities. The exemption should apply if all conditions in this paragraph are met.

Measures of interception and supervision

Preliminary remark

Paragraphs 128–134 on measures of interception and supervision in exercising visit and search are interrelated and should be read as a whole.

128   Belligerent States should promulgate and adhere to safe procedures for intercepting civil aircraft as issued by the competent international organisation.

128.1   This paragraph obliges belligerent States to promulgate and adhere to the guidance in the 'Manual Concerning Interception of Civil Aircraft' issued by the International Civil Aviation Organisation (ICAO), the competent international organisation.[185] As indicated in paragraph 125 and the commentary thereto, interception is an initial step in the visit and search of a civil aircraft. The ICAO manual contains detailed procedures for interception, including approach, manoeuvring, visual signals, sample voice transmissions, and the use of identification modes and codes. It also requires that all States publish a safe method of interception, establish rapid communications with air traffic services, and co-ordinate between air intercept aircraft and their ground control units.

---

185   See also Annex 2 to the Chicago Convention, International Standards, Rules of the Air.

129   Civil aircraft should file the required flight plan with the cognisant Air Traffic Service, complete with information as to registration, destination, passengers, cargo, emergency communication channels, identification modes and codes, updates en route and carry certificates as to registration, airworthiness, passengers and cargo. They should not deviate from a designated Air Traffic Service route or flight plan without Air Traffic Control clearance unless unforeseen conditions arise, e.g., safety or distress, in which case appropriate notification should be made immediately.

129.1   This paragraph is identical to paragraph 76 which sets forth the requirements to be fulfilled by civil aircraft engaged in international navigation. The commentary thereto applies. The information in the flight plan is important to belligerent forces and the intercepting military aircraft in attempting to exchange information, verify status, resolve ambiguities, clarify intentions, and determine whether reasonable grounds still exist to suspect that the civil aircraft is subject to capture. A complete and accurate flight plan filed by the civil aircraft may obviate the necessity for interception and visit and search.

130   Belligerents and neutrals concerned, and authorities providing air traffic services should establish procedures whereby commanders of warships and military aircraft are continuously aware of designated routes assigned to and flight plans filed by civil aircraft in the area of military operations, including information on communication channels, identification modes and codes, destination, passengers and cargo.

130.1   This paragraph is identical to paragraph 74 which places an obligation on belligerents and neutrals, including authorities providing air traffic services, to be aware on a continuous basis of designated routes assigned to and flight plans filed by civil aircraft in the area of military operations. The commentary thereto applies. Flight plan information is important to commanders of warships and military aircraft in determining which aircraft may or may not need to be intercepted, or whether a particular track corresponds to an assigned route and flight plan.

131   In the immediate vicinity of naval operations, civil aircraft shall comply with instructions from the combatants regarding their heading and altitude.

131.1   This paragraph repeats the rule in paragraph 73 on the customary right of a belligerent to control civil aircraft in the immediate vicinity of naval operations. It may be necessary to alter the heading or altitude of a civil aircraft to effect a safe interception.

132 **In order to avoid the necessity of visit and search, belligerent States may establish reasonable measures for the inspection of the cargo of neutral civil aircraft and certification that an aircraft is not carrying contraband.**

132.1 This paragraph is identical to paragraph 122 applicable to neutral merchant vessels. The commentary thereto applies.

133 **The fact that a neutral civil aircraft has submitted to such measures of supervision as the inspection of its cargo and grant of certificates of non-contraband cargo by one belligerent is not an act of unneutral service with regard to an opposing belligerent.**

133.1 This paragraph is identical to paragraph 123 applicable to neutral States and their merchant vessels. The commentary thereto applies.

134 **In order to obviate the necessity for visit and search, neutral States are encouraged to enforce reasonable control measures and certification procedures to ensure that their civil aircraft are not carrying contraband.**

134.1 This paragraph is identical to paragraph 124 applicable to neutral merchant vessels. The commentary thereto applies.

Section IV Capture of enemy vessels and goods

135 **Subject to the provisions of paragraph 136, enemy vessels, whether merchant or otherwise, and goods on board such vessels may be captured outside neutral waters. Prior exercise of visit and search is not required.**

135.1 According to international law enemy vessels of any category (irrespective of nature of their cargo and their destination) and their cargo are liable to capture if not specially protected.[186] Hence, also, private vessels such as yachts may be captured. Whereas enemy cargo on board enemy merchant ships can always be captured as prize,[187] neutral cargo on board enemy merchant vessels can only be captured if it is contraband, if the vessel is breaching a blockade, or if it travels in enemy convoy or actively resists visit and search.[188]

135.2 As regards the sea areas where enemy vessels may be captured, reference is made to the commentary on paragraph 10 and on Part II of the Manual.

---

186 With regard to efforts undertaken to exempt enemy private property from capture and condemnation see the references in Heintschel v. Heinegg, 'Visit, Search, Diversion, and Capture in Naval Warfare: Part I, The Traditional Law', pp. 305 ff. For capture of vessels and aircraft liable to attack see the preliminary remarks to Part V.

187 Canadian Draft Manual, para. 716 (1); NWP9, *The Commander's Handbook*, para. 8.2.2.1; German Manual, para. 1023.

188 Cf. Heintschel v. Heinegg, 'Visit, Search, Diversion, and Capture in Naval Warfare: Part I, The Traditional Law', p. 316.

136   The following vessels are exempt from capture:

(a)   hospital ships and small craft used for coastal rescue operations;

(b)   other medical transports, so long as they are needed for the wounded, sick and shipwrecked on board;

(c)   vessels granted safe conduct by agreement between the belligerent parties including:

    (i)   cartel vessels, e.g., vessels designated for and engaged in the transport of prisoners of war;

    (ii)   vessels engaged in humanitarian missions, including vessels carrying supplies indispensable to the survival of the civilian population, and vessels engaged in relief actions and rescue operations;

(d)   vessels engaged in transporting cultural property under special protection;

(e)   vessels charged with religious, non-military scientific or philanthropic missions; vessels collecting scientific data of likely military applications are not protected;

(f)   small coastal fishing vessels and small boats engaged in local coastal trade, but they are subject to the regulations of a belligerent naval commander operating in the area and to inspection; *and*

(g)   vessels designed or adapted exclusively for responding to pollution incidents in the marine environment when actually engaged in such activities.

136.1   As the legal aspects of the special exemption of enemy vessels from attack according to treaty and customary law (see paragraph 47) are essentially based on the same considerations, the Round Table considered it sufficient to list those categories of enemy vessels which under the existing law are also exempt from capture.[189] The exemption of the different categories are based on the following legal foundations:[190]

–   hospital ships, small craft used for coastal rescue operations and medical transports are protected under customary as well as under treaty law;[191]

---

189 Cf. Heintschel v. Heinegg, 'Visit, Search, Diversion, and Capture in Naval Warfare: Part I, The Traditional Law', pp. 311 ff.; 'Visit, Search, Diversion, and Capture in Naval Warfare: Part II, Developments since 1945', pp. 110 ff.

190 For further references see the commentary on paragraph 47.

191 Arts. 22 ff. GCII; Arts. 22 ff. API.

—   cartel vessels and other vessels guaranteed safe conduct by prior agreement between the belligerents have protected status because of the prior agreement;[192]

—   vessels on humanitarian missions, namely vessels engaged in relief actions, rescue operations and those carrying goods indispensable for the survival of the civilian population are protected under customary and treaty law.[193] However, exemption, in principle, depends upon the prior consent of the belligerents;

—   vessels charged with religious, non-military scientific or philanthropic missions are exempt from capture according to Article 4 of Hague Convention XI. That provision, in the opinion of the Round Table, is still valid. However, since scientific data may also be of likely military applications, not all such vessels may be accorded a specially protected status;

—   small coastal fishing vessels and small boats engaged in local coastal trade are protected under Article 3 of Hague Convention XI as well as by customary international law;[194]

—   ships engaged in the protection of the marine environment are protected neither under treaty nor customary law. This category, thus, is innovative. It should be recalled that, in the opinion of the Round Table, such vessels may not be considered military objectives. Hence, because of the important function they serve, it is believed to be logical to exempt them from capture as well.

136.2   There are two categories of ships that are not included in the list of exempt enemy vessels although they have appeared in earlier treaties: vessels in port at the outbreak of hostilities and mail ships. The Round Table has not included the former because it considered Hague Convention VI to have fallen into desuetude. The latter were never generally accepted as being exempt from capture[195] and the Round Table saw no reason to include them in the list.

---

192 See *inter alia* D. P. O'Connell, *The International Law of the Sea*, vol. II, p. 1123 (ed.) I. A. Shearer (Oxford, 1984); Oppenheim, *International Law*, vol. II, pp. 538 ff., 541 ff.; Colombos, *The International Law of the Sea*, paras. 660 f.; Art. 45 of the 1913 Oxford Manual.

193 Art. 70 API.

194 See I. A. Shearer, 'Commentary on Hague Convention XI', in N. Ronzitti (ed.), *The Law of Naval Warfare*, pp. 186 f.; Tucker, *The Law of War and Neutrality at Sea*, p. 96; Schramm, *Das Prisenrecht*, pp. 143 ff.

195 Only in isolated cases were mail ships exempt from capture. Such treaty obligations did not become embodied in customary international law. Schramm, *Das Prisenrecht*, p. 149; Oppenheim, *International Law*, vol. II, p. 480.

137   **Vessels listed in paragraph 136 are exempt from capture only if they:**

(a)   **are innocently employed in their normal role;**

(b)   **do not commit acts harmful to the enemy;**

(c)   **immediately submit to identification and inspection when required;** *and*

(d)   **do not intentionally hamper the movement of combatants and obey orders to stop or move out of the way when required.**

137.1   The vessels listed in paragraph 136 have never enjoyed an absolutely protected status. Firstly, exemption from capture (and attack) does not imply that those vessels may not be visited, searched or diverted in accordance with the above provisions. Secondly, they lose their protected status as soon as they do not comply with one of the conditions for their exemption. If they engage in acts harmful to the enemy they become military objectives and there is no longer any reason to exempt them from attack and capture. This follows from treaty as well as from customary law.[196] If they unintentionally hamper the movements of combatants they may be ordered to move out of the way. In this context it needs to be stressed that orders to stop or move out of the way may not be given arbitrarily. In particular, the safety of the vessels concerned has to be taken into due consideration.

138   **Capture of a merchant vessel is exercised by taking such vessel as prize for adjudication. If military circumstances preclude taking such a vessel as prize at sea, it may be diverted to an appropriate area or port in order to complete capture. As an alternative to capture, an enemy merchant vessel may be diverted from its declared destination.**

138.1   This paragraph is only applicable to enemy merchant vessels as defined in paragraph 13(i). Capture of such a vessel is complete when the prize is under the control of the captor.[197] Prior exercise of visit and search is not required provided positive determination of enemy status can be made by other means. The property does not pass to the captor until the prize has been condemned by a prize court of the captor.[198] The lawfulness of the act of capture is, however, not dependent upon later condemnation by a prize court. Condemnation by a prize court constitutes a valid and complete title. On the capture of an enemy warship or of another military objective,

---

196 See the commentary on paras. 49–52.
197 Colombos, *The International Law of the Sea*, para. 903; Oppenheim, *International Law*, vol. II, p. 474. Note that capture differs from other acts such as e.g. those amounting to no more than diversion into port for search. The distinguishing criterion is the intent of the belligerent. See also Tucker, *The Law of War and Neutrality at Sea*, pp. 344 ff. A prize is lost (a) when it escapes through being rescued by its own crew, (b) when the captor intentionally abandons it, or (c) when it is recaptured; see Oppenheim, *International Law*, vol. II, p. 494.
198 Oppenheim, *International Law*, vol. II, pp. 474 ff.; Berber, *Lehrbuch des Völkerrechts*, vol. II, pp. 195 ff.; Art. 112 of the 1913 Oxford Manual; US District Court for the Western District of Washington, *The Wilhelmina* [1948] 78 F. Suppl. 57.

both not being prizes as such, the property passes at once to the captor.[199] With regard to all other cases, it is a 'well-recognised rule that a prize must be brought into a convenient port for adjudication. The propriety or rather the necessity of acting upon this rule is based ... on the principle that the property of private persons must not be converted without due process of law.'[200] If the capture of a vessel 'is not upheld by the prize court, or if the prize is released without any judgment given, the parties interested have the right to compensation, unless there were good reasons for capturing the vessel'.[201]

138.2   Again, in view of recent State practice, the Round Table considered it desirable to include a rule on diversion. Two different situations may occur. On the one hand, an enemy vessel that is not exempt may be diverted to a certain sea area or port in order to be captured there. This will be the case when capture at sea is impossible or hazardous. On the other hand, it may suffice to keep the vessel concerned away from a certain sea area or port. In such a situation the belligerent's interests can be met by merely diverting the enemy vessel from its declared destination. This, however, is not a settled rule of international law but a proposal for progressive development.

139   Subject to paragraph 140, a captured enemy merchant vessel may, as an exceptional measure, be destroyed when military circumstances preclude taking or sending such a vessel for adjudication as an enemy prize, only if the following criteria are met beforehand:

    (a)   the safety of passengers and crew is provided for; for this purpose, the ship's boats are not regarded as a place of safety unless the safety of the passengers and crew is assured in the prevailing sea and weather conditions by the proximity of land or the presence of another vessel which is in a position to take them on board;

    (b)   documents and papers relating to the prize are safeguarded; *and*

    (c)   if feasible, personal effects of the passengers and crew are saved.

139.1   In principle, captured enemy merchant vessels must be taken into port in order to be adjudicated upon (unless they were captured as military objectives). When, however, circumstances render this course impossible, the prize may be destroyed. In State practice as well as in legal writings there had been a tendency to allow destruction

---

199   Oppenheim, *International Law*, vol. II, pp. 474 ff.; W. G. Downey Jr, 'Captured Enemy Property, Booty of War and Seized Enemy Property', 44 AJIL, pp. 488 ff. (1950); Colombos, *The International Law of the Sea*, para. 930. The same applies to goods on board such vessels if it is property of the enemy State. Private property on board such ships is subject to the law of prize.

200   Colombos, *The International Law of the Sea*, para. 925; see also P. Guttinger, 'Réflexions sur la jurisprudence des prises maritimes de la Seconde Guerre Mondiale', 25 RGDIP, pp. 54 ff. (1975).

201   Art. 64 of the 1909 London Declaration.

in nearly every case.[202] Indeed, it could be argued that according to the wording of the 1936 London Procès-Verbal relating to the Rules of Submarine Warfare[203] the destruction of merchant ships can be considered legal as long as passengers, crew and ship's papers have been placed in a place of safety.

139.2   Aside from general considerations of proportionality there are, however, many reasons why the destruction of merchant ships should be limited. In this regard one needs to take into consideration the fact that the capturing warship can only rarely be considered a place of safety. Moreover, enemy merchant vessels may be carrying neutral cargo which cannot be classified as contraband. For these reasons destruction of enemy merchant vessels must be treated as an exceptional measure and must be strictly limited.[204] Hence, mere reference to military exigencies does not suffice to justify the destruction. If enemy merchant vessels are not legitimate military objectives, they may, in case of military necessity, be destroyed after capture only if the safety of passengers and crew has been provided for. Documents and papers relating to the prize should be safeguarded and, if practicable, the personal effects of passengers should be saved. In any event a prize court has to adjudicate whether the destruction was lawful.[205] If the destruction was illegal, the owner of the vessel is entitled to full compensation.[206]

140   The destruction of enemy passenger vessels carrying only civilian passengers is prohibited at sea. For the safety of the passengers, such vessels shall be diverted to an appropriate area or port in order to complete capture.

140.1   Passenger vessels do not belong to any category of enemy vessels exempt from capture and, therefore, are generally subject to the same treatment as all enemy merchant vessels. If, however, passenger vessels are solely employed in carrying civilian passengers, reasons of humanity call for an absolute prohibition of destroying them at sea, even if the criteria in paragraph 139 are met beforehand. Subject to the principle of proportionality, the exemption from destruction applies only when the vessel is not carrying military personnel and/or military material. The incidental carriage of the personal effects of passengers and crew and other normal supplies of the vessel do not affect the prohibition contained in this paragraph.

---

202 See the examples given by Oppenheim, *International Law*, vol. II, p. 487.
203 Procès-Verbal relating to the Rules of Submarine Warfare Set Forth in Part IV of the Treaty of London of 22 April 1930, signed at London, 6 November 1936; text in LNTS, vol. 173 (1936), pp. 353 ff.
204 Colombos, *The International Law of the Sea*, paras. 909 ff.; Oppenheim, *International Law*, vol. II, p. 487.
205 Oppenheim, *International Law*, vol. II, p. 488.
206 In its award of 13 October 1922, the Hague Permanent Court of Arbitration (1923 AJIL, 363, 392 ff.) ruled that '... just compensation implies a complete restitution of the status quo ante based not upon future gains ..., but upon the loss of profits of the ... owners as compared with other owners of similar property'.

Section V Capture of enemy civil aircraft and goods

141 **Subject to the provisions of paragraph 142, enemy civil aircraft and goods on board such aircraft may be captured outside neutral airspace. Prior exercise of visit and search is not required.**

141.1 The 1923 Hague Rules of Aerial Warfare state that enemy private aircraft are liable to capture in all circumstances. This paragraph reflects this customary rule which is the same as that in paragraph 135 applicable to enemy merchant vessels and goods. Prior exercise of visit and search is not required, but interception is required as part of the capture procedure as specified in paragraph 144.

142 **The following aircraft are exempt from capture:**

(a) medical aircraft; *and*

(b) aircraft granted safe conduct by agreement between the parties to the conflict.

142.1 As a general rule, medical aircraft are exempt from capture. This is in accord with the practice of belligerents as reflected in the Canadian and United States military manuals. However, medical aircraft may be ordered to land for inspection. If the inspection discloses that the aircraft is not a medical aircraft or has breached certain conditions of flight (see paragraphs 174–183), it may be captured.[207]

142.2 The very nature of safe conduct by agreement between the belligerents exempts such aircraft from capture. However, the aircraft may be subject to inspection to verify adherence to the agreement, preferably before the aircraft begins the mission.

143 **Aircraft listed in paragraph 142 are exempt from capture only if they:**

(a) are innocently employed in their normal role;

(b) do not commit acts harmful to the enemy;

(c) immediately submit to interception and identification when required;

(d) do not intentionally hamper the movement of combatants and obey orders to divert from their track when required; *and*

(e) are not in breach of a prior agreement.

143.1 This paragraph contains the conditions that belligerents would expect medical aircraft and aircraft granted safe conduct to observe. Subparagraph (b), 'do not commit acts harmful to the enemy' should be strictly interpreted and applied only to significant acts that confer a distinct military advantage at the time.[208]

---

207 API Art. 30
208 See API Art. 28

144   **Capture is exercised by intercepting the enemy civil aircraft, ordering it to proceed to a belligerent airfield that is safe for the type of aircraft involved and reasonably accessible and, on landing, taking the aircraft as a prize for adjudication. As an alternative to capture, an enemy civil aircraft may be diverted from its declared destination.**

144.1   This paragraph is different from paragraph 138 applicable to enemy merchant vessels in that enemy civil aircraft cannot be captured while airborne. Belligerent forces must first intercept the enemy civil aircraft in accordance with safe provisions for interception (paragraph 128) and order it to proceed to a safe and accessible belligerent airfield. Upon landing, the enemy civil aircraft is to be taken as a prize for adjudication (unless it was captured as a military objective). The enemy civil aircraft may also be diverted from its declared destination as an alternative to capture.

145   **If capture is exercised, the safety of passengers and crew and their personal effects must be provided for. The documents and papers relating to the prize must be safeguarded.**

145.1   In the capture of an enemy civil aircraft, there is no exceptional measure that permits destruction of the aircraft while airborne analogous to paragraphs 139–140 applicable to captured enemy merchant vessels at sea. If, after landing, the capture of an enemy civil aircraft is exercised, the passengers, crew, personal effects, documents and papers must be safeguarded.

Section VI Capture of neutral merchant vessels and goods

146   **Neutral merchant vessels are subject to capture outside neutral waters if they are engaged in any of the activities referred to in paragraph 67 or if it is determined as a result of visit and search or by other means, that they:**

(a)   **are carrying contraband;**

(b)   **are on a voyage especially undertaken with a view to the transport of individual passengers who are embodied in the armed forces of the enemy;**

(c)   **are operating directly under enemy control, orders, charter, employment or direction;**

(d)   **present irregular or fraudulent documents, lack necessary documents, or destroy, deface or conceal documents;**

(e)   **are violating regulations established by a belligerent within the immediate area of naval operations;** *or*

(f)   **are breaching or attempting to breach a blockade.**

Capture of a neutral merchant vessel is exercised by taking such vessel as prize for adjudication.

146.1   In principle, neutral merchant vessels may not be captured, condemned, or destroyed.[209] Neutral merchant vessels may be captured in exceptional cases only. The right to capture neutral merchant vessels may be considered a legal reaction of a belligerent to a certain behaviour of the neutral merchantman[210] which, it may be added, does not as such constitute a violation of international law.[211]

146.2   As in the case of enemy merchant ships, the legality of capture of neutral merchant vessels is not dependent upon later condemnation by a prize court. It suffices for the captor to establish that 'at the moment of seizure circumstances were such as to warrant suspicion of enemy character, whether of vessel or of cargo, or of the performance of acts held to constitute contraband carriage, blockade breach, or unneutral service'.[212] Capture of neutral vessels does not serve to effect transfer of title in favour of the captor, but only places him in temporary possession of the property. The final decision on whether there is sufficient cause for confiscating the vessel and/or cargo lies with the competent prize court alone. Hence, the captor is obliged to take all reasonable measures in order to preserve the vessel and its cargo intact and to take it into the nearest port without undue delay.[213]

146.3   Carriage of contraband

Neutral merchant vessels engaged in the carriage of contraband, or reasonably suspected of being so engaged, are liable to capture[214] and, under certain conditions, may be condemned. The conditions under which a neutral merchant vessel may be condemned differ. In any event, condemnation is dependent on the decision of a duly commissioned prize court. For the purposes of the present proposal, it is sufficient to indicate that the carriage of contraband as such justifies capture. Hence, it is immaterial whether the master or owner knows that the cargo is contraband or whether the contraband 'reckoned either by value, weight, volume, or freight, forms more than half the cargo'.[215] Under certain conditions, carriage of contraband, according to paragraph 67(a) renders a neutral merchant vessel liable to attack. If a ship may legally be attacked, this implies that it may be captured as well. Nevertheless, it was considered necessary to have in this Section a rule on carriage of contraband as well, because the concept of contraband is being dealt with extensively in paragraphs 147–150.

---

209 See *inter alia* Hyde, *International Law*, vol. 3, pp. 2041 ff.; NWP9, *The Commander's Handbook*, para. 7.4.
210 With regard to the question whether a belligerent may capture and condemn neutral merchant vessels by way of reprisal in response to violations of the neutral flag State's duty of impartiality see Tucker, *The Law of War and Neutrality at Sea*, pp. 252 ff.
211 Berber, *Lehrbuch des Völkerrechts*, vol. II, pp. 223 ff.; Tucker, *The Law of War and Neutrality at Sea*, pp. 253 ff.
212 Tucker, *The Law of War and Neutrality at Sea*, p. 346.
213 Art. 48 of the 1909 London Declaration.
214 See Art. 37 of the London Declaration; Tucker, *The Law of War and Neutrality at Sea*, p. 276; Hyde, *International Law*, vol. 3, p. 2160; Oppenheim, *International Law*, vol. II, p. 826. However, a 'vessel may not be captured on the ground that she has carried contraband on a previous occasion if such carriage is in point of fact at an end' (Art. 38 of the London Declaration).
215 Art. 40 of the 1909 London Declaration.

146.4 Subparagraphs (b) and (c)

It is a well-established right of belligerents to prevent neutral vessels from transporting enemy troops.[216] The conditions rendering a neutral merchant vessel liable to capture in subparagraphs (b) and (c) have *inter alia* already been laid down in Articles 45 and 46 of the 1909 London Declaration. Of course, those provisions no longer serve as a general indication of the existing law. In State practice, because of the variety of acts included within the category of unneutral service, no generally accepted and comprehensive rules have developed.[217] Despite the difficulties arising from that fact, the Round Table was of the opinion that the activities enumerated in subparagraphs (b) and (c) justify capture. With regard to subparagraph (b) it must be stressed that the incidental presence of some enemy nationals who are members of the armed forces or who are going to enlist does not justify capture. Therefore, the voyage must be undertaken 'especially' for that purpose.[218] Capture according to subparagraph (c) would already be justified because the vessel concerned might be qualified as having enemy character.[219] Still, subparagraph (c) is maintained for clarification purposes.

146.5 Irregular documents etc.

The acts listed here give sufficient ground to suspect that the vessel concerned has enemy character and is, thus, liable to capture.[220]

146.6 Violation of regulations

Neutral merchant vessels are not normally obliged to obey any orders given by one of the belligerents. However, in the immediate area of naval operations, for example, in the vicinity of naval units, the belligerents' security interests outweigh the freedom of navigation of neutral merchant shipping. If neutral merchant vessels do not comply with such orders they may be presumed to have enemy character or hostile intent and may thus be treated as if they were enemy ships, provided the orders were not given arbitrarily.

146.7 Breach of blockade

Here the same considerations apply as with regard to subparagraph (e). If a belligerent has instituted a blockade in accordance with international law, it is entitled to prevent all vessels from entering or leaving the blockaded area or port. It should be noted that the normal result of breach of blockade is limited to capture. Only if, after prior warning, a vessel breaching a blockade intentionally and clearly refuses to stop may it be attacked in accordance with paragraph 67(a).

146.8　The last sentence of this paragraph reflects the customary rule that any prize has to be adjudicated upon. It follows that if the court finds that capture was not justified, the owner or operator of the vessel has a right to compensation.

216　That was already acknowledged in the treaties concluded between The Netherlands, Sweden and France in 1614 and between The Netherlands and the *Hanse* in 1615.

217　See *inter alia* Schramm, *Das Prisenrecht*, pp. 253 ff.

218　See *inter alia* Oppenheim, *International Law*, vol. II, pp. 833 ff. In the case of *The Friendship* the High Court of Admiralty in its decision of 19 August 1807 (1807) 6 C. Rob. 420 condemned *The Friendship* because it was to be considered a 'vessel engaged in the immediate military service of the enemy'.

219　See e.g. Canadian Draft Manual, para. 717.

220　See e.g. NWP9, *The Commander's Handbook*, para. 7.9.

147   Goods on board neutral merchant vessels are subject to capture only if they are contraband.

147.1   Paragraph 147 reaffirms the principle 'free ship – free goods'. All goods on board neutral merchant vessels, whether enemy or neutral, are in principle exempt from capture. This follows from the 1856 Paris Declaration Respecting Maritime Law. Hence, with the exception of the cases of blockade, of unneutral service and of resistance to visit and search, enemy and neutral goods on board neutral merchant vessels may only be captured if they constitute contraband.[221]

148   Contraband is defined as goods which are ultimately destined for territory under the control of the enemy and which may be susceptible for use in armed conflict.

148.1   In accordance with the traditional law on contraband and with State practice, two elements are necessary for an article to constitute contraband of war: it must be susceptible to belligerent use and it must be (directly or indirectly) destined for the enemy.[222] While there is obviously general agreement on the validity of this definition, determining which particular goods may be classified as contraband has always been a matter of controversy.[223]

148.2   The same holds true with regard to the distinction between three categories of articles which dates back to Hugo Grotius:[224] absolute contraband, conditional contraband and free goods. In State practice, the distinction between absolute and conditional contraband, though formally retained, has in fact been abolished and the rules originally designed to apply to absolute contraband alone have also been applied to conditional contraband. In the Second World War almost all goods were included in lists of absolute contraband.[225] This practice was justified by the doctrine laid down by Hall that 'contraband must vary with the circumstances of particular cases, and that in considering the inclusion of articles in the lists, the mind must chiefly be fixed upon

221 See *inter alia* Hyde, *International Law*, vol. 3, p. 2163; U. Scheuner, 'Konterbanderecht', in WVR II, pp. 290 ff.
222 Scheuner, *ibid.*, p. 290; Tucker, *The Law of War and Neutrality at Sea*, p. 263; Colombos, *The International Law of the Sea*, para. 706. See also Canadian Draft Manual, para. 721; NWP9, *The Commander's Handbook*, para. 7.4.1; German Manual, para. 1143.
223 Even though a number of (bilateral) treaties have been concluded in order to determine what articles belonged to which category, they did not contribute to a clarification of this question because of their differing content.
224 Hugo Grotius, *De jure belli ac pacis libri tres, Liber III, Caput I, V.*: 'Sunt enim res quae in bello tantum usum habent, ut arma: sunt quae in bello nullum habent usum, ut quae voluptati inserviunt: sunt quae et in bello et extra bellum usum habent, ut pecuniae, commeatus, naves, et quae navibus adsunt. ... In tertio illo genere usus ancipitis distinguendus erit belli status.'
225 See J. H. W. Verzijl, *Le droit des prises de la Grande Guerre* (Leyden, 1924); M. M. Whiteman, *Digest of International Law*, vol. 11, chapter XXXII (Washington, DC, 1968); A. Gervais, 'Le droit des prises maritimes dans la seconde guerre mondiale. La jurisprudence française (britannique, italienne, allemande) des prises maritimes dans la seconde guerre mondiale', RGDIP, 1948, pp. 82–161; 1949, pp. 201–74; 1950, pp. 251–316; 1951, pp. 481–546.

the characteristics of essentiality of the articles to the prosecution of the war'.[226] Further, States did not subscribe to an exclusive application of the doctrine of continuous voyage to absolute contraband.[227]

148.3   In the light of this development, the Round Table thought it most appropriate to merely define the two constitutive elements of contraband, to do without the distinction between absolute and conditional contraband, and to make the capture of goods dependent on their inclusion in a list (paragraph 149).[228] This does not mean that any goods may be declared contraband. Those articles that, as a minimum, may not be included in contraband lists are enumerated in paragraph 150.

148.4   The fact that the goods concerned must be 'ultimately destined' for the enemy implies two important consequences. First, the doctrine of continuous voyage applies to all goods legitimately included in a belligerent's contraband list. Secondly, the doctrine of contraband is not applicable to exports from enemy territory. With regard to the latter point, there was a division of views whether measures other than blockade may be used to block exports that by sale or barter sustain the enemy's war effort. Even though a number of participants supported the view that today the doctrine of contraband may be applied to exports from enemy territory, the Round Table at this stage felt unable to extend the traditional law to that effect. That, however, does not prejudice the authority of the UN Security Council under Chapter VII of the UN Charter.

149   In order to exercise the right of capture referred to in paragraphs 146(a) and 147, the belligerent must have published contraband lists. The precise nature of a belligerent's contraband list may vary according to the particular circumstances of the armed conflict. Contraband lists shall be reasonably specific.

149.1   Goods ultimately destined for the enemy and susceptible for use by his armed forces may be considered contraband as soon as they are included in a list. That list must be published prior to the act of capture. A view was put forward, however, that there is a right to capture munitions obviously intended for military use, even if there is no contraband list.

149.2   The second sentence takes account of the fact that contraband must vary with the circumstances of particular cases. It is impossible to define in advance what, in the light of the circumstances of a particular armed conflict, ought to be considered contraband. Hence, subject to paragraph 150, belligerents have considerable discretion to decide on lists they consider most appropriate for their needs. However, the third sentence obliges them to be as specific as possible so that neutral merchantmen are enabled to judge in advance whether or not the carriage of certain goods entails risks.

---

226 Colombos, *The International Law of the Sea*, para. 776 referring to Hall, p. 781.
227 See the examples given by Hyde, *The International Law of the Sea*, pp. 2130 ff., and by Oppenheim, *International Law*, vol. II, pp. 816 ff., 821 f.
228 It is expected that in the forthcoming edition of NWP9, *The Commander's Handbook*, the distinction between absolute and conditional contraband will be abandoned.

150 **Goods not on the belligerent's contraband list are 'free goods', that is, not subject to capture. As a minimum, 'free goods' shall include the following:**

(a) **religious objects;**

(b) **articles intended exclusively for the treatment of the wounded and sick and for the prevention of disease;**

(c) **clothing, bedding, essential foodstuffs, and means of shelter for the civilian population in general, and women and children in particular, provided there is not serious reason to believe that such goods will be diverted to other purpose, or that a definite military advantage would accrue to the enemy by their substitution for enemy goods that would thereby become available for military purposes;**

(d) **items destined for prisoners of war, including individual parcels and collective relief shipments containing food, clothing, educational, cultural, and recreational articles;**

(e) **goods otherwise specifically exempted from capture by international treaty or by special arrangement between belligerents;** *and*

(f) **other goods not susceptible for use in armed conflict.**

150.1 Paragraph 150 re-emphasises that goods not included in a belligerent's contraband list may not be considered contraband and thus may not be captured. Despite their descriptive denomination as 'free goods', they are not to be confused with those articles that, by their very nature, may never be captured. Those 'truly free goods' are enumerated in subparagraphs (a)–(d).

150.2 Subparagraphs (a)–(c) are mostly based on the 1949 Geneva Conventions and Additional Protocol I. While subparagraph (a) reflects Article 38 GCII and Article 23(1) GCIV, and while subparagraph (c) takes into account GCIII, the scope of protection of those goods enumerated in subparagraph (b) is wider than Article 59 GCIV. Subparagraph (d) takes into consideration that there may be international treaties in force between the parties to a specific conflict by which they are prohibited to consider certain articles contraband of war. Of course, belligerents are free to agree on any extension of 'free lists'. That is being taken care of in subparagraph (e). Finally, subparagraph (f) re-emphasises the rule laid down in paragraph 148 that goods not susceptible for use in armed conflict may not be included in contraband lists.

150.3 The regulations in paragraph 150 do not prejudice the authority of the UN Security Council under Chapter VII of the UN Charter.

151   **Subject to paragraph 152, a neutral vessel captured in accordance with paragraph 146 may, as an exceptional measure, be destroyed when military circumstances preclude taking or sending such a vessel for adjudication as an enemy prize, only if the following criteria are met beforehand:**

    (a)   **the safety of passengers and crew is provided for; for this purpose the ship's boats are not regarded as a place of safety unless the safety of the passengers and crew is assured in the prevailing sea and weather conditions, by the proximity of land, or the presence of another vessel which is in a position to take them on board;**

    (b)   **documents and papers relating to the captured vessel are safeguarded; *and***

    (c)   **if feasible, personal effects of the passengers and crew are saved.**

    Every effort should be made to avoid destruction of a captured neutral vessel. Therefore, such destruction shall not be ordered without there being entire satisfaction that the captured vessel can neither be sent into a belligerent port, nor diverted, nor properly released. A vessel may not be destroyed under this paragraph for carrying contraband unless the contraband, reckoned either by value, weight, volume or freight, forms more than half the cargo. Destruction shall be subject to adjudication.

151.1   In principle, the same considerations apply with regard to paragraph 151 as with paragraph 139. As already laid down in Article 49 of the 1909 London Declaration:

> [a]s an exception, a neutral vessel which has been captured by a belligerent warship, and which would be liable to condemnation, may be destroyed if the observance of Article 48 would involve danger to the safety of the warship or to the success of the operations in which she is engaged at the time.

Of course, before destruction, all persons on board and all the ship's papers and documents must be placed in safety.[229]

151.2   Until the last session in Livorno, this paragraph was in square brackets as some participants wished it deleted. In the light of past practice, these participants were concerned that belligerents would routinely resort to destruction of neutral vessels if there were a rule allowing the destruction of neutral prizes. It was suggested that neutral prizes would never need to be destroyed if they do not commit the acts listed in paragraph 67 which makes them in any event liable to attack. The relevance of the prohibition of the use of force and consequent protection of neutrals as embodied in the UN Charter was also mentioned in favour of deleting the paragraph. Again others were concerned about the environmental impact of such destruction which was not really

---

229 Art. 50 of the 1909 London Declaration; NWP9, *The Commander's Handbook*, para. 7.9.1; Canadian Draft Manual, para. 717; German Manual, para. 1148.

necessary. The majority, however, was not prepared to depart from customary law according to which, as an exceptional measure, the destruction of captured neutral vessels may be legitimate. It was felt that if the vessel was engaging in actions so prejudicial to the belligerent that it becomes liable to capture, it would be unreasonable to require the belligerent to release it in circumstances that absolutely preclude taking it into port. In any event, the legality of such destruction has to be adjudicated upon by the competent prize court.

152   The destruction of captured neutral passenger vessels carrying civilian passengers is prohibited at sea. For the safety of the passengers, such vessels shall be diverted to an appropriate port in order to complete capture provided for in paragraph 146.

152.1   There was general agreement that if a rule on the destruction of neutral passenger vessels is to be maintained, the conditions justifying destruction need to be more restrictive than those justifying the destruction of other vessels. Since a warship would normally not be in a position to put the passengers of such vessels in a place of safety, belligerents are obliged to divert the vessel in question. If, however, the criteria laid down in paragraph 151 are met and the passengers have been disembarked in port, destruction is not prohibited.

Section VII Capture of neutral civil aircraft and goods

153   Neutral civil aircraft are subject to capture outside neutral airspace if they are engaged in any of the activities in paragraph 70 or if it is determined as a result of visit and search or by any other means, that they:

(a)   are carrying contraband;

(b)   are on a flight especially undertaken with a view to the transport of individual passengers who are embodied in the armed forces of the enemy;

(c)   are operating directly under enemy control, orders, charter, employment or direction;

(d)   present irregular or fraudulent documents, lack necessary documents, or destroy, deface or conceal documents;

(e)   are violating regulations established by a belligerent within the immediate area of naval operations; *or*

(f)   are engaged in a breach of blockade.

153.1   The 1923 Hague Rules of Aerial Warfare provide that a neutral private aircraft is liable to capture if it engages in certain activities substantially the same as those set forth in this paragraph. This paragraph corresponds to paragraph 146 pertaining to the capture of neutral merchant vessels. The commentary thereto also applies here. See also paragraphs 93–104 on blockade and the commentary thereto.

154   **Goods on board neutral civil aircraft are subject to capture only if they are contraband.**

154.1   This paragraph corresponds to paragraph 147 pertaining to the goods on board neutral merchant vessels. The commentary thereto applies.

155   **The rules regarding contraband as prescribed in paragraphs 148–150 shall also apply to goods on board neutral civil aircraft.**

155.1   The commentary to paragraphs 148–150 is also applicable to this paragraph.

156   **Capture is exercised by intercepting the neutral civil aircraft, ordering it to proceed to a belligerent airfield that is safe for the type of aircraft involved and reasonably accessible and, on landing and after visit and search, taking it as a prize for adjudication. If there is no belligerent airfield that is safe and reasonably accessible, a neutral civil aircraft may be diverted from its declared destination.**

156.1   As with enemy civil aircraft, capture is exercised by intercepting the neutral civil aircraft in accordance with safe procedures of interception (paragraph 128) and ordering the aircraft to proceed for visit and search to a safe and reasonably accessible belligerent airfield. If there is no belligerent airfield that is safe and reasonably accessible, the aircraft can be diverted from its declared destination. See paragraphs 125–126 and the commentary thereto. This situation differs from that pertaining to an enemy civil aircraft, in that visit and search is required before capturing a neutral civil aircraft.

157   **As an alternative to capture, a neutral civil aircraft may, with its consent, be diverted from its declared destination.**

157.1   As indicated in paragraph 126 and the commentary thereto, both the belligerent forces and the neutral civil aircraft may prefer that the aircraft proceed to a new destination rather than proceeding to a belligerent airfield, landing and undergoing visit and search. This paragraph provides such an alternative, which requires the consent of the neutral civil aircraft concerned.

158   **If capture is exercised, the safety of passengers and crew and their personal effects must be provided for. The documents and papers relating to the prize must be safeguarded.**

158.1   Normally the capture of a neutral civil aircraft or of the goods it carries is made the subject of prize proceedings, in order that any neutral claims may be duly heard and determined. In some cases, if the aircraft is found to bear false external marks (or no marks), has disregarded the orders of belligerent forces, or is armed, the aircraft is liable to condemnation. If the condemnation is based on unneutral service or bearing false marks (or no marks), the aircraft may be destroyed if sending it for adjudication would be impossible or would endanger the safety of belligerent forces or the success of the belligerent operation. For obvious reasons of safety, there is no rule that permits destruction of a neutral civil aircraft while airborne analogous to destruction of a merchant vessel at sea. Before destroying the neutral civil aircraft on land, all persons on board must be placed in safety and all papers preserved. A neutral civil aircraft must not be destroyed except in the gravest military emergency, which would not justify the belligerent commander in releasing the aircraft or sending it for adjudication. The 1923 Hague Rules of Aerial Warfare reflect the customary rule as set forth above.[230]

230 HRAW, Arts. 49–60.

PART VI

PROTECTED PERSONS, MEDICAL TRANSPORTS AND MEDICAL AIRCRAFT

General rules

159 **Except as provided for in paragraph 171, the provisions of this Part are not to be construed as in any way departing from the provisions of the Second Geneva Convention of 1949 and Additional Protocol I of 1977 which contain detailed rules for the treatment of the wounded, sick and shipwrecked and for medical transports.**

159.1   The Round Table decided not to introduce into this document all the detailed provisions on the protection of the wounded, sick and shipwrecked that are to be found in the Second Geneva Convention of 1949 and Additional Protocol I. This document concentrates on the law applicable to the conduct of hostilities at sea as this is the area that has been the subject of the greatest uncertainty. The law applicable to the protection of the wounded, sick and shipwrecked at sea, however, is still governed by the Second Geneva Convention and Additional Protocol I and the rules therein are sufficiently clear. The provisions in Part VI of this document are therefore to be seen as additional to these treaty law provisions or as a clarification. The only exception to this is paragraph 171 which recommends a rule which is at variance with the Second Geneva Convention.

160 **The parties to the conflict may agree, for humanitarian purposes, to create a zone in a defined area of the sea in which only activities consistent with those humanitarian purposes are permitted.**

160.1   This paragraph is inspired by the 'Red Cross Box' that was agreed on by Argentina and the United Kingdom during the South Atlantic conflict in 1982. A neutral zone at sea was established, with a diameter of approximately twenty nautical miles, located on the high seas to the north of the Falkland/Malvinas islands. It enabled in particular the exchange of the British and Argentine wounded.

160.2   There is no provision of this type in the Second Geneva Convention, but the experts thought that it would be useful to encourage parties to the conflict to consider this possibility for humanitarian purposes. The 'Red Cross Box' was established in order to exchange the wounded, but any other humanitarian aim would be possible.

160.3   Although an agreement would be necessary, there is no need for any particular formality, and in the case of the 'Red Cross Box' the agreement was not made in writing. Once established, the zone need not exist indefinitely, but for the period of time agreed to.

160.4   The participants discussed at length which type of military activities should be permissible in this zone and which should be prohibited. It was easily agreed that the activities necessary to carry out the humanitarian work for which the zone was created, for example, military helicopter flights undertaken to transport the wounded to the hospital ships, are of course permitted. However, it was also agreed that acts must not be undertaken in this zone that would undermine the humanitarian action being undertaken, nor of course any acts that are specifically contrary to the terms of the agreement. Further, the area must not be used in ways that are inconsistent with the agreed purposes of the zone, such as using the area as a sanctuary for submarines, as this would be an abuse of the humanitarian agreement.

Section I Protected persons

Preliminary remarks

This section applies to the treatment of all persons falling into the power of a belligerent or neutral at sea.

161   **Persons on board vessels and aircraft having fallen into the power of a belligerent or neutral shall be respected and protected. While at sea and thereafter until determination of their status, they shall be subject to the jurisdiction of the State exercising power over them.**

161.1   The first sentence of this paragraph repeats the general humanitarian law provision that persons in the power of an authority are to be respected and protected. This means that they may not be ill-treated in any way and that the authority is under an obligation to assure that officials treat the persons correctly and that they are kept in healthy conditions. Further, if any of these persons are in need of medical treatment, this should be given in accordance with the needs of the individuals concerned and without any adverse discrimination.

161.2   The second sentence indicates the self-evident fact that whilst still at sea, and until their status is decided, they are subject to the jurisdiction of those into whose power they fell at sea. Therefore once on land, they will be kept until an authoritative body decides whether, for example, they can be interned as prisoners of war, whether they are civilians whose internment is absolutely necessary for security purposes, or whether they are to be liberated. The respect and protection of these persons is to continue once on land and it is clear that the determination of their status should take place as speedily as possible in order to avoid uncalled-for incarceration, especially in the case of civilians.

162 **Members of the crews of hospital ships may not be captured during the time they are in the service of these vessels. Members of the crews of rescue craft may not be captured while engaging in rescue operations.**

162.1   The protection of the crews of hospital ships from capture stems from Article 36(1) of GCII. The reasoning behind this protection is to ensure that the hospital ship is always operational, which would not be the case if it were deprived of its crew. The immunity continues even if the crew leaves the ship temporarily, or if there are at the time no sick or wounded on board. The immunity ceases once the crew is no longer assigned to the hospital ship.[231]

162.2   Originally, the draft text of this paragraph assimilated the crews of rescue craft to the crews of hospital ships. There is, however, no indication in GCII as to the status of the crew of rescue craft. If the rescue craft belongs to a neutral Power, only those members of the crew who have committed an act of hostility may be detained. Although a possible reason for protection of the crews of belligerent rescue craft would be the same as for the crews of hospital ships, namely, that the crew is necessary to maintain the rescue craft operational, it was pointed out that the vast majority of personnel manning such craft would be volunteers serving on a part-time basis. There could be other reasons for which the belligerents might wish to capture members of the crew. It was felt, however, that crews of rescue craft should at any rate be protected whilst engaging in rescue operations. The term 'engaging' is used in order to indicate that they are also protected when transiting to an area where they have to perform rescue operations.

162.3   The status of religious and medical personnel assigned to hospital ships is covered in paragraph 164.

162.4   With regard to the wounded and sick on hospital ships or rescue craft, their status depends on whether they are civilians, members of the armed forces or neutrals:

–   enemy civilians may not be surrendered to a belligerent warship nor captured, but if they find themselves in the power of the adverse forces, they are covered by the Fourth Geneva Convention and API;[232]

–   members of the enemy's armed forces may be surrendered to warships of the adverse belligerent, provided that they are in a fit state to be moved and that the warship can provide adequate facilities for necessary medical treatment.[233] When they fall into enemy hands they are prisoners of war;[234]

---

231 *ICRC Commentary on Geneva Convention II for the Amelioration of the Condition of Wounded, Sick and Shipwrecked Members of Armed Forces at Sea*, p. 204.
232 API Art. 22.
233 GCII Art. 14.
234 GCII Art. 16.

– civilian neutral persons cannot be surrendered nor captured.[235] Members of the armed forces of a neutral power may be surrendered to a belligerent warship,[236] but subsequently left at liberty.[237]

163   Persons on board other vessels or aircraft exempt from capture listed in paragraphs 136 and 142 may not be captured.

163.1   The vessels covered by this paragraph are those listed in subparagraphs (b)–(g) of paragraph 136. In most cases, there are no specific treaty or even clear customary rules relating to the status of persons on these vessels.[238] However, the experts were of the opinion that all persons, whether they be the crew, specialised personnel or passengers, on board vessels that are exempt from capture should logically be themselves also exempt from capture.

163.2   If they should nevertheless fall into the hands of the adverse party, members of the enemy armed forces are entitled to prisoner-of-war status, civilians are to be treated in accordance with the Fourth Geneva Convention and persons of neutral nationality are to be liberated unless they have committed an act of hostility or belong to the enemy armed forces.

163.3   The wounded and sick that are on medical transports covered by subparagraph (b) are to be treated in the same way as those under subparagraph (a).[239]

163.4   This provision applies to medical aircraft and to aircraft granted safe conduct. The reasoning is the same as that with vessels, namely, that as the aircraft are exempt from capture, all the persons on board, whatever their function, are likewise exempt.

163.5   There are, however, two exceptions to this rule which arise in the case of medical aircraft that land in enemy territory:

– the crew of enemy medical aircraft may be detained as prisoners of war;[240]

– the wounded, sick or shipwrecked belonging to the adverse forces may be detained as prisoners of war.[241]

---

235 API Art. 22.
236 GCII Art. 14 provides for the surrender of such persons 'whatever their nationality'.
237 Under customary law, armed forces of a neutral power are to be left at liberty unless they have committed an act of hostility or are in fact members of the armed forces of the belligerent. In the latter case they are entitled to prisoner-of-war status, unless they are mercenaries or spies.
238 There is a reference to the inviolability of the personnel of cartel vessels in Article 65 of the Oxford Manual, which is, however, not a binding document.
239 See commentary to para. 162 of the Manual.
240 GCII Art. 39. According to the *ICRC Commentary*, it was intentionally decided to have a different rule to that of the crews of hospital ships, because of the fear of espionage.
241 *Ibid.*

163.6   There is no indication in treaty law as to whether there is a change in the status of persons on board vessels or aircraft which have violated one or more of their conditions of exemption.[242]

163.7   It is suggested that the religious, medical and relief workers that were innocently undertaking their work should continue to enjoy the same protection that they would have had if the vessel had not forfeited its exempt status. The same is true for innocent passengers and for the wounded, sick and shipwrecked.

163.8   With regard to the crew of the vessels or aircraft, it is suggested that they retain their protected status unless they forfeited the exempt status of the vessel or aircraft by committing an act of hostility. In this case, they may be detained as prisoners of war.

164   Religious and medical personnel assigned to the spiritual and medical care of the wounded, sick and shipwrecked shall not be considered prisoners of war. They may, however, be retained as long as their services for the medical or spiritual needs of prisoners of war are needed.

164.1   Religious and medical personnel on hospital ships may not be captured during the time they are in service of the hospital ship.[243]

164.2   The religious and medical personnel, whether military or civilian, on any medical transport or in the merchant navy[244] are to be respected and protected[245] if they fall into the hands of the enemy.[246]

164.3   These personnel cannot be prevented from continuing to look after the wounded and sick in their care if they consider this necessary.[247] Once they finish, they are to be sent back to their own country and, where appropriate, to the forces to which they were attached.[248]

164.4   The capturing power, however, may also choose to retain some of this personnel if it considers this necessary for the medical or spiritual needs of the prisoners of war. Once on land, the treatment to be accorded to this medical and religious personnel is governed by Articles 28–32 of the First Geneva Convention of 1949.[249] They are not to be considered as prisoners of war, but are to be repatriated as soon as their services are no longer necessary. Whilst they are retained, they are at least to benefit from the protection provided by the Third Geneva Convention[250] and specific facilities are provided for them by Article 28 of the First Geneva Convention.

---

242 I.e. if these vessels or aircraft are not behaving in conformity with the conditions listed in paras. 48, 54 and 55.
243 GCII Art. 36(1).
244 See *ICRC Commentary on Geneva Convention II for the Amelioration of the Condition of Wounded, Sick and Shipwrecked Members of Armed Forces at Sea*, p. 208.
245 On the meaning of these terms, see the commentary to para. 161.
246 GCII Art. 37 and API Arts. 22 and 23(5).
247 *ICRC Commentary*, p. 207.
248 GCII Art. 37(1) and commentary thereto in *ICRC Commentary*, p. 208.
249 GCII Art. 37(3) and commentary thereto in *ICRC Commentary*, p. 211.
250 Arts. 28 and 30 of GCI.

165   **Nationals of an enemy State, other than those specified in paragraphs 162–164, are entitled to prisoner-of-war status and may be made prisoners of war if they are:**

(a)   **members of the enemy's armed forces;**

(b)   **persons accompanying the enemy's armed forces;**

(c)   **crew members of auxiliary vessels or auxiliary aircraft;**

(d)   **crew members of enemy merchant vessels or civil aircraft not exempt from capture, unless they benefit from more favourable treatment under other provisions of international law;** *or*

(e)   **crew members of neutral merchant vessels or civil aircraft that have taken a direct part in the hostilities on the side of the enemy, or served as an auxiliary for the enemy.**

165.1   (a)   members of the enemy's armed forces

It is a general customary rule that members of the armed forces of the adverse party may be made prisoners of war whether they are found on enemy or neutral vessels or aircraft and whether they are members of the crew or passengers.[251]

165.2   (b)   persons accompanying the enemy's armed forces

The Third Geneva Convention provides that persons who accompany the armed forces with the authorisation of those forces, but without actually being members thereof, are entitled to, or may be made prisoners of war.

165.3

Examples given are civilian members of military aircraft crews, war correspondents, supply contractors and members of labour units or of services responsible for the welfare of the armed forces.[252] This is not an exhaustive list and anyone who falls within the general definition is included in this category, whether they are found on enemy or neutral vessels and whether they are members of the crew or passengers.

165.4   (c)   crew members of auxiliary vessels or auxiliary aircraft

This category was introduced in order to make it clear that such persons have prisoner-of-war status and may be made prisoners of war although they are not expressly mentioned in Article 4.A. of the Third Geneva Convention. If crew members of auxiliary vessels are not themselves officially members of the armed forces, they would not fall into Article 4.A.(1) and they are not members of crews of the merchant marine or civil aircraft that under Article 4.A.(5) may benefit from the more favourable treatment referred to in category (d) below. Many crews of auxiliary vessels which are not members of the armed forces would fall into Article 4.A.(4) of the Third Geneva Convention, but as some might not, for example, because they may not have the

---

251   For example, Art. 47 of the London Declaration Concerning the Laws of Naval War of 1909 states that: 'Any individual embodied in the armed forces of the enemy who is found on board a neutral merchant vessel, may be made a prisoner of war, even though there be no ground for the capture of the vessel.'

252   GCIII Art. 4.A.(4).

identity card referred to in that provision or because the auxiliary vessel may not be in the vicinity of warships, it was considered useful expressly to include the crews of auxiliary vessels as having prisoner-of-war status in order to remove any possible doubt.

165.5   (d)   crew members of enemy merchant vessels or civil aircraft not exempt from capture, unless they benefit from more favourable treatment under other provisions of international law
The crews referred to here are those of enemy merchant vessels, passenger vessels, civil airliners, and civil aircraft that are not exempt from capture under paragraphs 136 and 142 and are not religious or medical personnel referred to in paragraph 164.

165.6   These persons are at least entitled to prisoner-of-war status by virtue of Article 4.A.(5) of the Third Geneva Convention which indicates that the following are prisoners of war:

> Members of crews, including masters, pilots and apprentices, of the merchant marine and the crews of civil aircraft of the Parties to the conflict, who do not benefit by more favourable treatment under any other provisions of international law.

165.7   The reference to the possibility of more favourable treatment is in order to preserve the possibility of crews being given the benefit of the original rule in Article 6 of Hague Convention XI of 1907 which reads as follows:

> The captain, officers and members of the crew, when nationals of the enemy State, are not made prisoners of war, on condition that they make a formal promise in writing, not to undertake, while hostilities last, any service connected with the operations of the war.

165.8   The *ICRC Commentary to the Third Geneva Convention* states that the alternative of prisoner-of-war status was introduced because of the practice in the Second World War of requiring enemy merchant ships to participate in hostile operations. Captured merchant seamen were sometimes treated as prisoners of war and sometimes as civilian internees (who did not then have the benefit of the Fourth Geneva Convention). The proposal to grant them prisoner-of-war status in this type of situation was accepted, but with some difficulty, and with the proviso of the possibility of better treatment.[253]

165.9   Unless the merchant vessel or civil aircraft is taking part in hostile operations, as merchant vessels were in the Second World War, there is no reason why the crew should not benefit from the more favourable treatment and be released.[254] The captor will need to make an assessment of whether the crew of the merchant vessel is likely to undertake activities that will help the military action of the enemy, and if he considers that internment is necessary for his security, the crew is entitled to prisoner-

---

253 *ICRC Commentary to the Third Geneva Convention*, (ed.) Jean S. Pictet, 1960, pp. 65–6.
254 The German Manual ZDv 15/2, para. 1032, provides for the release of the crew if they undertake not to undertake any service connected with the armed conflict and if their ship was not undertaking any activity bringing it within the definition of a military objective.

of-war status.

165.10 (e) crew members of neutral merchant vessels or civil aircraft that have taken a direct part in the hostilities on the side of the enemy, or served as an auxiliary for the enemy

The NWP9A provides that although the crews of captured neutral merchant vessels or civil aircraft are normally to be released, they may be detained as prisoners of war if they take a direct part in hostilities on the side of the enemy or serve as an auxiliary. The reasoning is that this is possible because this behaviour has made the neutral vessel or aircraft assume the character of an enemy warship or military aircraft.[255]

165.11 It is evident that if crews of neutral nationality can be detained as prisoners of war in these circumstances, the same is true of members of the crew of enemy nationality.

165.12 Crew members of State vessels who do not fall into categories (a)–(e), for example on State-owned fishery-protection vessels or non-military police vessels, fall under paragraph 167 and are to be treated in accordance with the Fourth Geneva Convention.

166   Nationals of a neutral State:

    (a)   who are passengers on board enemy or neutral vessels or aircraft are to be released and may not be made prisoners of war unless they are members of the enemy's armed forces or have personally committed acts of hostility against the captor;

    (b)   who are members of the crew of enemy warships or auxiliary vessels or military aircraft or auxiliary aircraft are entitled to prisoner-of-war status and may be made prisoners of war;

    (c)   who are members of the crew of enemy or neutral merchant vessels or civil aircraft are to be released and may not be made prisoners of war unless the vessel or aircraft has committed an act covered by paragraphs 60, 63, 67 or 70, or the member of the crew has personally committed an act of hostility against the captor.

166.1   (a)   who are passengers on board enemy or neutral vessels or aircraft

Customary law provides that passengers of neutral nationality on board enemy merchant vessels or aircraft are to be released, apart from the relatively unlikely event that they are members of the enemy's armed forces in which case they may be detained as prisoners of war. The same will be the case for a passenger who has personally committed an act of hostility.[256] If, on the other hand, it is suspected on reasonable

---

255 NWP9A, *The Commander's Handbook*, para. 7.9.2.
256 See NWP9A, *The Commander's Handbook*, para. 8.2.2.1 and the German Manual ZDv 15/2, para. 1033. If a neutral has committed an act of hostility on behalf of the enemy as a

grounds that the passenger concerned is a serious security risk to the captor, that person may be detained but is to be treated in accordance with the Fourth Geneva Convention.[257]

166.2 Authorities are silent on the status of neutral passengers on board neutral vessels, but the participants were of the opinion that practice supports the requirement to release them unless they happen to be members of the enemy's armed forces[258] or have themselves personally committed an act of hostility against the captor.

166.3 **(b)   who are members of the crew of enemy warships or auxiliary vessels or military aircraft or auxiliary aircraft**
Such persons are likely to be members of the enemy's armed forces, who are entitled to prisoner-of-war status under Article 4.A.(1) of the Third Geneva Convention, or are persons accompanying the armed forces within the meaning of Art. 4.A.(4) such as supply contractors. Crews of auxiliary vessels and auxiliary aircraft are similarly entitled to prisoner-of-war status as indicated in the commentary to paragraph 165(c).

166.4 **(c)   who are members of the crew of enemy or neutral merchant vessels or civil aircraft**
Article 5(1) of Hague Convention XI of 1907 provides that:

> When an enemy merchant ship is captured by a belligerent, such of its crew as are nationals of a neutral State are not made prisoners of war.

An exception is made for vessels which have participated in acts of hostility against the captor, in which case the crew can be made prisoners of war.[259]

The participants were of the opinion that if such an enemy vessel or aircraft has committed any of the acts listed in paragraph 60 or 63 of the Manual (which would render such vessels military objectives), this amounts to an 'act of hostility' for the purpose of this rule. In this case, all of the crew may be made prisoners of war. However, if the vessel has not committed such an act, only those members of the crew who have personally committed an act of hostility against the captor may be detained.

166.5 The crew members of captured neutral merchant vessels or civil aircraft may not be detained. The only exception made is in the case of the vessel or aircraft committing acts listed in paragraphs 67 or 70 of the Manual which would render such a vessel liable to attack. In this latter case, the crew may be detained as prisoners of war.[260] If the vessel has not committed such an act, only those members of the crew who have personally committed an act of hostility against the captor may be detained.

---

mercenary within the meaning of Art. 47 of Additional Protocol I, and is not a member of the armed forces, he is not entitled to prisoner-of-war status, but is in any event entitled to the protection accorded in Art. 75 of that Protocol.
257   See commentary to para. 167 below.
258   For the case of mercenaries, see footnote 256.
259   Para. 8.2.2.1. of NWP9A, *The Commander's Handbook*, refers to those that have participated in acts of hostility or resistance against the captor, and para. 1032 of the German Manual ZDv 15/2, refers to the situation where the ship falls within the definition of a military objective.
260   NWP9A, *The Commander's Handbook*, para. 7.9.2.

167 **Civilian persons other than those specified in paragraphs 162–166 are to be treated in accordance with the Fourth Geneva Convention of 1949.**

167.1   This rule applies to all civilians, wherever they are found and whatever their function, with the exception of the specific rules indicated in paragraphs 162–166. This will mean in practice that such persons are to be respected and protected and may not be interned unless this is absolutely necessary for security reasons.[261]

167.2   Nationals of a neutral State which has normal diplomatic relations with the captor are not formally protected by the Fourth Geneva Convention. However, they should not be treated in any way less favourably than persons protected by that Convention, and are in any event covered by Article 75 of Additional Protocol I, the international minimum standard and by human rights law.

168 **Persons having fallen into the power of a neutral State are to be treated in accordance with Hague Conventions V and XIII of 1907 and the Second Geneva Convention of 1949.**

168.1   Hague Convention V provides for the treatment of belligerents that are in neutral territory. It will also apply in practice to those on neutral State vessels or aircraft. It does not cover the situation of belligerents on vessels in a neutral State's territorial waters, as this is covered by Hague Convention XIII.

168.2   A neutral State that receives on its vessels, aircraft or territory troops belonging to the belligerent armies shall intern them and shall treat them humanely. It may decide to leave the officers at liberty if they undertake not to leave the neutral territory without permission.[262]

168.3   If a neutral State receives escaped prisoners of war on its vessels, aircraft or territory, it is to leave them at liberty.[263]

168.4   If a neutral State receives sick or wounded belligerents on its vessels, aircraft or territory, it is to ensure that they do not take part again in military operations.[264]

168.5   Civilians of belligerent nationality on neutral territory are to be left at liberty.[265]

---

261 Fourth Geneva Convention Art. 42. The Round Table decided to clarify the status of such persons, in particular with regard to civilians of enemy nationality on enemy merchant vessels. Various authorities indicate that such persons are 'subject to the discipline of the captor'. The Round Table was of the opinion that this is insufficient and that although it is true that they are subject to the jurisdiction of the captor until their status is determined, they are protected by the Fourth Geneva Convention.
262 Arts. 11 and 12.
263 Art. 13.
264 Arts. 14 and 15.
265 Customary law.

168.6   Articles 21–23 of Hague Convention XIII regulate the treatment of the crew of belligerent ships that it detains pursuant to its neutral duties,[266] as well as the treatment of the crews of prizes, and of the prize crew, that is, those which captured the prize.[267]

168.7   In principle, a belligerent may not take a prize into a neutral port. An exception to this rule is one of *force majeure,* that is, unseaworthiness, stress of weather, lack of fuel or insufficient provisions. Once this is alleviated, the prize must leave.

168.8   If it does not do so, or if the prize was brought in for reasons other than *force majeure,* the neutral State must use the means at its disposal to release the prize as well as its crew and any passengers (that is, those originally on board the merchant vessel before being captured). The neutral State must also intern the prize crew, that is, the officers from the belligerent warship which captured the merchant vessel.[268]

168.9   Article 5 of the Second Geneva Convention indicates that neutral Powers are to apply, by way of analogy, the provisions of the Second Geneva Convention to the wounded, sick and shipwrecked, as well as to medical or religious personnel that are received or interned in their territory.[269]

168.10   In addition to this general rule, there are two specific rules relating to the duties of neutral States in the Second Geneva Convention:

–   if the wounded, sick or shipwrecked are taken on board a neutral warship or a neutral military aircraft, the neutral State concerned shall ensure that they can take no further part in the hostilities when international law requires this;[270]

–   if the neutral State agrees to let wounded, sick and shipwrecked persons land at its ports, it must guard them so that they do not take part again in hostilities, where this is required by international law.[271] The only exception is if there is a different agreement between the neutral and the belligerent States concerned, that is, both the party of origin of the shipwrecked and the adverse party.[272]

168.11   Article 40 of the Second Geneva Convention and Article 31 of Additional Protocol I of 1977 indicate that if wounded, sick or shipwrecked belligerents carried on belligerent medical aircraft are disembarked on neutral territory, the neutral State must see to it that they are detained where so required by international law, that is, in accordance with Hague Convention V.

---

266 See paras. 15–22 of the Manual.
267 In the context of this paragraph, a prize is a merchant vessel that has been captured by one of the belligerents.
268 Arts. 21 and 22.
269 See paras. 162–164 and the commentary thereto.
270 Art. 15. With regard to the rules of international law, see the rules contained in Hague Convention V above.
271 This is regulated by Hague Convention V; see commentary above.
272 Art. 17; see the commentary to this Article in *ICRC Commentary on Geneva Convention II for the Amelioration of the Condition of Wounded, Sick and Shipwrecked Members of Armed Forces at Sea,* p. 119.

Section II Medical transports

Preliminary remarks

The rules relating to the protection of medical transports are to be found in the Second Geneva Convention of 1949 and Additional Protocol I of 1977. The paragraphs in this Section make some clarifications to this law or some suggestions by way of progressive development. The rules relating to the exemption from attack or capture of these vessels are to be found in paragraphs 47 and 136.

169   In order to provide maximum protection for hospital ships from the moment of the outbreak of hostilities, States may beforehand make general notification of the characteristics of their hospital ships as specified in Article 22 of the Second Geneva Convention of 1949. Such notification should include all available information on the means whereby the ship may be identified.

169.1   Article 22 of the Second Geneva Convention requires, as a condition of the protection of hospital ships, that their names and descriptions be notified to the parties to a conflict ten days before those ships are employed.

169.2   The notification does not have to be precisely ten days before they are used, but can take place at an earlier date. This paragraph makes this point clear and also indicates that the existence of the ships can be notified even before the conflict occurs, so that they are protected from the moment that they need to be used.[273] The importance of this is that there may be casualties needing treatment on the very first day of the hostilities, and therefore it would be unreasonable to have to wait until the first day of the hostilities to give the notification which would only confer protected status ten days later.

169.3   Article 22 of the Convention indicates that the notification is to be given to the parties to the conflict, which means as a minimum to the adverse party or parties. However, if the notification is made before a conflict erupts, it is more likely to be sent to States in general or to the probable parties to a foreseeable conflict. It is recommended, however, in the case of such general notification before a conflict, to remind parties to the conflict of the notification once hostilities have begun.

169.4   The Convention requires that the notification contain the name of the hospital ship, its registered gross tonnage, the length from stem to stern and the number of masts and funnels.

169.5   Paragraph 169 of this document proposes that the notification include all available information that will help identify the ship. This takes into account the various methods of identification including the new methods referred to in paragraph 172.

---

273 For example, the United States circulated a notification of its two hospital ships, the *USNS Mercy* and the *USNS Comfort* to all States party to the Geneva Conventions on 16 November 1990, indicating that they were present in the waters off the Arabian Peninsula. This was done in view of the likely renewal of the hostilities in the second Gulf war, which indeed took place the following January.

169.6   It is suggested that in addition to the facts indicated in Article 22 of the Second Geneva Convention, the following information be included in the notification:

–   the call sign or other recognised means of identification of the hospital ship;[274]

–   radio frequencies guarded and languages used;

–   whether the hospital ship is accompanied by other medical transports, for example, medical helicopters;

–   whether it is equipped with means of defence;[275] *and*

–   the position of the hospital ship, its intended route and estimated time en route and of departure and arrival as appropriate.[276]

170   Hospital ships may be equipped with purely deflective means of defence, such as chaff and flares. The presence of such equipment should be notified.

170.1   The Second Geneva Convention is silent on the question of possible means of defence of the hospital ship itself. Article 35 indicates that the crews of these ships may be armed for their own defence or that of the sick and wounded.

170.2   The Round Table thought that as there is no prohibition on hospital ships defending themselves, it would be unreasonable not to allow them to do so as long as it is in a way that cannot be interpreted as being potentially aggressive. In particular, with modern means of warfare, it is quite likely that a missile could be deflected from a military target using its deflective means of defence, and that the missile would then find a ship without such means, namely, the hospital ship. As hospital ships are likely to be in the vicinity of warships, the chances of their being hit in this way are quite high and not allowing them this means of defence would mean that they are more likely to be hit than warships, which would be an absurd result. However, it should be kept in mind that deflective means are far from infallible and in most cases depend upon associated sensors and a trained crew to be effective. Therefore both the hospital ships and the belligerents will need to continue to take the necessary precautionary measures to avoid these ships being hit.

170.3   This paragraph is formulated in a way as to leave no doubt that hospital ships can only use deflective means of defence, and not means that could be used in an offensive fashion, such as anti-aircraft guns. This is necessary to preserve the obviously innocent nature of the vessel. The examples of chaff and flares were included in order to give an idea of what the Round Table meant by deflective means and therefore other means are possible. In particular it is likely that in the future new methods will be developed and they will be usable as long as they are in keeping with the purpose of this paragraph.

---

274 See commentary to para. 172 of the Manual. Information could also be given on the acoustic signature of the ship.
275 See para. 170 and commentary thereto.
276 This last category of information will probably only be appropriate for more detailed notification after the general notification has been made.

171   **In order to fulfil most effectively their humanitarian mission, hospital ships should be permitted to use cryptographic equipment. The equipment shall not be used in any circumstances to transmit intelligence data nor in any other way to acquire any military advantage.**

171.1   This paragraph indicates a different rule to that in the Second Geneva Convention. Article 34(2) of this Convention states that:

> hospital ships may not possess or use a secret code for their wireless
> or other means of communication.

This provision was introduced for the first time in 1949 and was meant to ensure that hospital ships did not abusively use their apparatus to communicate information of a military nature, in particular intelligence such as sighting reports. It was felt that the mere presence of equipment capable of using a secret code undermined the integrity of the vessel.

171.2   However, the general wording of this provision, that is, a total prohibition of the possession of a secret code, has caused difficulties. In particular, British forces in the South Atlantic conflict in 1982 found that having to give orders to their hospital ships in the clear risked giving away their own positions or likely movements of combatant forces.[277] The solution used was to abstain from informing hospital ships about the movements of the fleet, and to make the ships wait in the 'Red Cross Box' that was created.[278] This was possible because of the geography of the area, but might not be a possible solution in other situations.

171.3   The fear of giving military secrets away by communicating instructions to hospital ships in the clear means that hospital ships may not be informed in detail of the medical evacuations in which they are required to participate, nor about the military situation and the dangers in the area in which they are operating. To perform their mission, hospital ships need to be in the right place at the right time. In practice, belligerent commanders control the movements of hospital ships by high priority radio messages. Technology has changed since the adoption of the Geneva Conventions. All messages to and from warships, including unclassified messages, are nowadays automatically encrypted when sent and decrypted when received by communication equipment that organically includes the crypto function. Hospital ships, therefore, should have the same type of communication equipment to avoid delays in receiving vital information caused by having separate and outdated radio equipment that does not have the integral crypto function.

171.4   The participants were of the opinion that as the inability to receive encrypted information jeopardises the ability of hospital ships to operate effectively, the rule ought to concentrate on the sending of military intelligence. Therefore, in order to fulfil their humanitarian mission effectively, hospital ships should be permitted to use cryptographic equipment (modern terminology for a secret code) which in modern

---

277   See P. Eberlin, 'Identification of hospital ships and ships protected by the Geneva Conventions of 12 August 1949', *International Review of the Red Cross*, November–December 1982, p. 315 at p. 324; Admiral Sir J. Woodward, *One Hundred Days*, 1992, p. 26.

278   See para. 160 of the Manual and the commentary thereto.

technology is an integral part of most communications systems. This cryptographic equipment may not be used for any purpose other than the humanitarian tasks of the vessel, obviously not to transmit intelligence data, nor for any other incompatible purpose.

171.5   There was a great deal of discussion as to whether this paragraph should indicate that hospital ships 'may' use cryptographic equipment or 'should be permitted to' use such equipment. A very narrow majority of the participants decided in favour of 'should be permitted to' because of the fact that present law still prohibits the use of such equipment and that this law has not fallen into desuetude. They were of the opinion that the text needed to reflect this fact and that the participants were encouraging a change in the law.

171.6   A way of checking the correct use of this equipment would be the presence of a qualified neutral observer, which is provided for in Article 31(4) of the Second Geneva Convention. It is obvious that the neutral observer must be able to check that the information transmitted, whether encrypted or not, does not contain intelligence data nor other information which may enable the acquisition of military advantage.

172   Hospital ships, small craft used for coastal rescue operations and other medical transports are encouraged to implement the means of identification set out in Annex I of Additional Protocol I of 1977.

172.1   It has been recognised for some time that marks on vessels are insufficient to ensure the identification of medical transports. Recent tests at sea on the visibility of the emblem have shown that red crosses of 2x2 metres are only visible and recognisable up to a distance of 700 metres in good weather. In general, the red crescent emblem is much less visible than the red cross.[279]

172.2   Annex I of Additional Protocol I has introduced three new methods of identification in order to benefit from new technologies. It is recommended that several methods of identification be used, as no one system is fully reliable. In particular, radio communication and electronic identification may be adversely affected by electronic warfare measures.[280]

172.3   New methods of identification are likely to become available in due course. Additional Protocol I incorporates a procedure[281] for the regular review of Annex I in order to assess whether amendments are appropriate to take new developments into account. It is hoped that by virtue of this procedure, medical transports will be in a position to use the most effective up-to-date means of identification.[282]

---

279 G. Cauderay, 'Visibility of the distinctive emblem on medical establishments, units and transports', 277 *International Review of the Red Cross*, 1990, p. 295 at pp. 315–16.
280 See comments by the USA to the Meeting of Technical Experts on the revision of Annex I of Additional Protocol I convened by the ICRC on 20–24 August 1990, Report, Geneva, December 1990.
281 Art. 98.
282 For more detailed guidance on technical means of identification of medical transports, see *Manual for the Use of Technical Means of Identification*, International Committee of the Red Cross, 1990.

172.4   Annex I was amended as a result of the first review of this type and the amendments entered into force on 1 March 1994. We will now refer to the methods of identification in Annex I as indicated in the new amended version.[283]

172.5   Article 7 of Annex I of Additional Protocol I provides for the use of a *flashing blue light*. Although this method of identification is primarily meant for medical aircraft and hospital ships, its use by other medical transports is also a possibility. Tests have shown that the use of a flashing blue light considerably increases the visibility of a medical vessel at dusk and at night: at the greatest distances the light appears to be white, but it turns blue at about 10 kilometres.[284] It is possible to install more powerful lights on hospital ships.

172.6   Paragraph 2 of Article 7 on the use of the flashing blue light by hospital ships and other medical vessels reads as follows:

> In accordance with the provisions of Chapter XIV, para. 4 of the International Maritime Organisation (IMO) International Code of Signals, vessels protected by the Geneva Conventions of 1949 and the Protocol should exhibit one or more flashing blue lights visible from any direction.

172.7   The International Code of Signals stipulates that the visual range of the flashing blue light shall be as high as possible and not less than three nautical miles.

172.8   It should be noted that the choice of a blue light was made because all other possible colours were already used in navigation. It was recognised that the blue light is used in some countries for their ambulances or police vehicles and that this could not be forcibly changed.

Article 7(3) of Annex I takes this into account as follows:

> In the absence of a special agreement between the Parties to the conflict reserving the use of flashing blue lights for the identification of medical vehicles, ships and craft, the use of such signals for other vehicles, ships and craft is not prohibited.

172.9   Article 8 of Annex I to Additional Protocol I provides for a *radio signal* consisting of a radiotelephonic or radiotelegraphic message preceded by a distinctive priority signal that is restricted exclusively to medical units and transports. The Parties may, either in agreement with each other or acting alone, designate and publish selected national frequencies to be used by them for such communications.

172.10   The use of radiocommunications is governed by the Radio Regulations of the International Telecommunication Union (ITU) and the World Administrative Radio Conference held in 1979 accorded the radiocommunications of medical units and

---

283 The amendments entered into force for all States party to Additional Protocol I except for Sweden which did not accept the wording of new Arts. 7 and 8 (former Arts. 6 and 7) and Jordan which wishes to retain the original wording of para. 1(c) (formerly Art. 1).
284 Cauderay, 'Visibility of the distinctive emblem on medical establishments, units and transports', at pp. 314–17.

transports the same degree of priority as the urgency and safety transmissions governed by Articles 40 and N40 of the Radio Regulations.

172.11 ·Under Articles 40 and N40 of the Radio Regulations, the distinctive signals are as follows:

> In radiotelegraphy: XXX XXX XXX YYY
> In radiotelephony: PAN PAN PAN PAN PAN PAN MAY-DEE-CAL.[285]

172.12 A system of *automatic radio identification* has been introduced which parties to a conflict could agree to make use of. It does not appear in Annex I that came into force in March 1994, because it was not yet available during the meeting of technical experts that met in 1990 to recommend amendments to the original Annex I.

172.13 This system is referred to as a 'transponder system using digital selective calling techniques for use with vessel traffic services and ship-to-ship identification'. It was introduced in 1992 by Recommendation 825 of the then CCIR International Radio Consultative Committee (now called the Radiocommunication Bureau) of the ITU. This method is in use in areas where 'vessel traffic services' are in operation. The system involves the use by all vessels of a transponder which, when questioned by shore-based systems or those on other vessels, will automatically transmit on VHF channel a symbol number indicating its identity.

172.14 Table 3 of Recommendation 825 attributes the symbol number 58 to medical transports as defined in the Geneva Conventions and Additional Protocols.[286]

172.15 Article 9 of Annex I provides for the use of *radar transponders*. Although the principal purpose of Article 9 is to provide for the identification of medical aircraft by the use of Secondary Surveillance Radar,[287] paragraph 2 encourages medical transports other than aircraft to identify themselves using radar transponders:

> Protected medical transports may, for their identification and location, use standard aeronautical radar transponders and/or maritime search and rescue radar transponders.

> It should be possible for protected medical transports to be identified by other vessels or aircraft equipped with secondary surveillance radar by means of a code transmitted by a radar transponder, e.g. in mode 3/A, fitted on the medical transports.

---

285 Radio Regulations, Art. 40, paras 3196, 3197, 3210. Section II of this Article is devoted to Medical Transports referred to as follows: 'The term "medical transports" as defined in the 1949 Geneva Conventions and Additional Protocols, refers to any means of transportation by land, water, air, whether military or civilian, permanent or temporary, assigned exclusively to medical transportation and under the control of a competent authority of a party to the conflict or of neutral States ... when these ships, craft and aircraft assist the wounded, the sick and the shipwrecked' (para. 3209).
286 ITU, 1992–CCIR Recommendations (new and revised as of 22 September 1992) at p. 197, Table 3 at p. 201.
287 See para. 175 of the Manual and the commentary thereto.

The code transmitted by the medical transport transponder should be assigned to that transport by the competent authorities and notified to all the Parties to the conflict.[288]

172.16 If hospital ships and other medical vessels wish to be specifically identified using a transponder, appropriate frequencies, modes and codes would have to be established by the ITU and IMO. Although this possibility is being studied in order to enhance the safety of navigation in congested areas, the designation of radar codes for vessels has not at the time of writing been achieved.

172.17 This method of identification is not dependent on agreement between the parties to the conflict, but notification is required and this is essential for its efficacy. The mode that is cited as an example, that is 3/A, was indicated because it is the one that is common to both military and civilian surveillance radars.

172.18 *Acoustic underwater identification* is provided for by paragraph 3 of Article 9 of Annex I as follows:

It should be possible for medical transports to be identified by submarines by the appropriate underwater acoustic signals transmitted by the medical transports.

The underwater acoustic signal shall consist of the call sign (or any other recognised means of identification of medical transport) of the ship preceded by the single group YYY transmitted in morse on an appropriate acoustic frequency, e.g. 5kHz.

Parties to a conflict wishing to use the underwater acoustic identification signal described above shall inform the Parties concerned of the signal as soon as possible, and shall, when notifying the use of their hospital ships, confirm the frequency to be employed.

172.19 This provision was not in the original version of Annex I adopted in 1977, but has been introduced into the new Annex I which came into force in 1994.

172.20 It has been evident for some time that hospital ships and other medical vessels need to be able to be identified by submarines and that visual means of identification are of very limited use in this regard. Identification is usually undertaken by submarines by means of the recognition of acoustic signatures. However, this system is not infallible: several ships of identical design are sometimes ordered which therefore have very similar acoustic signatures, and further these signatures are not immutable for they may alter depending on the load of the ship, its age or any damage or modifications. This method requires sophisticated equipment used by specialists and, of course, the signature of each ship needs to be pre-recorded.

172.21 The purpose of the use of underwater acoustic signals by medical vessels is to allow a more reliable means of identification for these vessels using equipment that is

---

288   Art. 9(2) of Annex I to Additional Protocol I.

not difficult to acquire or use. The signalling system can either be towed by the vessel or installed in its hull, the latter system having less chance of being damaged.[289]

172.22   The use of this system does not depend on the agreement of the parties, and parties using this system simply need to notify the signal to the parties to the conflict and confirm the frequency to be employed. Such a signal can also be used by medical transports belonging to neutral States or humanitarian organisations.

173   These means of identification are intended only to facilitate identification and do not, of themselves, confer protected status.

173.1   The exemption from attack or capture of medical vessels is based on their function, namely, that their purpose is to rescue the shipwrecked and to give medical care to the sick and wounded. It is in order to give protection to these categories of persons that protection from attack and capture is given to the vessels, subject to certain procedures and regulations that have been instituted in order to assure the *bona fide* use of these vessels.

173.2   The method of identification used by a vessel cannot therefore of itself confer protected status, for the status is based on its function and not on its appearance alone.

173.3   This principle is indicated in Article 1(2) of Annex I as follows:

> These rules do not in and of themselves establish the right to protection. This is governed by the relevant Articles in the Conventions and the Protocol.

173.4   The methods of identification provided for in Annex I are optional and therefore a vessel that does not use them is entitled to protection as long as it conforms to the conditions indicated in the Second Geneva Convention and Additional Protocol I of 1977 (without the Annex). Paragraph 173 of this document merely encourages parties to use these optional methods because they give a much better chance in practice of a correct identification of their function by a belligerent.

173.5   The other aspect of importance is that vessels which have not fulfilled the conditions in the Second Geneva Convention and Additional Protocol I may not use these methods of identification and expect to be protected. Further, if they use them in order to obtain falsely the confidence of a belligerent with the intention of committing acts of hostility, they are guilty of perfidy. However, belligerents must not assume that these new signals are being used perfidiously. If such a signal is noticed, the presumption must be that it is a *bona fide* use, unless there is serious evidence to the contrary. In this case, the belligerent concerned must take all feasible measures to verify the true nature of the vessel, following the procedures indicated in paragraphs 46 and 49–52 of the Manual.

---

289 See P. Eberlin, 'Underwater acoustic identification of hospital ships', 267 *International Review of the Red Cross*, 1988, p. 505 at pp. 510–17; more recent models have been developed since the publication of this article.

Explanation

Section III Medical aircraft

174 **Medical aircraft shall be protected and respected as specified in the provisions of this document.**

174.1   The various provisions on medical aircraft reflect customary law, the practice of belligerents and treaties (1949 Geneva Conventions and 1977 Additional Protocol I).

175 **Medical aircraft shall be clearly marked with the emblem of the red cross or red crescent, together with their national colours, on their lower, upper and lateral surfaces. Medical aircraft are encouraged to implement the other means of identification set out in Annex I of Additional Protocol I of 1977 at all times. Aircraft chartered by the International Committee of the Red Cross may use the same means of identification as medical aircraft. Temporary medical aircraft which cannot, either for lack of time or because of their characteristics, be marked with the distinctive emblem should use the most effective means of identification available.**

175.1   This paragraph prescribes the basic marks for medical aircraft as set forth in the 1949 Geneva Conventions.[290] The distinctive emblem may not be used by any other aircraft, except aircraft chartered by the ICRC. Unlike hospital ships, there is no requirement that the aircraft be painted white all over. However, they frequently are so painted for maximum visual identification, particularly medical aircraft that are permanently assigned medical missions. In any event, the distinctive emblem (red cross or red crescent) must be red on a white background, however small the background. Annex I to Additional Protocol I[291] provides that temporary medical aircraft which cannot, either for lack of time or because of their characteristics, be marked with the distinctive emblem may use the distinctive signals described in Annex I.[292] These will be discussed below. The provision authorising the assignment of aircraft temporarily to medical missions was inserted to assist States who cannot procure aircraft, particularly helicopters, exclusively for medical tasks. However, aircraft temporarily assigned to medical missions must comply with all the provisions pertaining to medical aircraft while performing that mission.

175.2   Article 7 of Annex I provides that the light signal, consisting of a flashing blue light as defined in the *Airworthiness Technical Manual of the International Civil Aviation Organisation* (ICAO Doc. 9051), is established for the use of medical aircraft to signal their identity. No other aircraft shall use this signal. Medical aircraft using the flashing blue light should exhibit such lights as may be necessary to make the light signal visible from as many directions as possible.

---

290 GCII Art. 39
291 API Annex I, Art. 6(4)
292 Arts. 7–9. See also commentary to para. 172.

242

175.3   Article 8 of Annex I provides that medical aircraft may use the radio message[293] preceded by the distinctive priority (urgency) signal earmarked for all medical transports and described in the Radio Regulations of the International Telecommunication Union (ITU) and in Annex 2 to the Chicago Convention.[294] These messages and distinctive signals have the same priority as other safety and distress radio signals. In the future, an automatic radio identification system may be developed which uses a transponder and digital selective calling techniques.[295] Such a system would benefit medical helicopters with a limited crew and many tasks to perform.

175.4   In accordance with Article 9 of Annex I, the Secondary Surveillance Radar (SSR) system, as specified in Annex 10 to the Chicago Convention

> may be used to identify and to follow the course of medical aircraft. The SSR mode and code to be reserved for the exclusive use of medical aircraft shall be established by the High Contracting Parties, the Parties to a conflict, or one of the Parties to a conflict, acting in agreement or alone, in accordance with procedures to be recommended by the International Civil Aviation Organisation.

The belligerents may, by special agreement among them, establish for their use a similar electronic system for the identification of medical aircraft. At the time of writing there are an insufficient number of codes to permit their permanent assignment to medical aircraft.

176   Means of identification are intended only to facilitate identification and do not, of themselves, confer protected status.

176.1   Article 1(2) of Annex I of Additional Protocol I specifically includes the admonition in this paragraph.[296] Technology may greatly enhance the means to identify medical aircraft, but in a dynamic, unpredictable and often confused battle area, identification will never be easy. Medical aircraft must comply with all other provisions to enjoy protection and respect.

177   Parties to the conflict are encouraged to notify medical flights and conclude agreements at all times, especially in areas where control by any party to the conflict is not clearly established. When such an agreement is concluded, it shall specify the altitudes, times and routes for safe operation and should include means of identification and communications.

177.1   This paragraph supplements paragraph 54 which states that medical aircraft are exempt from attack if they are acting in compliance with an agreement as specified in this paragraph. As indicated in the commentary to paragraph 54, protection for

---

293 Art. 8(2) indicates that the message shall be transmitted in English and shall include data such as the vehicle's position, intended route, estimated times, flight altitude, guarded frequencies, languages used and SSR modes and codes.
294 See also commentary to para. 172.
295 See commentary to para. 172.
296 See also commentary to para. 173

medical aircraft, when flying in areas where military control by either belligerent is in doubt or only partially assured, or where the opposing belligerent does have control, can be fully effective only by prior agreement between the belligerents. Agreements are encouraged and, as a prudent military measure, a belligerent commander should attempt to reach agreement with the opposing side on the employment of medical aircraft. It should be recognised that a low-flying, hard-to-identify helicopter may be perceived to be a threat to a warship. Notification of medical flights is also encouraged, especially if the medical aircraft fly within weapons range of the opposing belligerent. Agreements and notification should be formulated in accordance with Article 29, Additional Protocol I and ICAO procedures. Identification and communication methods are discussed in paragraph 175 and the commentary thereto.

178 **Medical aircraft shall not be used to commit acts harmful to the enemy. They shall not carry any equipment intended for the collection or transmission of intelligence data. They shall not be armed, except for small arms for self-defence, and shall only carry medical personnel and equipment.**

178.1   This paragraph states the customary rule as reflected in Additional Protocol I regarding restrictions on the operations of medical aircraft.[297] If a belligerent suspects that a medical aircraft is in breach of the rules in the paragraph, it may order the aircraft to land for inspection.[298]

179 **Other aircraft, military or civilian, belligerent or neutral, that are employed in the search for, rescue or transport of the wounded, sick and shipwrecked, operate at their own risk, unless pursuant to prior agreement between the parties to the conflict.**

179.1   Belligerent military forces employ armed, sea-air rescue (SAR) helicopters to search for and rescue downed airmen. These helicopters are not marked with the distinctive emblem and operate at their own risk. Other search and rescue aircraft, belligerent or neutral, armed or unarmed, must operate under an agreement with the belligerents to enjoy protection, unless they qualify as medical aircraft in all respects.

180 **Medical aircraft flying over areas which are physically controlled by the opposing belligerent, or over areas the physical control of which is not clearly established, may be ordered to land to permit inspection. Medical aircraft shall obey any such order.**

180.1   This paragraph reflects the customary rule as set forth in the Geneva Conventions and Additional Protocol I. Article 14 of Annex I to Additional Protocol I provides that if an intercepting aircraft is used to verify the identification of a medical aircraft in flight or to require it to land, the standard visual and radio interception procedures in ICAO regulations shall be used by both aircraft. The procedures for inspection and actions thereafter are set forth in Article 30, Additional Protocol I.

297 Art. 28
298 See API Art. 30.

181   **Belligerent medical aircraft shall not enter neutral airspace except by prior agreement. When within neutral airspace pursuant to agreement, medical aircraft shall comply with the terms of the agreement. The terms of the agreement may require the aircraft to land for inspection at a designated airport within the neutral State. Should the agreement so require, the inspection and follow-on action shall be conducted in accordance with paragraphs 182–183.**

181.1   This paragraph reflects the substance of the rule in Article 31, Additional Protocol I regarding medical aircraft flying over neutral airspace.

182   **Should a medical aircraft, in the absence of an agreement or in deviation from the terms of an agreement, enter neutral airspace, either through navigational error or because of an emergency affecting the safety of the flight, it shall make every effort to give notice and to identify itself. Once the aircraft is recognised as a medical aircraft by the neutral State, it shall not be attacked but may be required to land for inspection. Once it has been inspected, and if it is determined in fact to be a medical aircraft, it shall be allowed to resume its flight.**

182.1   This paragraph reflects the substance of the rule in Article 31, Additional Protocol I regarding medical aircraft flying over neutral airspace. Interception and diversion for landing should follow ICAO procedures.[299]

183   **If the inspection reveals that the aircraft is not a medical aircraft, it may be captured, and the occupants shall, unless agreed otherwise between the neutral State and the parties to the conflict, be detained in the neutral State where so required by the rules of international law applicable in armed conflict, in such a manner that they cannot again take part in the hostilities.**

183.1   This paragraph reflects the substance of the rule in Article 31, Additional Protocol I regarding medical aircraft flying over neutral airspace.

---

299 See para. 128 and commentary thereto.

INDEX

acoustic underwater identification 240–
2
air traffic services
  and civil aircraft: interception of 34,
    204; precautions regarding 22, 23,
    165
  and civil airliners 92
aircraft
  basic rules 15, 121–2
  exempt from attack 18–19, 142
  exempt from capture 36, 211
  granted safe conduct 18, 19, 36, 142,
    144
  precautions regarding civil aircraft
    22–3, 123–4, 163–6
  provisions in the Manual 69
  rights of transit passage 105
  and the wounded, sick and shipwrecked
    43, 244
  see also auxiliary; civil; medical;
    military; neutral (aircraft)
airliners see civil airliners
airspace
  blockades of 177
  see also neutral airspace
Annex I of Additional Protocol I 1977
  see identification
archipelagic sea lanes passage 12–13,
  99–100, 101, 102–3, 105
  belligerents in transit passage
    through 106
  mining 26, 174
  and neutral States 12, 104, 105–6
archipelagic States 105
archipelagic waters 11–13, 80, 81, 93,
  94, 95, 99, 100, 104, 105
  right of innocent passage through
    108
artificial islands 14
attack
  defining 9, 84, 86–7
  precautions in 16, 122–4
  see also exemption from attack
auxiliary aircraft
  civil aircraft acting as 20
  crew as prisoners of war 42, 228–9,
    230, 231

deception by 28, 184
defining 10, 85, 91
and international straits 12, 13, 102–
  3, 104
and neutral airspace 11, 97
neutral civil aircraft as 162
rights of passage 104
auxiliary vessels
  crew as prisoners of war 42, 228–9,
    230, 231
  defining 9, 85, 90
  innocent passage of 13, 98, 103–4,
    107
  and international straits 12, 13, 102–
    3, 104
  merchant vessels acting as 20, 161
  and neutral waters 12, 98, 100–1
  passage through territorial sea 12, 99
  right to attack 68
  rights of passage 104
  and ruses of war 28
  transit passage of 12–13, 103–4

basic rules
  of armed conflict 15–16, 113–22
  visit and search: of civil aircraft 201–
    2; of merchant vessels 195–7
belligerent medical aircraft 44, 97, 245;
  see also medical aircraft
belligerent military aircraft
  interception, visit and search of civil
    aircraft 33, 201–2
  and neutral airspace 97
belligerent naval operations, effect on
  neutrals 62; see also neutral States;
  neutral waters
belligerent States
  and civil aircraft 22–3, 164–6;
    intercepting 34, 203–5
  continental shelf 80, 108–9
  exclusive economic zone 80, 108–9
  inspection of merchant vessels 32,
    200
  and mine-laying 172–3; see also
    mines
  and neutral waters 99–102
  territorial sea 104

247

Printed in the United Kingdom
by Lightning Source UK Ltd.
108600UKS00002B/67-70